P9-CDG-792

WITHDRAWN

DOING
WELL
&
DOING
GOOD

DOING
WELL
===&===
DOING
GOOD

• • •

The Challenge to the Christian Capitalist

• • •

RICHARD JOHN NEUHAUS

DOUBLEDAY

New York   London   Toronto   Sydney   Auckland

PUBLISHED BY DOUBLEDAY

a division of Bantam Doubleday Dell Publishing Group, Inc.
666 Fifth Avenue, New York, New York 10103
DOUBLEDAY and the portrayal of an anchor with a dolphin
are trademarks of Doubleday,
a division of Bantam Doubleday Dell Publishing Group, Inc.

Book design by Patrice Fodero

Library of Congress Cataloging-in-Publication Data

Neuhaus, Richard John.
Doing well & doing good : the challenge to the Christian capitalist /
Richard John Neuhaus.
p.   cm.
ISBN 0-385-42502-3
1. Sociology, Christian (Catholic)   2. Economics—Religious aspects—Catholic
Church.   3. Capitalism—Religious aspects—Catholic Church.   4. Social ethics.
5. Liberty—Religious aspects—Catholic Church.   6. Church and social problems—
Catholic Church.   7. Catholic Church—Doctrines.   8. Catholic Church.   Pope
(1978– : John Paul II). Centesimus annus.   I. Title.   II. Title: Doing well and
doing good.
BX1753.N484   1992
261.8′5—dc20   92-8752
CIP

Printed in the United States of America

October 1992

First Edition

To
Peter and Brigitte Berger
with gratitude
for the constancy of friendship
in the turnings of turning it around

CONTENTS

Introduction: What This Book Is About, and Why   1

Part One

Chapter One: Economics and How the
World Is Turning Out   17
Chapter Two: A Choice of Capitalisms   45

Part Two

Chapter Three: Living the Tradition   75
Chapter Four: A Social Gospel   107

Interlude

Chapter Five: Reading the Signs of the Times   135

Part Three

Chapter Six: Human Freedom and
the Free Economy   167
Chapter Seven: Property and Creativity   187
Chapter Eight: The Potential of the Poor   209
Chapter Nine: Society and State   239
Chapter Ten: The Many and the One   261
Appendix: Centesimus Annus   285
Index   305

Introduction

. . .

WHAT THIS BOOK IS ABOUT, AND WHY

This is a book about doing well and doing good, about taking care of business and taking care of one another. It is far from obvious that those concerns go together. In fact, it is commonly assumed that they are in tension, if not in irreconcilable conflict. It is often said, or at least implied, that we must make a choice between doing well and doing good, between concern for business and concern for people. There are indeed tensions, and there are indeed choices to be made, but this book explores the reasons why, all things considered, there is not a necessary opposition between doing well and doing good, between taking care of business and taking care of one another. Far from these interests being opposed, they may actually need one another.

This is also—in fact, it is most importantly—a book about the moral challenge of living in a free society. Freedom is not freedom from challenges. Most human beings over the course of history have not lived in free societies. Even today, most human beings do not live in free societies. Freedom is not the "natural" condition of humanity, nor is it self-evidently justified. Freedom is always under challenge and must give an account of itself. Which is to say that people who would live freely must give an account of themselves.

Our subject is economic freedom, but this book is about much more than economics. That is because economic behavior is inseparably intertwined with other social spheres, notably the political and the cultural. At the heart of the sphere we call culture is the moral and the spiritual. And so, precisely because our subject is economic freedom, this is also a book about democracy and the moral truths by which freedom is—or can be—ordered to justice.

In some ways, giving a moral account of freedom should be easier after the Revolution of 1989 in Central and Eastern Europe. With the collapse of Communism, the chief alternative to the free society has been devastatingly discredited. The theory and practice of "real socialism" has been consigned, as Marxists used to say, to the dustbin of history. Around the world, societies are awakening from the nightmare of socialism and turning with eager hope to democratic models of freedom, including economic freedom. After the long, shadowed years of the cold war it seems that the democracies have been vindicated with a suddenness and lucidity that almost nobody expected. In such a circumstance, we might think it very easy to give a moral account of the free society. We might even think that such an account is unnecessary, that freedom is a self-evident good that is now evident to everybody.

In fact, however, it may now be *more* difficult to give a moral account of freedom. During the cold war we had, so to speak, the great benefit of a clear and present danger, and of a clear and present contrast. Whatever the failures of our own society, it was manifest to all but the willfully blind that it was immeasurably preferable to the chief alternative. A free society was justified by contrast with a slave society, and the slave societies were there for all to see.

In this century, the democratic idea has been revivified by two unmistakable contrasts, National Socialism and Communism. Also in the democracies, the theory and practice of freedom was under vigorous intellectual attack during the 1930s, when it seemed apparent to many that the future was being pioneered by the likes of Mussolini, Hitler, and Stalin. With the exposure and defeat of the horrors of Fascism and Nazism in World War II, the democratic idea seemed mightily vindicated, although not a few continued to pin their hopes for the future on Communism.

As of this writing, Communism is not yet finished. In countries such as China, Vietnam, and Cuba aged despots vow to keep the faith. But they are now viewed by almost the entire world not as the wave of the future but as lifeless relics becalmed in the stagnant backwaters of history. Communism is finished as a global force, as an aggressive idea harnessed to moral energies and military force. Unlike any time since at least 1917, then, the free society is not self-evidently justified by contrast with an ideologically aggressive alternative to the free society. This makes it more imperative, not less imperative, that we be able to give a moral account of freedom. It also makes it more difficult. For all the terrible human costs involved, the conflicts with Nazism and Communism provided moral and intellectual justification on the cheap. Now, and, let us hope, for the foreseeable future, we do not have global monsters to convince us that our way of ordering our life together is worthy of moral commitment.

The free society—otherwise known as constitutional or representative democracy—is not the obvious or taken-for-granted way of ordering public life. This democratic regime is a human contrivance, an achievement that is never entirely achieved. The American Founders understood that, inscribing on the Great Seal of the United States their hope that this would be a *novus ordo seclorum*—a new order for the ages. At Gettysburg, Lincoln reflected on the Civil War as a great testing of whether this nation or any nation so conceived and so dedicated can long endure. Democracy is a continuing experiment. It may seem odd to speak of America as an experiment. After more than two centuries, it is, after all, the oldest, largest, most powerful, and in many ways most stable republic in human history. Yet the American proposition is as audacious today as it was when Jefferson penned liberty's creed, beginning with the words, "We hold these truths . . ."

The experiment will continue so long as the truths are held. When Americans can no longer persuasively articulate the truths of freedom, they will discover to their dismay that there are many ways to order society other than the way of freedom. In the absence of Stalins and Hitlers, the chief enemy of freedom is our own indifference to the truths of freedom. G. K. Chesterton's observation that America is a nation with the soul of a church will remain true so long as America understands itself as an experiment offering the hope of a *novus ordo seclorum*. America is the first creedal nation in human history. America did not just happen. It was professed into being. In that sense, America is the first universal nation, for all who are convinced can join in professing its creed—as indeed its creed is professed in the remotest corners of the world.

We may be made nervous by talk about an American creed. We should be made nervous by it. We know about the darker side of a universal mission called "manifest destiny." We know about the American Way of Life as a "civil religion" that can too easily turn into idolatry. That happens when we forget that the truths we hold are truths that keep the experiment under unremitting judgment. The Founders did not invent the truths they held. Their contribution was in daring to construct a constitutional order according to truths that had a long and conflicted history. Their ideas were a sometimes curious mix of the Scottish Enlightenment and Calvinist Christianity, shaped by the emergence of democratic insight among English dissenters, and colored by their idealization of republican Rome and Periclean Athens. The result has been aptly described as a Puritan-Lockean Synthesis. From that they produced a constitutional order of social contract encompassed by covenantal purpose and obligation.

It is not enough simply to repeat the formulations that they used to give an account of this experiment joining social contract and historical covenant. While the words of the Constitution have continuing legal force, they cannot by themselves secure the future of the experiment. The ideas of freedom need to be thought through and given fresh expression with each generation, and never more so than now. Otherwise, the Constitution's guarantees of freedom become, as James Madison said, nothing more than parchment barriers against tyranny.

In this century, eminent Americans have proposed various ways of thinking through again the ideas that can sustain a free society. There was John Dewey's proposal for "a common faith" that might replace the traditional religion that he supposed to be dead. Walter Lippmann called for a "public philosophy," John Rawls expounded an elegant "theory of justice," and Richard Rorty invites us to join him in espousing a "liberal irony" that, he believes, can nurture the moral solidarity necessary for a democratic society. The list of intellectual worthies who have produced conceptual schemes of similar purpose can be readily extended.

Among the problems with all those efforts is that they had little resonance with the democracy that they were intended to serve. They produced interesting ideas for debate among mainly academic elites. A few thousand people, for instance, have read Rawls' very impressive *A Theory of Justice*, and there may be a thousand or more interpretations of what it means. It is in the nature of a theory of democratic justice that it should offer truths that can be held by the people who are the democracy. Otherwise it is not very democratic. Democracy cannot be morally legitimated by ideas that are not understood or accepted by the people.

At least in America, the ideas of democracy must be in conversation with the moral intuitions sustained and articulated by religion. Tocqueville said religion is the first political institution in American democracy. That is even more true today than it was in the 1830s. Give or take two or three percentage points, all the relevant survey research tells us that 90 percent of the American people claim to be Christian or Jewish, and 95 percent say they believe in God. Comparably overwhelming percentages say that morality is derived, directly or indirectly, from religion. In sum, in 1992 as in 1776, the Judeo-Christian tradition provides the "meaning system" or the "plausibility structure" of American moral discourse, personal and public. (I am aware that there are those who protest the term "Judeo-Christian tradition," insisting that there are only Jewish and Christian traditions. I believe it is accurate to speak of a Judeo-Christian tradition, but that is an argument for another time.)

"We hold these truths," the Founders declared, and the future of this constitutional order depends upon those truths being held and articulated in a way that can sustain the Puritan-Lockean Synthesis. In great moments of national crisis, effective leaders have understood the need to cast their arguments within the conceptual framework and vocabulary of a biblical tradition that resonates with the American people. Abraham Lincoln has rightly been called the greatest "public theologian" of the American experiment, and he expounded a doctrine of national judgment and redemption that will, I expect, stir the hearts and minds of Americans so long as the experiment continues. Woodrow Wilson failed to sell the League of Nations, but his essentially religious vision and rhetoric moved the nation toward a sense of global community and duty. To the distress and puzzlement of his political opponents, Ronald Reagan, no churchgoer himself, won the support of most Americans in large part because he communicated respect for their moral and religious sensibilities. Those who fail to communicate as effectively will, of course, complain that he "exploited" those sensibilities.

Probably the best example from recent history is Martin Luther King, Jr. It was a grace of my life to work personally with Dr. King for several years as a liaison between his Southern Christian Leadership Conference and other social movements of the time. I was struck at the time by how often the media and many activists missed the heart of Dr. King's message. During his public speeches, the television lights and cameras would go on when he touched on some specifically political topic of the day, and would go off when he explained, in explicitly biblical and Christian terms, his understanding of the driving ideas of the civil rights movement, centered in human dignity, creation, redemption, forgiveness, and the promise of the Kingdom. A few days after his death on April 4, 1968, a large memorial service was held at a Roman Catholic church in Harlem. The reporter on that evening's television newscast noted that it was a religious service. He concluded, "And fittingly so, for, after all, Dr. King was the son of a minister."

The moral transgressions in his personal life notwithstanding, Dr. King was above all a Christian minister in his public presentation of himself and his cause. He understood the need to "catch the conscience of the king"—meaning the American people and their leaders—by appealing to the truths by which people felt themselves conscientiously bound. His effectiveness, like Lincoln's, was the result of skillfully synthesizing the American and the biblical stories, drawing on the Old Testament and New alike. The great "I Have a Dream" speech at the Lincoln Memorial in August 1963 will, I trust, be recognized many years from now as a powerful and almost perfect articulation of the Puritan-Lockean Synthesis. Dr. King was fond of saying, "Whom you would change you must first love, and they must know that you love them." Dr. King communicated a love of the American experiment and persuasively appealed to the truths that most Americans, almost desperately, want to believe that they hold.

To be sure, there are those who claim that Lincoln, King, Reagan, and a host of others simply and cynically manipulated moral rhetoric to accomplish their purposes, for good or evil. Appeal to morality is no more than public "boilerplate" and "rhetorical fluff" designed to disguise other intentions. Those who interpret the world this way find it hard to believe that those whom they admire could possibly believe what they themselves do not believe. Nor can they credit with a moral or spiritual intention those whom they distain. Thus the narrow-eyed "hermeneutics of suspicion" quite thoroughly "deconstructs" the tradition of moral discourse by which democracy has been shaped. It is impossible to disprove a negative. Although it is utterly implausible, we cannot disprove the claim that, for instance, Lincoln neither believed in God nor despised slavery. Even the most obtusely skeptical practitioner of the hermeneutics of suspicion, however, might nonetheless recognize the social and political *utility* of moral discourse in our public life. They might allow that, hypocrite though they think him to be, a Lincoln used and had to use the truths the people held.

Reviving and sustaining the idea of a free society, including a free economy, depends, then, upon our ability to draw from the font of popular moral beliefs and sensibilities, which in America are essentially religious in character. It is therefore only natural that we look to those institutions that are the chief communal bearers of moral and religious tradition. We may well wonder whether the religious institutions of America are up to the task. In the pages that follow, we will be looking at various aspects of the religious situation.

Briefly, the leadership of the mainline-oldline churches of Protestantism is today deeply demoralized, and in many cases seems to have soured on the American experiment. Such leadership will be of limited help in revivifying the idea of the free society. The evangelical and fundamentalist churches are generally flourishing, but have not yet developed the critical mass of intellectual and cultural leadership required to shape a popular understanding of the American project. Despite the relentlessly secularizing mindset of most Jewish organizations, there is heartening evidence today of an emerging generation of Jewish thinkers who are determined to bring religion into a closer conversation with the ordering of our public life.

That brings us to Roman Catholicism in America. This book is in large part about the distinctively Catholic contribution to our public deliberation on the *novus ordo seclorum*. Because all Americans have a deep stake in that deliberation, the subject is most definitely not of interest only to Catholics. Our focus will be on Catholic social teaching, and most specifically on the remarkable encyclical of 1991, *Centesimus Annus* ("The Hundredth Year"), which marked the centenary of another encyclical, *Rerum Novarum* ("The New Things"). The 1991 encyclical of Pope John Paul II has sparked a perhaps unprecedented measure of general interest. This author's essay, "The Pope Affirms the 'New Capitalism,'" appeared in *The Wall Street Journal* on May 2, a day after the encyclical was officially issued. Perhaps because of where the essay appeared, some readers assumed that *Centesimus* was an unqualified endorsement of capitalism. But the Pope was endorsing the *new* capitalism, and the essay ended with the observation that "the work of the new capitalism has hardly begun."

This encyclical, like others of recent popes, is addressed not only to the Catholic faithful but "to all people of goodwill." All people of goodwill have good reason to be informed about what the popes are saying on questions that affect all of us. At least one out of four Americans is Roman Catholic. Despite the media's exaggerated portrayal of the dissolution of Catholic allegiance in recent decades, for the great majority of Catholics loyalty to the pope is no light matter. There are over a billion Catholics in the world, with thousands of bishops, and hundreds of thousands of priests and members of religious orders. The Catholic Church is undoubtedly the largest and most widespread institution of moral instruction in the contemporary world.

Of course, a relatively small number of people read papal encyclicals, and many who read them do so only to disagree with them. But it is reasonable to believe that the redirection signaled by, for instance, *Centesimus Annus* will, through the myriad institutions of Catholicism, work its way into the thinking of millions of people, both here and in the farthest corners of the planet. Even those who are suspicious of or hostile to Catholicism will want to know what is helping to shape the cultural and moral mentality of our time. Beyond that, I hope readers will want to engage the arguments proposed in Catholic social teaching. They are emphatically *public* arguments in both substance and implication. As we shall see, *Centesimus* is not shy about advancing explicitly Christian truth claims, but its subject matter is the human condition and why that condition requires the free society and the free economy.

Samuel P. Huntington, professor of political science at Harvard University, has written about the "third wave" of democracy in the modern world. The first wave, lasting from the 1820s to the rise of the dictatorships mentioned above in the 1920s, was essentially a North American and European phenomenon that had its roots in the American and French revolutions. The second wave, resulting from the Allied victory in World War II, produced democracies in West Germany, Italy, Austria, Japan, and Korea, and strengthened democratic trends in Turkey, Greece, and much of Latin America. Both those waves, Huntington notes, were driven by countries—and most notably the United States—in which Protestant Christianity was dominant. In fact, until recently many scholars have contended that there is a necessary and integral connection between Protestantism and democracy. There is impressive historical evidence in support of that claim.

A third and continuing wave of democracy began with the end of the Portuguese dictatorship in 1974. The third wave is overwhelmingly Catholic. Spain turned to democracy, and the wave swept through South America, then into Central America, and in the 1980s into East Asia, with the Philippines, that region's only Catholic country, throwing off the dictatorship of Marcos. All this leading up to the Revolution of 1989 in Central and Eastern Europe, with Poland and Hungary in the vanguard. "The future of the third wave," writes Huntington, "thus depends on the extent to which Western Christianity expands into societies where it is now weak or absent and on the extent to which democracy takes root in societies that are not predominantly Christian . . . Western Christianity is clearly not a prerequisite for democracy—witness Greece, India, Sri Lanka,

Israel, and Japan. Yet apart from these countries, very few non-Western Christian societies have sustained democratic politics for any length of time." If Huntington is right, and I believe his argument is persuasive, the prospects of democracy and Christianity may be interlinked in complicated ways. In Eastern Europe, Orthodox Christianity will be critically important to the future of democracy. Almost everywhere, the future of democracy is tied to the influence of Roman Catholicism.

That is merely an observation, and in no way an exclusivistic claim. In world-historical perspective, the two expressions of Christianity that are on the move and expanding rapidly are Catholicism and the evangelical/fundamentalist communities. Frequently, and most notably in Latin America, they move against one another. In at least some Latin American countries, traditional Catholic establishments are on the defensive. On the world scene, a more or less centralized and hierarchical Catholicism claims three times the membership of the highly fissiparous evangelical/fundamentalist groupings. But, if we can mentally step back from the immediacies of the present, it may be that, in ways that elude our sure discernment, these two forces are working in tandem to advance not only faith in the God of Abraham but also the democratic project to which that faith gave birth and gives continuing foundation.

The role of Catholicism in the Revolution of 1989 is beyond reasonable dispute. People in Central and Eastern Europe are astonished and incredulous when told that many in the West credit Mikhail Gorbachev with the collapse of Communism. They allow that Gorbachev made a great contribution by not sending in the troops to quell the uprising, as the Soviet Union had so often and so brutally done in the past. But the uprising in Poland and elsewhere is universally attributed to the influence of John Paul II. The millions of people who turned out and publicly stood up when he visited Poland shortly after his pontificate began in 1978 signaled the sure beginning of the end of the years of tyranny. The scant attention paid the religion factor in most Western analyses of the dramatic developments in Eastern

Europe reflects a deep-seated secular prejudice that assures a
continuing clash between elite perceptions of reality and the
cultural forces that shape our world.

I know that despite everything said here, some readers will
still resist the idea that the Catholic Church might have anything of importance to say about the problems of democracy in
the modern world. The Church, they have been trained to believe, is the last major holdout against modernity, and against
democracy in particular. That prejudice can find ample support
from history, and especially from the history of the Counter-
Reformation, which lasted from the sixteenth century to the
Second Vatican Council that ended in 1965. Catholicism is still
critical of certain versions of modernity and is determinedly set
against democracy as the normative principle for ordering the
internal life of the Church. The argument here, however, is that
Catholic social teaching proposes a fresh way of thinking about
modernity and about democracy in the public order. It is a way
of thinking that could contribute powerfully to reviving and sustaining the idea of the free society, including the free economy.

I have tried to make the structure of the book quite simple
and straightforward. There are ten chapters. The first two chapters deal with perennial problems in thinking about economics,
morality, and religion—especially as those problems arise in the
context of American public discussions. Chapters Three and
Four address common questions and misunderstandings about
Catholic teaching and the role of "magisterial" teaching in the
social sphere. They are designed to prepare the way for examining the theoretical and practical significance of *Centesimus Annus*
for a whole range of public policy disputes in American life.
That examination is found in Chapters Six through Ten. Before
getting to that discussion, however, there is the interlude of
Chapter Five, "Reading the Signs of the Times." It is no *mere*
interlude. It is about John Paul's understanding of the Revolution of 1989, and how those events enable us to think about
history in terms of human dignity and providential purpose.

So there are four parts to our discussion: economics and

moral reflection (Chapters One and Two), Catholic social teaching (Chapters Three and Four), an interlude on the Revolution of 1989 (Chapter Five), and what all this might mean for ordering our common life together in greater justice and friendship (Chapters Six through Ten). Please note that this book presents itself as nothing more than *an* interpretation of Catholic social teaching, and of *Centesimus Annus* in particular. As the reader might expect, I find the interpretation persuasive, indeed compelling. But it is offered as part of a continuing conversation. I am gratefully aware that it is not the last or the definitive word on the subjects that it addresses. So that readers may test the interpretation for themselves, I have included as an appendix the condensed version of the text of *Centesimus Annus*. It is a document that will for a long time, I believe, help to advance the third wave of democracy. (Please note that the following chapters quote from the complete text of the encyclical, which is available from Catholic News Service, 3211 4th Street NE, Washington, DC 20017.)

Much of what follows deals with economics, and the author is keenly aware that he is not an economist. Of course, neither is the Pope. That's one answer. The more serious answer is that there is little in the argument here that depends on narrowly economic expertise, that where such expertise is required the author has drawn on those better informed than he, and, finally, he would be grateful to be corrected wherever he has erred. Needless to say, that goes for the entire argument of the book. Knowing the ways of readers and reviewers, the author has absolutely no doubt that he will be given occasion for such gratitude.

There is the matter of gender and language, about which there is a great deal of understandable sensitivity these days. Suffice it that words such as *himself* and *men* are simply abbreviations for *himself and herself, men and women*, etc.

I am especially indebted to the following who read the manuscript in whole or in part and offered many helpful criti-

cisms and suggestions: Matthew Berke of *First Things*, Midge
Decter of the Institute on Religion and Public Life, Avery Dul-
les of Fordham University, Ian Markham of Exeter University,
Michael Novak of the American Enterprise Institute, James
Nuechterlein of *First Things*, and George Weigel of the Ethics
and Public Policy Center. I trust that they will recognize their
contributions and their respective responsibilities. My thanks
also to Eli Posner for much help, and to my secretary and col-
league Davida Goldman, who, as usual, assisted in keeping this
project on its scheduled track.

NOTES

Page 10. Samuel Huntington, "Democracy: The Third Wave," *National Interest*, Summer 1991. The article is developed more fully in his subsequent book,
The Third Wave: Democratization in the Late Twentieth Century, Oklahoma,
1991.

Page 10. For a masterful account of the connections between democracy and
Protestant Christianity, see A. D. Lindsay, *The Modern Democratic State*, Oxford, 1943.

— Part One —

Part One

Chapter One

. . .

ECONOMICS AND HOW
THE WORLD IS
TURNING OUT

The reader may well wonder whether religion, and Christianity in particular, has anything very important to say about economics. A measure of such suspicion is justified. In recent decades, the professional intellectuals of religion, those who are called theologians, often seem not quite sure what to do with themselves. Sciences and technologies of a thousand sorts have expanded their "expertise" to explain and control ever-vaster reaches of reality. Theologians often feel pushed to the sidelines. In an effort to maintain, or recapture, a sense of relevance, religious thinkers have produced a rash of what might be called generic theologies. Thus we have books beyond number setting forth theologies *of* science, theologies *of* work, theologies *of* play, theologies *of* sex, theologies *of* whatever.

Our purpose is not to offer a theology of economics. What follows is an invitation to think theologically *about* the free society, and about the free economy that such a society requires. Thinking theologically is not the exclusive preserve of theologians. Theology might be described as disciplined reflection on

God and His relationship to the world, and what that means for how we ought to live. Economics, politics, and social policy are by no means the most important questions in life. But they are important. To the extent that Christians think about them, they should want to think about them *Christianly*. That is not necessarily because the Christian revelation tells them things about, say, economics that they could not know from other sources. Rather, they want to think about these matters Christianly because being Christian is, presumably, the most important thing in their lives. At least they say it is the most important thing when they gather in communal worship, and, we must assume, most Christians want to believe that it is.

Christianity is a comprehensive "meaning system." One need not be a Christian to understand much of the *what* and the *how* of the world's workings. But if we ask questions about what it all means, if we ask questions about the *why* of things, Christianity responds with quite distinctive answers. The answers are in the form of assertions about creation, covenant, sin, grace, redemption, church, and life eternal. If the form of Christianity in question is recognizably orthodox, these assertions are intended to be *truth claims* about how reality really is. These truths provide what might be called a cognitive context within which we evaluate other truth claims that are not distinctively Christian.

Christians are not—or should not be—schizophrenic. That is to say, we do not put on our "Christian hat" when in church or in time set aside for prayer, and then resume our "secular hat" when going about the business of everyday life. The most elementary Christian confession of faith is "Jesus Christ is Lord." He is lord of all, or he is lord not at all. He is lord also of the marketplace. That does not mean that everything done in the economic marketplace is done according to his will. Economic behavior, like all human behavior, is deeply distorted by sinfulness. Economic behavior, like all human behavior, frequently refuses to acknowledge the lordship that, Christians are convinced, will one day be evident to all.

Christians are, so to speak, people ahead of time. They are the people who acknowledge now what will one day be acknowledged by all (with either great sorrow or immeasurable joy), namely, that Jesus Christ is Lord. Christians are the people who live and work now on that premise. We are constantly reminded, as Saint Paul says, that we walk by faith and not by sight. In a world distorted by sin—also by our own sinfulness!—we cannot always discern God's will with indisputable certainty. Individually and communally, our life is one of ongoing discernment, of the quest to understand. Also in the confused structures and patterns of behavior that we call economics, our understanding of Christian truth is always being tested, even as we test other claims to truth by the standard of Christian revelation.

A VERY BIG SUBJECT

The subject of Christian economic responsibility may seem a bit intimidating at first. After all, economics is a very big subject. Like other categories, such as "health" or "education," economics can be inflated to the point where it seems to include just about everything we can think of. The history of the term indicates the expansiveness of the subject. The Latin word *oeconomicus* refers to divine dispensations or the general arrangement of everything that is. Christian theologians, for example, refer to the "divine economy," meaning both the internal life of God—Father, Son, and Holy Spirit—and the external way in which God has arranged the whole creation. In discussing economics in these pages, however, we are referring to something considerably more modest. (Although, to be sure, Christians would insist that what we are discussing cannot be understood fully apart from the life and purposes of God.)

Our subject has its roots in two Greek words, *oikos* (house) and *nomos* (manager or ruler). A pertinent biblical word is *steward*. The steward is someone who takes care of things, who keeps the household in good order. "Stewardship" says very nicely what we mean by economic responsibility. Jesus had a great deal to say about stewards, both good and bad stewards. Whether we are talking about a huge corporation, a corner boutique, or the family budget, the subject is stewardship or economic responsibility. The global household of humanity is composed of innumerable households. While all of us are to be concerned for the global household, each of us has a little household for which we are responsible.

The managers of gigantic transnational corporations may feel that the entire future of humanity depends upon what they do. In the *really* big picture, however, each of us has but a small piece of the action, so to speak. Small does not mean unimportant, however. In the biblical view of things, the importance of our *oikonomos* is found not in its measurable effect upon the world but in its being a service rendered to God. As the fifteenth-century Thomas à Kempis wrote in *The Imitation of Christ*, "No man ruleth safely but he that is ruled willingly." The Christian who is engaged in economic activity understands that he is responsible to the Ultimate Economist, who is none less than God.

In this chapter we consider some of the reasons why many Christians have a hard time thinking *Christianly* about economics. One reason is that economics is a reality so immense and with so many dynamics that seem to be indifferent to religious or moral truth. The other reasons are closely related to the first. Economics itself seems to be a most doubtful science. If we cannot even understand what is happening in the sphere of economics, how on earth can we make religious or moral sense of it? A third reason follows. Because it is so hard to get a handle on economics, and because economic behavior seems to be motivated by base self-interest, the entire subject seems to lack moral dignity.

Other spheres of human activity—politics, literature, the arts, family life—lend themselves to soaring visions of the true, the good, and the beautiful. It is not easy to wax inspiring about economics. Finally, many people are hesitant about thinking

Christianly about economics because much Christian thought about economics has turned out to be nonsense, and very destructive nonsense at that. Still today, those who traffic in grand moral visions tend to exhibit a contempt for the real world of economic behavior, and especially for behavior in the free economy that is usually called capitalism. It is very much worth our effort to try to understand why this should be the case.

This is not a textbook on economics. Of the writing of such textbooks there is no end. Everybody who took Economics 101 in college learned that economics is the science that deals with the production, distribution, and consumption of commodities. Economics is often called "the dismal science," and many people are inclined to think it is more an art than a science. Some go further and say that it resembles nothing so much as a kind of superstition. I confess to harboring a robust skepticism about economics as a science. Those who read the business section of the newspaper or watch television programs such as "Wall Street Week" may be forgiven for thinking that economic prognosticators are very much like ancient shamans reading the entrails of pigeons.

Economists frequently dismiss the ideas of other economists with whom they disagree by saying that they are indulging in "theology." Turnabout may be fair play. Any economists reading this will, I hope, forgive me for repeating a question that I first heard in the company of economists. It goes like this: We all know that medicine came from witchcraft, chemistry came from alchemy, and astronomy came from astrology. What do you suppose will ever come from economics?

THE SUBJECTIVITY OF SOCIETY

Far from being anything like an exact science, economics has to do with calculations, guesses, risks, surprises, and serendipities of all sorts. Pope John Paul II has a very useful phrase in this connection. He repeatedly speaks about "the subjectivity of soci-

ety." When we talk about society we sometimes tend to put it in
the upper case—as in Society. Society thinks this or thinks that,
we say. Society should do this or that, we say. Pretty soon this
"Society" takes on the appearance of a thing or a person with a
will of its own. In Marxist terminology, society is "reified." That
is, we begin to attribute to an abstraction a life of its own, as
though Society were an agent of action. The "subjectivity of
society" underscores the truth that society is composed of persons who are the agents or subjects of human action. Society is
also composed of many societies, beginning with the family and
extending to other associations of a maddening variety. The
multiplicity of persons and associations that make up society is
key to understanding economics—especially the economics of
advanced societies that operate by the free market.

A young economist at Harvard University told me this story
several years ago. "I used to be a socialist. I read everything
there was to read about socialism. I knew socialist theory and
practice upside down and backwards and forwards. I really understood socialism. That's when I decided to become a capitalist. I could never respect an economic system that I could understand."

For many others, socialism, especially in its Marxist forms,
continues to have a powerful appeal, and precisely for the reason
that the Harvard economist rejected it. The appeal will no doubt
outlive the supposed collapse of socialist theory and practice in
recent years. Anthony Daniels, a distinguished student of Marxism, explains why this should be the case.

Why should the philosophy of a man who died a century ago,
whose prophecies have been confounded, and whose followers
have caused some of the greatest catastrophes in history, remain
the single most important intellectual influence in the world today,
more important by far than that of men of more profound insight?
Marxism answers several needs. It has its arcana, which persuade

believers that they have penetrated to secrets veiled from others, who are possessed of false consciousness. It appeals to the strongest of all political passions, hatred, and justifies it. It provides a highly intellectualized rationalization of a discreditable but almost universal and ineradicable emotion: envy. It forever puts the blame elsewhere, making self-examination unnecessary and self-knowledge impossible. It explains everything. Finally, it persuades believers that they have a special destiny in the world. For disgruntled intellectuals, nothing could be more gratifying. The end of Marxism is definitely not nigh.

A dramatically different approach to economics, and perhaps to life, is reflected in a whimsical report by a New York writer of liberal disposition who decided to take a flutter on the stock market. He bought a prestigious stock that immediately went into a free fall. "There is only one rule," he writes, "buy low, sell high. All the rest is double talk." His broker told him that it was going to be a "difficult earnings quarter," and consoled him that the market was "shedding its downside risk." " 'Uh-huh,' I said, understanding nothing, so I bought more. I also found an epigram I believed in: 'Even a dead cat bounces.' " What has he learned from all this? "Chiefly, that the stock market is the greatest game imaginable. I have played board games seriously since I was twelve. Nothing matches the grand terror and wicked joy of trading. I'm not up against dice, or my Mac's blips; I'm up against the entire known universe. Out there is every dollar since 1776 and every sharpie since Beelzebub, and here I am waiting for another opening bell." He has also learned "that no one knows what's going to happen—not next quarter or next uptick. No one remembers what happened either: the market has no memory or loyalty and, scariest of all, no more self-preservation than a typhoon." In sum: "I've learned not to be somber about capitalism. Bear market, bull market, technical bounce, blow-off: How can anyone who talks like this be anything but irony writ large?"

Such testimonials remind us not to be too somber about economics, and about capitalism in particular. While the Pope does not typically write in an ironic vein, the above testimonial is related to John Paul's insistence that our thinking about economics must attend to real, concrete human beings and how they behave. Not just how we think they *should* behave, but how they actually *do* behave. Real people do not easily fit into the procrustean beds of grand theories. Economic theorists, too, are sometimes like Procrustes, the wicked son of Poseidon, who forced travelers to fit into his bed by stretching their bodies or cutting off their legs. The "subjectivity of society" means that we start by taking people where they are and as they are. To be sure, we do not stop there. People, beginning with ourselves, can always be more than they are. They can and should become more truly themselves by moving beyond what they are. But we should be very cautious in thinking that we can prescribe how people should behave economically. Human nature possesses its own integrity.

Some aspects of human nature are a given, a datum, that we are called to respect. To say that we respect patterns of behavior does not mean that we approve of them. It does mean that we don't brush them aside as unimportant, or refuse to pay them the attention they deserve. The role of real, concrete human beings in the "subjectivity of society" is obscured by some familiar ways of talking about economics. Just as we "reify" Society, as though society were a thing with a mind of its own, we tend to reify "the economy" or "the market." Every day news reports tell us that "the economy is sick" or "the economy is reviving." We hear that "the market gained confidence" or that "the market was made nervous" by some development or another. It is a convenient shorthand way of talking, but in fact there is no "the economy" and there is no "the market." There are only millions of people making millions of decisions every day. Decisions about what to buy, what to sell, what to offer for sale, whether to work at this or that, whether to invest here or there, whether to save or whether to spend.

As war is too important to be left to the generals, it is at least equally true that economics is too important to be left to the economists. Put differently, in a limited sense we are all economists. There is hardly a person among us who is not deeply involved, one way or another, in economics. Our activity as economic man, *homo economicus*, is not the main thing in most of our lives. And for that we can be grateful. But it is an important dimension of our lives, and, in Christian teaching, this dimension of life, too, should be brought under the lordship of Christ. That requires Christians to become more reflective about what they might otherwise take for granted or simply ignore altogether. Even when our economic work is conceived as a game, we play to a celestial gallery. Because the subject of economics is so immense, and because human understanding of it is so uncertain, a measure of lightheartedness is in order. Lightheartedness is not unrelated to faith.

Anatole France tells the story of the young monk who wanted to express his devotion to the Blessed Virgin. In his first week as a postulant he witnessed the impressive skills of the other monks. Some of them sang beautifully, others were virtuosos on their musical instruments, yet others were learned theologians or accomplished poets. All that this young monk had learned to do really well was to juggle. And so, in the dead of night, he furtively made his way to the altar, hoping the other monks would not see him and make fun. He brought his sackful of wooden mallets and balls and there, before the altar, he juggled for Our Lady. The only thing some people know how to do really well is to make money. It is not an unworthy thing to offer up.

Recall, too, the fellow in Molière's *Le Bourgeois Gentilhomme* who, in the course of a conversation about language, exclaimed, "Good heavens! For more than forty years I have been speaking prose without knowing it." So also, for years many people have been significant economic agents without knowing it. The sociologist of knowledge Alfred Schutz wrote about the importance of what he called "Aha experiences." An "Aha experience" is when a taken-for-granted aspect of life is first brought to consciousness. We say that something or the other suddenly "dawned" on us. After such a dawning, after such an "Aha experience," the reality in question assumes the character of "of courseness." "*Of course* that's the way it is," we say. "How could I not have seen it before?" Thinking about the free economy in terms of moral responsibility can be something of an "Aha experience."

Being in Business

While the "subjectivity of society" means that we are all involved in economics, some are more involved than others. Some are, as we say, "in business." That's another odd word. It comes from the Middle English *bisy*, meaning busy, plus *nesse*. So business is busyness, and most of us may think that our lives are altogether too much taken up by busyness. In ordinary usage, however, we say that someone is in business if he is in a line of work that we associate with producing and selling goods. We do not ordinarily say that a doctor or priest or college professor or artist is "in business." If we do say that he is in business, a criticism is usually implied. It is no compliment to say that a pastor runs a parish or a doctor practices medicine "like a business." There is a shadow, a moral ambivalence, surrounding the word "business." And that is one reason why many people who are "in business" find it hard to view their work as an integral part of their religious commitment, as something that is done in service to God and neighbor. Here we encounter what we referred to as the third reason for our difficulty in thinking about economics Christianly: economics seems so lacking in moral dignity.

It is important to understand why business is under a shadow of moral suspicion. For the last twenty years, Gallup has asked the American people about the institutions in which they have the most confidence. Religion is almost always at the top of the list (in 1990 the military edged it out), and "Big Business" is *always* at the bottom. Big Business even trails the communications media, and most Americans are very skeptical of the media. I expect it makes a difference that Gallup asks about "Big Business." Many Americans tend to be suspicious of bigness, as in, for example, "Big Government." Big Business suggests giant entities such as General Motors, IBM, and Sony. If Gallup asked about "Small Business," it would no doubt get a higher approval rating. "Small Business" suggests the cheese shop down the road, or maybe the neighbor who sells and installs carpets. Having said that, however, there is still something a little dubious about "business" as such. It is, well, so mundane.

Business does not have the social status of more "elevated" professions practiced by, for example, scientists, doctors, clergy, and university professors. Of course, there are a good many people in business who would protest that statement, but their protest usually betrays a large measure of defensiveness. In any event, we are speaking of the general attitude in our culture. To be "in the professions" is several notches up from being "in business." Professionals *profess* something, they stand for something. The person in business, on the other hand, stands for nothing more than taking care of business. At least that is the way many view the matter. Taking care of business, it is thought, amounts to nothing more than looking out for Number One.

Those who rail against greed and selfishness in economic life typically have capitalism as the target of their outrage. But it is more accurate to see the source of the problem in human nature. Socialism indirectly acknowledged this by its declared aim to create a New Man, a new human nature brought about by changing the structure of economic relationships. Long before Russia's disastrous experiment with socialism, and in a society that was anything but capitalist, Dostoevsky wrote this magnificent passage in *The Brothers Karamazov* in which the Elder Zosima describes the economic behavior of his time:

"The world has proclaimed freedom, especially of late, but what do we see in this freedom of theirs: only slavery and suicide! 'You have needs, therefore satisfy them, for you have the same rights as the noblest and richest men. Do not be afraid to satisfy them, but even increase them'—this is the current teaching of the world. And in this they see freedom. But what comes of this right to increase one's needs? For the rich, *isolation* and spiritual suicide; for the poor, envy and murder, for they have been given rights, but have not yet been shown any way of satisfying their needs. We are assured that the world is becoming more and more united, is being formed into brotherly communion, by the shortening of distances, by the transmitting of thoughts through the air. Alas, do not believe in such a union of people. Taking freedom to mean the increase and prompt satisfaction of needs, they distort their own nature, for they generate many meaningless and foolish desires, habits, and the most absurd fancies in themselves. They live only for mutual envy, for pleasure-seeking and self-display. To have dinners, horses, carriages, rank, and slaves to serve them is now considered such a necessity that for the sake of it, to satisfy it, they will sacrifice life, honor, the love of mankind, and will even kill themselves if they are unable to satisfy it. We see the same thing in those who are not rich, while the poor, so far, simply drown their unsatisfied needs and envy in drink. But soon they will get drunk on blood instead of wine, they are being led to that.

Elder Zosima is indicting neither capitalism nor socialism, but the human greed and foolishness evident always and everywhere. It is a bleak picture that illuminates aspects of human behavior, no matter what the economic and political system of the moment. Also today, nobody should deny that there are indeed a lot of greedy, grasping people in business who are doing nothing more than looking out for Number One. But is business itself to be defined mainly or exhaustively by reference to greed? I think not. Unfortunately, too many people who are in business have been persuaded that their work is as grubby and self-serving as the detractors of the business world claim. Little wonder that such people have a hard time taking their work with religious seriousness, never mind offering it up to the glory of God.

I cannot vouch for the truth of the story, but it was told me by someone who said she was there. Nelson Rockefeller, then governor of New York, was on a panel at a Southern university. The subject was "Government and Business: The Moral Challenges." Rockefeller had held forth on the moral responsibility of business and government to respond to the needs of the poor and, more generally, to create a more just society. After he sat down, a questioner in the audience, a Methodist minister, delivered himself of his indignation. How could Rockefeller, the heir of one of the greatest fortunes in human history, dare to pretend that he was concerned about the poor and outcast? In a hungry world, how could a man who possessed money beyond counting and great political power even hold up his head in public? This was joined to some choice biblical citations about the unhappy fate of the rich come the Judgment. As he was getting up to go to the podium for his response, Rockefeller muttered something to a companion on the dais, not realizing that the microphone in front of him was live. The mutter was carried throughout the auditorium: "There's that damn Christian ethic again."

Many people in business are capitalists with a bad conscience. Like Rockefeller, they view "the Christian ethic" as something of an embarrassment, even a damning indictment of what they do economically. Their Sunday-morning piety and their Monday-to-Friday work are radically out of sync with one another. As we shall see, there was and there is good reason for many capitalists to have a bad conscience. Historically and at present, much philanthropy can be understood in terms of "conscience money." The rich feel guilty about what, in their heart of hearts, they think of as their ill-gotten wealth. Large corporations, too, are conspicuous in making gifts to the community and supporting activities such as public television and the arts associated with high culture. Of course, such support is good for public relations. Down deeper, however, one suspects that there is an uneasy conscience. "We recognize our obligation to give something back to the community," says the CEO of a big corporation upon announcing a grant to a regional theater company. The assumption behind that is that the corporation has been *taking* from the community, and probably taking unfairly. It is an odd way of thinking about business.

A VERY MIXED RECORD

There is no doubt that capitalism has a mixed moral record. In *Rerum Novarum* ("The New Things"), the 1891 encyclical that initiated modern Catholic social teaching, Leo XIII was positively scathing in his denunciation of the sins of capitalism. And we will be examining the sharp moral challenges raised to capitalists and capitalism by John Paul II in his 1991 encyclical, *Centesimus Annus* ("The Hundredth Year"). While John Paul makes a clear distinction between the "primitive" capitalism that marked the early periods of industrialization and the "new" capitalism that has responded positively to the criticisms raised by

Leo XIII and others, his critique of human behavior in the capitalist economies of today is, of necessity, very pointed.

Christianity—especially Protestantism in its Calvinist form—played an important part in the emergence of capitalism. At the same time, Christianity has been the most relentless critic of capitalism. In some ways, this is neither unusual nor objectionable. It may even be laudable. The Christian message directs human beings to strive toward great achievement, and the same Christian message insists that all such achievements be kept under critical judgment. This dual role of Christianity as generator and critic of capitalist achievement is by its very nature unstable. In large sectors of Christianity in the last hundred years and more, the critical dimension has clearly gained the upper hand. This is true not only in the case of Christian thinkers, but of others who draw upon the cultural and moral capital of Christianity.

In the several religious communities, and in our culture generally, there is today a profound bias against an economic system that is thought to operate on the sordid basis of unbridled selfishness. Industrialization and the market that motored it was and is viewed as somehow unworthy of, even antithetical to, human dignity. In the early nineteenth century, William Blake asked, "And was Jerusalem builded here / Among those dark Satanic mills?" It was a rhetorical question. The answer, obviously, was no. Blake pledged, "I will not cease from mental fight, / Nor shall my sword sleep in my hand, / Till we have built Jerusalem / In England's green and pleasant land." Among the obstacles that the sword must sweep aside were those dark Satanic mills of capitalism.

In America, the attitude of the churches toward capitalism was varied. Around the corner from where I live in Manhattan is St. George's, an Episcopalian church looking out over Stuyvesant Square. Engraved on its marble walls are the names of vestrymen, vergers, and other parish officials from the early nineteenth century up through the first decades of the twentieth. It is a veritable honor roll, or dishonor roll, of the legendary "robber barons" of the "gilded age," leading off with J. P. Morgan, all of whom bankrolled the Episcopal Church and its notable architecture scattered throughout the city. In *The Age of Innocence* and other novels, Edith Wharton chronicled an "Old New York" society, largely Episcopalian, that one might think was on friendly terms with capitalism. But that appearance is deceptive, for she made clear that her old New Yorkers harbored a deep resentment against the "new money" made from "trade," money deals, and an "excessive penchant for work." The attitude of her old New Yorkers toward the bustle of capitalism would come to be embraced by the intellectual elites of the country and those who wanted to join those elites—including the clergy of the oldline churches, and not least of all Episcopalian clergy.

In the last several decades there has been much complaint about leftist clerics who rail against the capitalism from which, through the generosity of capitalists, they derive their living. Such condemnations of capitalism are frequently condemned as "hypocritical." That is much too simple. In any event, ecclesiastical animus toward the economic system on which ecclesiastics also depend is nothing new. Given the class location of some churches, it is hardly surprising that there is a symbiotic relationship between elite culture and clerical attitudes. Nor should a clerical animus toward the free economy be reductively explained by reference to sociological factors alone. Inherent in Christianity, as we have seen, is the imperative to criticize forcefully (some would say "prophetically") the world that is, which is a long way from being the world that should be.

A MATTER OF CLASSES

There is a great difference between the elite culture and the popular culture. Here, too, generalizations pose difficulties. A nineteenth-century British visitor remarked that America is so large and so various that any generalization made about it can be supported by ample evidence. But, as a generalization, one can safely say that elite culture in America has been intensely hostile to capitalism and the market economy. Coming closer to our own time, in the 1960s the elite who were supposedly in the avant-garde of social change styled themselves as the "counterculture." Lionel Trilling of Columbia University, a staunch critic of that avant-garde, termed it the "adversary culture." Later, social scientists began to analyze the elite culture by referring to it as "the knowledge class," and the discussion of that phenomenon continues to this day.

The knowledge class, sometimes called the new knowledge class, is composed of those members of society who make their living by trading in knowledge, or at least in ideas. They are contrasted with the business class, the people who make and trade in goods and services. The specialty of the knowledge class is *symbolic* knowledge. That is to say, they are experts in the symbols, metaphors, and ideas by which we interpret reality. They do not deal in merely technical knowledge, such as an engineer or a banker may possess. The members of the knowledge class are, in a word, intellectuals.

A mark of the accredited intellectual is that he assumes an essentially adversarial posture toward the society of which he is part. At the same time, according to this theory, the knowledge class is enthusiastic about the expansion of government programs of all sorts. That is because so many members of this class get their salaries and status from the government, notably through universities and government agencies in which they serve as *experts*. What they have to sell is their expertise, and the easiest people to sell that to are other experts who are, in turn, selling their expertise. Given this circumstance, the obvious thing to do is to expand the world of certified expertise, and the obvious way to do that is to expand the sphere of government programs and funding. Needless to say, this course is pursued in service of the "public good"—it having been decided that "public" means "governmental." An additional link between the knowledge class and government is forged by the determination to "rationalize" society. As we will discuss later in connection with social policy and the poor, the state is the great rationalizer because it must, of necessity, operate in a way that is largely indifferent to the social particularities that mark "the subjectivity of society." That the knowledge class strongly tends toward statism is, as Marxists used to say, "no accident."

In addition, the knowledge class has a steep interest in not submitting its product to the test of a broader market. That is because the ordinary people who make up the general population may not recognize the superiority of the ideas offered by the intellectuals. The members of the knowledge class make no secret of the fact that they have an exceedingly low opinion of the ideas (usually called "prejudices") of ordinary people. Among the particularly odious opinions widely held by ordinary people is that there is nothing wrong with making money through economic enterprise. Such people are likely to think that it is a legitimate question to ask even of a distinguished intellectual, "Has he ever met a payroll?" Their vulgarity knows no bounds.

Knowledge-class theory can be both illuminating and the stuff of polemical fun. It is theory, needless to say, produced by people who are themselves members of the knowledge class. Knowledge-class theorists are doubly accredited as intellectuals since, although small in number, they constitute a kind of adversary culture to the adversary culture. They are usually viewed by other intellectuals as traitors to their class, and so they may well be. They are sometimes called neoconservatives, as distinct from other conservatives who are not thought capable of coming up with interesting theories. Neoconservatives are accused of having gone over to the opposition, namely, to the side of the business class. It is regularly pointed out, usually in tones sinister, that neoconservative intellectuals are often funded by foundations that are sympathetic to the free economy, rather than, like more reputable intellectuals, living the morally pure life off government money or foundations devoted to statist solutions for our many social problems.

The Genteel Tradition

While the new knowledge class is new in some respects, the hostility of intellectuals to capitalism has a venerable lineage. In *Humanism and Capitalism* Bernard Murchland surveys the American roots of that hostility. From about 1840 onward, German philosophy, combined with the English influence of Coleridge, Carlyle, and the Romantics, produced a profound alienation from the way the modern world was turning out. Looking back on that period, Van Wyck Brooks wrote in 1936, "They all agreed regarding the state of the world. It was a cold unfeeling civilization, bred by commercial interests and isolation." In a world produced by money and markets, asserted Henry David Thoreau, most men "lead lives of quiet desperation." It is a catching phrase but, as Murchland points out, Thoreau could hardly have known about such things. "I went to the woods," wrote Thoreau, "because I wished to live deliberately, to front only the essential facts of life." The essential facts of life to be confronted did not include how most men live.

The anticapitalist spirit of American high culture was nicely caught by George Santayana in a 1911 lecture titled "The Genteel Tradition in American Philosophy":

The truth is that one-half of the American mind, that not occupied intensely in practical affairs, has remained, I will not say high-and-dry, but slightly becalmed; it has floated gently in the backwater, while alongside, in invention and industry and social organization the other half of the mind was leaping down a sort of Niagara Rapids. This division may be found symbolized in American architecture: a neat reproduction of the colonial mansion . . . stands beside the skyscraper. The American Will inhabits the skyscraper; the American Intellect inhabits the colonial mansion. The one is the sphere of the American man; the other, at least predominantly, of the American woman. The one is all aggressive enterprise; the other all genteel tradition.

The bifurcation between aggressive enterprise and genteel tradition is analyzed by Ann Douglas in *The Feminization of American Culture*. The "finer things of life," including literature, the arts, and religion, were by the end of the last century increasingly thought to belong to the woman's domain. Men were off taking care of the grubby business that paid for the finer things. Philanthropy was conscience money, but it was also a tribute paid to the higher tastes of "the fairer sex." Men patronized the arts and even went to church in order to demonstrate that they were superior to their daily work. Those men who devoted their full time to the genteel tradition were seen as not necessarily effete but they were certainly not, well, "manly."

Murchland's conclusion about the influence of the genteel tradition on attitudes toward economic enterprise is sobering:

> No society in history has ever supported its intellectuals as has democratic capitalism. The reason for commerce's support of culture is clear: both are organized on the principle of freedom. Freedom of thought is sustained by freedom of the market; indeed, the former is very often impossible without the latter. Nowhere better than in societies where commerce thrives does materiality get translated into the ideal goods of culture and spirituality; nowhere do individual efforts so quickly merge into public benefits. If capitalism has done so much in the teeth of open hostility from so many intellectuals, imagine what might be the case had they supported it.

The elite culture's long-standing alienation from economic free enterprise is in many ways a Protestant phenomenon. The mainline of American cultural history is closely associated with the "brand name" churches such as the Congregational, Presbyterian, and Episcopalian. In the history of ideas and how they have worked themselves out also in the economic sphere, Calvinism of all varieties has played a particularly important role. Max Weber's argument about the connection between Calvinism, the Protestant work ethic, and the rise of capitalism has been debated in books beyond numbering. Whether or not he was always right in the way he construed the connections, there is little doubt that what we now call democratic capitalism was shaped in a Protestant, and usually Calvinist, milieu. Democratic capitalism was a northern European and North American development. Despite the nascent capitalism of Italian city-states, the evolution that Michael Novak has so influentially described as *The Spirit of Democratic Capitalism* did not take hold in the Mediterranean world or in Latin America. At least up until now, Catholic cultures have not been conducive to the nurturing of free-market enterprise. That is one reason why *Centesimus Annus* is of such potential significance. A Catholic social doctrine and spirituality that affirm democratic capitalism could reinvigorate an appreciation of economic enterprise that is no longer supported by the religious traditions that gave it birth.

EVER-SHIFTING ALIGNMENTS

I have written elsewhere about the ways in which the Protestant mainline has become the oldline and is fast becoming the sideline. (See *The Naked Pubic Square*, 1984.) It has now become a commonplace that mainline or liberal Protestantism is in the doldrums—as measured by morale, membership, institutional vitality, and cultural influence. Regrettably, some Christians outside the ambit of oldline Protestantism exhibit an unseemly *Schadenfreude* in this decline. I believe this is a mistake strategically. It is also not very nice.

Oldline Protestantism played the critical role in the shaping of the American experiment, and will almost certainly have an important part to play in the future. Defining figures such as Ralph Waldo Emerson, Walt Whitman, Thoreau, and John Dewey, while they were not orthodox Protestants, were all products of oldline Protestantism. They defined themselves by their dissent from it, and the relevance of their dissent assumed its continuing vitality. The whole of American cultural history, including our attitudes toward economics, was given its shape by thinkers who were but one step away from the Protestant pulpit. They drew upon the cultural and moral capital of oldline Protestantism as though it were inexhaustible. If it is not exhausted, that capital is now radically depleted. It is understandable that people look around for other sources of moral energy that might sustain a free society, including a free economy.

Commenting on *Rerum Novarum*, John Paul says that we should view that encyclical as "an invitation to 'look around' at the 'new things' which surround us and in which we find ourselves caught up, very different from the 'new things' which characterized the final decade of the last century" (¶ 3). While he has specific reference to the nature of capitalism a century ago, we can understand that invitation more broadly. Among the new things in the American context are the shifting alignments among culturally formative religious traditions. Of most particular note is the cultural ascendancy of evangelical Protestantism and Roman Catholicism.

It would be a mistake, I believe, to think that evangelicals and Catholics will simply replace the Protestant oldline. Close to 90 percent of the American people say that they are Christian, and at least a third of them identify with churches in the Protestant oldline. That is not likely to change in the foreseeable future. It is true that as national entities, institutions such as the Presbyterian Church (U.S.A.), the Episcopal Church, and the United Methodist Church are in a free fall that show no signs of having hit bottom. At the same time, however, in these communions there are thousands of local churches that are centers of vibrant growth and discipleship. Among the "new things" for which we must hope is that a rethinking of the morality of economic enterprise will be thoroughly ecumenical. It is almost impossible to imagine (try hard enough and you can imagine anything) that the oldline will ever again be the culturally formative mainline. Nonetheless, we should want liberal Protestantism also to be a full participant in the moral reconstruction of the economic base of American life and of America's role in the world.

Cultural and political alignments, along with the labels that attend them, are not forever. Liberalism, for example, was once "the vital center" described by Arthur Schlesinger, Jr., in a 1949 book by that title. Twenty years later it was "radicalized," which occasioned the emergence of neoconservatism and neoliberalism, both claiming continuity with the older liberalism. Twenty or thirty years from now such terms may show up only on tests in college history courses. The devising of labels is inevitable. It is a kind of shorthand, and often a short-circuiting of thought, in "positioning" people, attitudes, and arguments. In identifying ourselves and in distinguishing ourselves from others—the two being much the same thing—we do well not to make too heavy an investment in labels.

A M A T T E R   O F   C O N S E Q U E N C E

This is not to suggest that it is unimportant where we position ourselves with respect to the parties, attitudes, and arguments that are in play around great issues. After the Revolution of 1989 in Central and Eastern Europe and the collapse of Communism, for instance, it is important to sort out what these developments mean for some of the great questions that have so preoccupied us also in the West. Among those great questions, on which Christians, too, have been sharply divided, is the question of the relative merits of socialism and capitalism—and of permutations of both. We cannot just lightly brush socialism aside as a mistake, and then blithely move on as though it were a matter of no great consequence.

John Paul says that Leo XIII recognized that socialism *as an idea and ideal* was fatally flawed. It carried within it the seeds of the human catastrophe that would come to awful fruition in what John Paul calls the "real socialism" that followed the Communist revolution of 1917. In the last several decades, those who are called liberation theologians have commonly said that they are not Marxists, they simply employ "Marxist analysis" in understanding what is wrong with the world and how to set it right. The point of John Paul is that it is precisely the analysis that is dead, and deadly, wrong.

Those who criticize *Centesimus* from the left protest that John Paul refers to "socialism" in an undiscriminating way. Thus a publication of the World Council of Churches declares:

> [In *Centesimus*] socialism is equated with the totalitarian state and attributed to an atheism closely linked to rationalism and the Enlightenment. Even if this were true of Marxist socialism, which is arguable, it is absurd to restrict the term socialism in this way. Whatever one may think of it, there is a tradition of democratic socialism, and also a Christian socialist tradition, of which the encyclical seems unaware.

Readers of *Centesimus* can determine for themselves whether John Paul is "unaware" of various traditions of socialism. Not only does he deal with the core ideas common to all proposals and practices that have been called socialist, but, as we shall see, he treats extensively the problems posed by the so-called mixed economies of modern welfare states.

The word "socialism" is a talisman also for many Christian thinkers. They can bring themselves to recognize that this socialist experiment or that socialist experiment has failed, but never socialism itself. Right up to the Revolution of 1989, and

better perceived, deviations are corrected, the courage to
~rk for what is good is reinforced" (¶ 25).

In this view, trust in God's patience is not passivity but pre-
~ely "courage to work" for change. The familiar maxim that
~ should pray as though everything depended upon God and
~rk as though everything depended upon us should, I have
~ten thought, be reversed. Given the monumentally sad state of
~e world, rational beings can only work to improve it if they
~ork as though everything depended upon God. And prayer,
~ne might suggest, is not sufficiently urgent unless we pray as
~ough everything depended upon us.

The sin of presumption that was socialism supplanted such
~rayer and such work. Again, we are speaking about "real social-
~sm." We should not be surprised that there will be, no doubt
~or a long time, people holding out for their version of "ideal
~ocialism"—variously called democratic socialism, socialism
~with a human face, or a "third way" between socialism and capitalism. Others, who have disenthralled themselves from socialist
language of any sort, still cling to the fragments of the socialist
dream by declaring that whatever else they may not be, they are
certainly anticapitalist. Pushed yet further, they will take their
absolutely last stand by adamantly refusing to say that they favor
capitalism.

We should not push them unmercifully. It takes time to adjust to new realities. John Paul offers alternative language for
those who are not yet able to bring themselves to an explicit
affirmation of capitalism. He talks about a "business economy,"
or a "market economy," or simply a "free economy." By whatever name, however, the reality referred to is what most people
mean by capitalism. Even better is democratic capitalism, for
that term captures the dynamic interaction of the economic, the
political, and the cultural that is at the heart of the argument of
Centesimus Annus. It would be a most serious mistake to think
that the affirmation of capitalism means an uncritical endorsement of, for instance, the political and economic system of the
United States. As will become evident in the pages that follow,

beyond, many Christians were determined not
truth about socialism. Although not a Christian,
spoke also for many Christians when he declared,
the name of our dream." Nobody in his right
about capitalism. One may dream about having spe
cess in a capitalist system, but capitalism, unlike soc
presented itself as the remedy for our discontents v
wounded by sin.

A SIMPLE AND RADICAL SOLUTIC

Socialism did present itself, in the words of John Paul,
"simple and radical solution" (¶ 12). It was powerfully
to the utopian impulse in the human heart, an impulse
hardly been extinguished by virtue of the Revolution
Nobody should deny that the world as it is is highly un
tory. That, presumably, is why Christians pray daily,
kingdom come," and that is why we are called to work
amelioration of suffering and injustice. It is sometimes sa
the message of the coming kingdom is the Christian fo
utopianism. Christianity, however, is the opposite of utop
is eschatological. Faith is fixed on that which God will d
cording to his promise in Christ. Utopianism, says John
turns politics into a "secular religion." "By presuming to an
pate judgment here and now, man puts himself in the plac
God and sets himself against the patience of God" (¶ 25).
The Christian vision, also in the sphere of economics, is
of working with and not against the patience of God. "W
sacred Scripture teaches us about the prospects of the Kingdo
of God is not without consequences for the life of tempo
societies . . . [with] all their imperfection and impermanenc
The Kingdom of God . . . throws light on the order of huma
society, while the power of grace penetrates that order and give
it life. In this way the requirements of a society worthy of man

democratic capitalism poses an ambitious agenda of reform. Neither the United States nor any other developed Western country represents adequately the "free economy" for which the Pope is calling.

Like 1066, 1517, 1776, 1789, 1914, and 1945, so it seems almost certain that Anno Domini 1989 will be inscribed in history as one of those dates marking a genuinely new era. President Bush and others have spoken about a "new world order." Nobody is very sure about what that means, but it does seem that something like a new world order is afoot. There are no doubt many pieces to such a new order, but one critical piece is economics. The free economy is apparently the order of the future in this postsocialist world. A great deal rides on that supposition, especially for the many millions of people in the poor nations and for the poor in developed societies.

In this chapter we have considered some of the reasons why Christians have difficulty in thinking *Christianly* about economics. There is the immensity of the subject itself, and the uncertainty of the science that presumes to address it. Even more complex are the strains of religious thought that have, on the one hand, generated and nurtured capitalism while, on the other, have relentlessly attacked economic enterprise and deprived it of moral legitimacy. These strains of religious thought interact in a mutually reinforcing way with entrenched attitudes among our cultural elites, sometimes called the new knowledge class. Now we want to discuss how some of these conflicting dynamics have worked themselves out, and are working themselves out, in American religious and political thought, with specific reference to Catholicism in America.

NOTES

Page 22. Anthony Daniels, "He's Not Dead, Yet," *The Spectator*, May 11, 1991. For a more thorough discussion of Marxism's perduring appeal, see his book *The Wilder Shores of Marx*, 1990, published in the United Kingdom by Hutchinson.

Page 23. John Calvin Batchelor, "Confessions of a Capitalist Naif," *New York Times*, June 8, 1991.

Pages 28–29. Fyodor Dostoevsky, *The Brothers Karamazov*, translated by Richard Pevear and Larissa Volokhonsky, North Point Press, 1990.

Page 34. For a succinct discussion of knowledge-class theory, see Chapter 3, "Class: The Ladder of Success," in Peter Berger's *The Capitalist Revolution*, Basic Books, 1986.

Page 36. Ann Douglas, *The Feminization of American Culture*, Knopf, 1977.

Page 36. Bernard Murchland, *Humanism and Capitalism: A Survey of Thought on Morality*, American Enterprise Institute, 1984.

Page 40. Ronald Preston, "The Pope's New Social Encyclical," in the World Council of Churches publication *One World*, August/September 1991.

Chapter Two

• • •

A CHOICE
OF CAPITALISMS

The new era inaugurated by the death of "real socialism" invites us to undertake a thorough clearing of our minds. But old ideas, like old dreams, die hard. We grow accustomed to patterns of thought, and even when they have been discredited we are reluctant to let them go until we have a confident hold on better ways of thinking to take their place. This is perfectly understandable and not necessarily a sign of moral culpability. In a big and confusing world, nobody likes to feel lost at sea without some fixed points of reference by which he can locate himself. Certain symbolic words have played an important role in providing a kind of "cognitive chart" for the perplexed. The chart may not tell us how to get to land, but simply to possess such a chart is a great comfort in our perplexity. Among such words, few have been so important to so many people in this century as the word "socialism."

Winston Churchill probably did not utter even half of the clever sayings attributed to him, but this, too, he is alleged to have said: "If a young man isn't a socialist before he's thirty, there's something wrong with his heart. If he's a socialist after thirty, there's something wrong with his head." Socialism witnessed to the "idealism" that we want to associate with youth. Many who were no longer young insisted that they were socialists, if for no other reason than to demonstrate that they were still young at heart. Very often, the socialism in question did not have much in the way of content, but to be for socialism was testimony that one had not "sold out."

At a dinner party a few years ago there was a noted theologian who indicated that he didn't think very highly of socialism. Our hostess was offended. As the conversation proceeded, she made clear that by socialism she did not mean the collective ownership of property, the equalization of incomes, the state monopoly on social services, or a command economy directed from the top. By socialism she meant, rather, "a society in which people care about one another." If that is what is meant by socialism, our noted theologian allowed, he was glad to be called a socialist. She seemed greatly relieved that he had a conscience after all.

While socialism was over those years a soft, almost vacuous, sentiment for many, for other Christians it was a very definite program for the radical reordering of society in all its parts. One thinks, for example, of the "hard socialism" associated with liberation theology in Latin America and elsewhere. There were liberation theologians who said they were only employing "Marxist analysis" in order to understand the plight of the poor, but, with remarkable consistency, they were to be found on the side of Marxist-Leninist revolutions wherever they arose around the world.

CHASING THE FUTURE

It is hard now to remember that only a few years ago many of the best and the brightest among Christian thinkers were confidently declaring that socialism was the wave of the future. In this view, the United States was a capitalist, imperialist, militarist power implacably resisting "the inevitable tide of history." America was quite simply and devastatingly declared to be on "the wrong side of the global revolution." Those who shared this disposition were "political pilgrims" in never-ending search for the holy grail of "true socialism"—their loyalties and hopes traveling from Moscow to Havana to Hanoi to Maoist China to the Sandinistas in Nicaragua. Again and again, the revolution was "betrayed," but the revolution itself was never called into question. Such political pilgrims are still among us. Wags in the Vatican have been heard to observe that the last Marxist in the world will be an American nun in Latin America. Those who say that have probably never been to Harvard.

On the cognitive chart of recent Western culture, "socialism" was the name for the alternative to the way things were. The unsatisfactory state of the way things were was attributed to "capitalism." It seemed necessary to many to have a "systemic analysis" of what was wrong with the world. It was not sufficient to observe that the seven deadly sins—pride, covetousness, lust, envy, gluttony, anger, and sloth—were pretty much ubiquitous throughout human history, no matter how society was organized. Since the deadly sins in all their virulent variations were manifestly alive in American life, it was supposed, there had to be something radically and "systemically" disordered in this society. Marxism, in both soft and hard versions, provided an explanation. The root cause was economic and it was summed up in one word—capitalism. The conceptually available alternative to capitalism was, of course, socialism. And thus it came about that to be in favor of socialism "of one sort or another" was to take a principled stance against vice and in support of virtue.

To be sure, for many Christians it was not just a matter of demonstrating moral bona fides or declaring oneself in favor of the proposition that the world should be a much nicer place. The young Paul Tillich, for example, spoke for many when he declared, "Any serious Christian must be a socialist." Among both Protestants and Catholics, Tillich was one of the most influential theologians of the twentieth century. Tillich's socialism was not simply idealistic attitudinizing. He undoubtedly meant what he wrote:

> Religious socialism calls the capitalistic system demonic, on the one hand, because of the union of creative and destructive powers present in it; on the other, because of the inevitability of the class struggle independent of subjective morality and piety. The effect of the capitalist system upon society and upon every individual in it takes the typical form of "possession," that is, of being "possessed"; its character is demonic.

The sway of capitalism in world history was nothing less than an "evil empire," to use the phrase Ronald Reagan would later apply to the Soviet Union. Of course, there were many thinkers, also on the left, who early on recognized the fatuity of socialism. The influential economist John Maynard Keynes, who has left us so ambiguous a legacy, wrote in 1925: "Marxian Socialism must always remain a portent to the historians of opinion —how a doctrine so illogical and so dull can have exercised so powerful and enduring an influence over the minds of men, and through them, the events of history."

But for most "progressive" Christian leadership in the several churches, from the nineteenth century until very recently, socialism was the conceptually available alternative to what was wrong with the capitalism that they knew. R. H. Tawney, William Temple, Harry Ward, the early Reinhold Niebuhr, John Bennett, and even the great Karl Barth are among the host of Protestant social thinkers who agreed with Tillich that any serious Christian must be a socialist. One pithy and oft-repeated assertion captured this article of faith: "Socialism is the economics of which Christianity is the religion." Nobody should deny the power of the spirituality of socialist solidarity.

Christian thinkers who directly challenged socialist faith and piety were putting their intellectual careers into deep jeopardy. When, in 1982, the lay Catholic theologian Michael Novak published *The Spirit of Democratic Capitalism*, almost the entire Christian intellectual establishment, Catholic and Protestant, got out bell, book, and candle to banish the heretic from their midst. Today the gravamen of Novak's argument is much more widely accepted. His works are read avidly in Poland, which is trying to move as quickly as possible from a socialist to a capitalist order. Although the detailed history of the writing of *Centesimus Annus* is not known, it seems very likely that Novak's work was an influence in shaping the argument of this Polish pope. One might think that Novak would now be much celebrated by his intellectual peers, and that may come with time. But at present it appears that the only intellectual offense greater than having challenged conventional wisdoms is to have been too right too early. Novak was a premature antisocialist.

ECONOMIC INFLATION

The positive argument for capitalism is unacceptable to many because they have an inflated notion of economics itself. That is to say, under the influence of Marxist thought, people became accustomed to describing entire social orders as "capitalist" or "socialist." Contra Marx, however, those terms refer not to the entirety of a social order but only to the economic dimension of it. The economic is important, to be sure, but it is not all-important. The dimension we call political, one might argue, is at least as important, and the cultural is more important than both. It is true that the spheres that we call economic, cultural, and political overlap and interact in complicated ways, but making distinctions—not, be it noted, separations!—between the spheres is critically important if we are to free ourselves from our present confusions.

Those who seized upon socialist concepts and rhetoric in order to have a place to stand, as it were, from which they could criticize the societies of which they were part were by no means entirely wrong. American society, for instance, is sorely in need of sustained and careful criticism. The argument for democratic capitalism is a thoroughly reformist argument. As Novak and others have persistently contended, democratic capitalism is not the submission to the free and unfettered market that is favored by those who call themselves libertarians. It is not what most people mean by laissez-faire capitalism. Nor is commitment to democratic capitalism a defense of the status quo. Rather, democratic capitalism is an ongoing experiment in adjusting the relationship between three "systems"—the political, the economic, and the moral-cultural.

People who have now lost the cognitive securities once provided by their socialist attachments need not fear that this means they have lost their capacity to criticize what must be criticized in society. The place to take a critical stand, however, is no longer with the catastrophe of "real socialism" nor with the mythology of "ideal socialism" but with the moral-cultural traditions that bring all societies under judgment. One of the truly monumental human misfortunes of the last century is that Marxism succeeded in presenting itself as the only intellectually respectable perspective by which modern societies could be subjected to critical judgment.

The churches, Protestant and Catholic, share a large measure of responsibility for this misfortune. With few exceptions, Christian leadership denied the moral legitimacy of democratic capitalism. Of course, there were significant disagreements among such Christians. The chief differences, however, were over whether to favor the hard or soft versions of socialism—or, in the case of many Catholics, whether to reject modernity *tout court* in favor of sundry traditionalist, anarchist, syndicalist, or distributist schemes (cf. Hilaire Belloc, G. K. Chesterton, Dorothy Day, and, it must acknowledged, some papal pronouncements). The only agreement, as fixed as religious dogma, was that capitalism was irredeemably wrongheaded and would have to go.

For good and necessary reasons, "critical consciousness" is deemed very important in the intellectual life. The misfortune is that Marxism was granted a copyright on critical consciousness. In progressive Christian circles, analysis that was "systemic" and "critical" was assumed to be Marxist analysis. In hard-core liberationism, Christian theology seemed eager to commit suicide by embracing the doctrine that theology—along with ideas of divine revelation, the spiritual life, and eternal salvation—was but the "superstructure" that either served or hindered the *really real world* that was the class struggle revealed by Marxism. Now it is becoming obvious to all but the purblind that these bizarre constructions of reality have been, as the Marxists used to say, consigned to the dustbin of history.

Critical consciousness is now being freed from its long captivity to Marxist delusion. With this change comes a fresh capacity to criticize what needs to be criticized in the social orders of which we are part. In one important respect, however, such criticism is now more difficult. There is no alternative paradigm, called socialism, to which we can readily point. Our problems are really our own, they have no easy answers, and they will be with us for the duration. There is a parallel with the way that people cope or refuse to cope with their personal problems. Faced by myriad difficulties, many claim that they are the victims of some dreadful genetic or social injustice, that their problem is that they are not somebody else. So it was convenient to say that our problems were due to our being a capitalist society, and the remedy was to become a socialist society. That convenient "remedy" is no longer available, neither in practice nor in theory. There is no "somebody else" for us to be. Even more sobering, those other societies that once proposed themselves as the paradigm by which we could remake ourselves into somebody else are in a desperate hurry to become like us.

WHAT SHOULD NOT BE MISSED

When *Centesimus Annus* was issued on May 1, 1991 (May Day will never be the same), the press generally reported it as a "sharply qualified" endorsement of the free market. If we are to believe some reporters, it was in fact an attack on capitalism. Journalistic attention focused on what the Pope had to say about "consumerism." And indeed he was nothing if not forthright about the evils of consumerism. What was usually missed in early reports and later interpretations of the encyclical, however, is that the threat that consumerism poses to the affluent is one result of the success of the market economy. In other words, John Paul is making an economic argument, but, more importantly, he is also making a cultural and moral argument. He is not so much criticizing an economic system as he is warning against the excesses that the efficient working of that system makes possible.

Among the responses to Marxism, John Paul writes, is that of "the affluent or consumer society." "It seeks to defeat Marxism on the level of pure materialism by showing how a free-market society can achieve a greater satisfaction of material human needs than Communism, while equally excluding spiritual values. In reality, while on the one hand it is true that this social model shows the failure of Marxism to contribute to a humane and better society, on the other hand, insofar as it denies an autonomous existence and value to morality, law, culture and religion, it agrees with Marxism in the sense that it totally reduces man to the sphere of economics and the satisfaction of material needs" (¶ 19).

Consumerism is, quite precisely, the consuming of life by the things consumed. It is living in a manner that is measured by "having" rather than "being." As John Paul makes clear, consumerism is hardly the exclusive sin of the rich. The poor, driven by discontent and envy, may be as consumed by what they do not have as the rich are consumed by what they do have. The question is not, certainly not most importantly, a question about economics. It is first of all a cultural and moral problem requiring a cultural and moral remedy. "Of itself," the Pope writes, "an economic system does not possess criteria for correctly distinguishing new and higher forms of satisfying human needs from artificial new needs which hinder the formation of a mature personality" (¶ 36).

John Paul's spirited critique is directed against all who would, as he says, reduce human beings to the merely economic. It is therefore directed against both Marxists and those whom he at one point calls "radical capitalists." Those who advocate "radical capitalism," including those in America who call themselves libertarians, often tend to the view that the entire society can and should be ordered by market choices. In the European context, that view is commonly identified with "liberalism." *"Rerum Novarum,"* the Pope writes, "criticizes two social and economic systems: socialism and liberalism" (¶ 10). And John Paul leaves no doubt that he joins fully in that criticism.

The sociologist Peter Berger has written impressively about the intellectual task of "debunking the debunkers." Intellectuals have commonly understood their job to be that of showing people that the world, and the way they behave in the world, is not what they think it is. The job of the intellectual is to debunk the assumptions of the less enlightened. Among the debunking projects that many intellectuals prosecute most gleefully is that of demonstrating that how we live and order our life together is finally a matter of economics. We may think that we are making cultural and moral decisions of consequence, but that is simply an indulgence of "false consciousness." Our lives are, in fact, but the playthings of economic forces. The structure of economic relationships is the phenomenon and everything else is only "epiphenomenal." Thus are our pretensions to the dignity of being moral agents debunked. In *Centesimus Annus*, John Paul fits quite nicely Berger's definition of the intellectual as a debunker of the debunkers.

It is the moral and cultural, and finally the religious and spiritual, that matter most, he insists. When, for instance, he excoriates consumerism, he is talking about human sinfulness, a phenomenon that cannot be reduced to economic analysis of either the left or the right. He calls for a thorough deflation of the economic, the inflation of which has bedeviled so much thought in this century. "These criticisms," he writes, "are directed not so much against an economic system as against an ethical and cultural system. The economy in fact is only one aspect and one dimension of the whole of human activity." When producing and consuming goods becomes the meaning of life, "the reason is to be found not so much in the economic system itself as in the fact that the entire sociocultural system, by ignoring the ethical and religious dimension, has been weakened and ends by limiting itself to the production of goods and services alone" (¶ 39).

THE NEW OLD AND OLD NEW

This T-shirt legend was espied in a suburban mall: I SHOP, THEREFORE I AM. Only the most materialistic of cretins would not be offended. But is this, then, all that the Pope is saying? Is he in this encyclical taking twenty-seven thousand words simply to reiterate the maxim of Jesus that "man does not live by bread alone"? Isn't he saying anything *new?* If something isn't new, we are inclined to think that it must not be very interesting. In fact, most of the really interesting questions in life—beginning with the meaning, if any, of life itself—are far from new. The greatest novels, plays, and philosophical treatises have been devoted to the restatement of great truths that should be obvious but obviously are not, such as, "Man does not live by bread alone." At one level, then, we might say that the Pope is not saying much that is new.

It may not be new, but it is new to many people. It may not be new, but it is of immeasurable importance and interest. It is new that a pope is saying what this Pope is saying. It is new that it is being said in the context of the "new things" at this edge of the third millennium. It is new in that only now with the collapse of socialism is it possible to debunk the puffed-up conceits and pretensions of an imperiously economic analysis of the human condition. Without such a debunking, ironically enough, it is not possible to do justice even to the economic factor. "Socialism" and "capitalism" were, at least as presented by socialist theorists, huge conceptual abstractions that claimed to explain everything, and ended up by confusing everything. Only by relativizing economics, by knocking it down to its proper size, can we get a grasp on economics. Only then can we understand how the economic factor interacts with other, and immeasurably more important, dimensions of human existence.

Only after economics itself has been put into its place, so to speak, does John Paul proceed with his careful affirmations. "It would appear that on the level of individual nations and of international relations the free market is the most efficient instrument for utilizing resources and effectively responding to needs." He then immediately adds, "But there are many human needs that find no place on the market" (¶ 34). And, as we shall see, the needs that cannot be left to the market are the needs most essential to human dignity and fulfillment.

Even in terms of what an economic system can do, capitalism is at present not doing the job that it should. "We have seen," the Pope writes, "that it is unacceptable to say that the defeat of 'real socialism' leaves capitalism as the only model of economic organization" (¶ 35). Socialism, he makes abundantly clear, cannot be an alternative model. But the model presented by capitalism as it operates now is failing in important tasks, notably in the task of including the world's poor in what John Paul calls the circle of productivity and exchange. The urgent message of this encyclical is that the work of democratic capitalism has hardly begun. In the real world to which the Pope directs our attention, it would seem that despite his disclaimer, capitalism is "the only model of economic organization." The possible confusion on this point is clarified as he goes on to indicate that there is capitalism, and then there is capitalism.

"Can it perhaps be said," the Pope asks himself and us, "that after the failure of communism capitalism is the victorious social system and that capitalism should be the goal of the countries now making efforts to rebuild their economy and society?" It depends on what is meant by capitalism. "If by 'capitalism' is meant an economic system that recognizes the fundamental and positive role of business, the market, private property, and the resulting responsibility for the means of production, as well as free human creativity in the economic sector, then the answer is certainly in the affirmative, even though it would perhaps be more appropriate to speak of a 'business economy,' 'market economy,' or simply 'free economy.'"

John Paul hastens to add, "But if by 'capitalism' is meant a system in which freedom in the economic sector is not circumscribed within a strong juridical framework that places it at the service of human freedom in its totality and that sees it as a particular aspect of that freedom, the core of which is ethical and religious, then the reply is certainly negative" (¶ 42). Here, then, are two economic systems, both called capitalism. The first is to be affirmed, also as "the goal of the countries now making efforts to rebuild their economy and society." The second is to be rejected.

In this view, our moral responsibility is to work for an ever-closer approximation of the first capitalism. The second capitalism may work fine in some purely economic functions, but it refuses to let the purely economic be relativized by the priority of the cultural, especially the "ethical and religious." We will be coming back to what John Paul thinks are legitimate and illegitimate limits on the market economy, but the noteworthy point here is that *the choice is between two capitalisms.* Socialism is simply not in play as an option. At least for a time, until the utopian impulse again erupts and proposes another "simple and radical solution" for the problems attending the human condition—although it seems unlikely that the solution will then be called socialism.

CAPITALIST BAGGAGE

It will not escape the attention of the reader that John Paul's affirmation of capitalism is very carefully phrased. He says it "would perhaps be more appropriate" to speak of the business economy, the market economy, or simply the free economy. One suspects he is not merely expressing an aesthetic preference here. The term "capitalism," as we have seen, carries an enormous weight of historical baggage. In the view of many people, the cold war was a conflict between freedom and unfreedom. In the view of others, it was a struggle between capitalism and socialism. Both views are no doubt simplistic, since there are numerous factors engaged in an international conflict of such complexity. One might be inclined to think, however, that the first simplism is closer to the truth than the second.

In any event, the integrity and credibility of the Church's witness require that it maintain a measure of critical distance, never letting itself become unqualifiedly identified with or captive to one party in temporal conflicts. In the conflict between freedom and unfreedom, there is no doubt about where the Church stands. To the extent that in the cold war, the West represented freedom and the East unfreedom, the Church unquestionably declared itself for the West. If the conflict is construed in terms of socialism versus capitalism, John Paul, it seems, is strongly for capitalism. Yet the suggestion is that he prefers to affirm "the free economy." The reason for the preference, apparently, is that much that happens in the name of capitalism is morally unacceptable. One might observe, however, that the free economy *is* capitalism, and capitalism *is* the free economy. At least that is what proponents of capitalism have always asserted. We may call it the free economy rather than capitalism, but, precisely because it is free, it facilitates and often encourages people choosing the evils that John Paul deplores.

So is more involved here than simply a quibble over terminology? After the passing of the nightmare of "real socialism," the proponents of capitalism will no doubt continue to champion "capitalism" precisely because it is the way of the "free economy." John Paul is clearly aware that given the alternatives thrown up by the experience of the modern world, the way of the free economy is the way of capitalism. Yet he must prefer the language of free economy rather than that of capitalism in order to maintain a measure of critical distance; in order, putting it very bluntly, to make clear that the Catholic Church is not a religiomoral cheering squad for capitalism's new world order. The Church's witness, directed always to the coming Kingdom of God, must never be uncritically identified with any existing or proposed social order short of that goal. It was a great mistake for Christians to say that "socialism is the economics of which Christianity is the religion." It would also be a great mistake for the Church to say that "capitalism is the economics of which Christianity is the religion."

Whether called the free economy, the market economy, or the business economy, capitalism will never be morally satisfactory. The bracing message of *Centesimus* is that no economic system—or political or cultural system—will be satisfactory short of the genuinely new order of the Kingdom. The free economy leaves people free to do bad things. In many respects it panders to base instincts. In addition, it must be admitted that the business economy does not appeal to the moral imagination in the way that politics can appeal to a transforming vision of a new humanity. Profit-seeking, for instance, is in itself neither pretty nor edifying. Yet, as John Paul says, profits are necessary to the functioning of the free economy. Further, there is no way a market economy can be prevented from pandering to the human propensity for making debasing choices. Political and cultural forces can discourage people from making wrong choices, but that must be done in a way that does not destroy the free market itself.

There is, then, an inescapable dilemma here. *Centesimus* invites us to face it unflinchingly. The free market is the economic order appropriate to humanity in all its ambiguity. Human beings are endowed with reason, virtue, and grace but are also wounded by sin and inclined to evil. The market has no morality of its own; it simply reflects the morality and immorality of those who participate in it. The common good (emphatically a moral category!) therefore depends upon the vitality of the political and, above all, moral-cultural spheres. The political, driven by the moral-cultural, can to a limited extent tame and direct the economic, but it must do so in a way that does not enervate the freedom of the free market. Contrary to the beliefs of both socialists and libertarians, there is no way out of this complicated interaction between the economic, the political, and the cultural. The interaction of spheres requires constant attention, which is one reason why the order is called *democratic* capitalism. Its workings are always to be subjected to the robust and often raucous debate that is appropriate in a democratic polity.

A M I L L E N N I A L   V I S I O N

We have all heard it said that the Catholic Church thinks in terms of centuries. It is in the business not of historically contingent judgments but of eternal verities. Some readers of *Centesimus Annus* may find it disconcerting that John Paul does in fact devote much of his reflection to the historically contingent, especially to the events surrounding the Revolution of 1989. At the same time, however, it is obvious that he is thinking in terms of centuries. Most particularly, he is thinking of the first century of the coming third millennium. In numerous statements throughout his pontificate this Pope has referred to the coming third millennium in a manner that some observers have described as mystical. That is probably not the right word for it, but John Paul clearly senses that something momentous is afoot in the context of world history. He has alluded to the third millennium as a time that holds high promise of "a new springtime" for everything from world evangelization to Christian unity. And so also in the present encyclical he evokes that sense of promise with respect to the expansion of democratically free societies benefiting from the free economy.

The long-term future of democratic and economic freedom requires that the logic of freedom be secured in the faith and piety of the Christian people. The Pope calls for what might be described as a spirituality of freedom, including economic enterprise. Here we must be careful. It is necessary to avoid the "sacralizing" of any social order—also the order of democracy and the market economy—in a way that could lead to making that order an "idol." The Church has lived and flourished under many different social systems. We need to be reminded that Christian faith has often been most vibrant under the worst of social systems. From the persecution of the early Church in the Roman Empire to the millions of martyrs under the evil empire that was Communism, Christian witness to the Light of the World has often been most luminous in times of deepest darkness.

Some might draw the perverse conclusion that it therefore follows that Christians should welcome despotic and unjust regimes because they present such marvelous opportunities for the testing of the faith. The romantic appeal of a "return to the catacombs" is a perennial temptation for immature Christians. Indulging such romanticism may provide a *frisson* of radical discipleship, but it is to ignore our most elementary duty of love for our neighbor. Setting aside romantic daydreams, we are called to the more everyday and demanding work of establishing social orders that are in accord with "the defense of the human person and the safeguarding of human dignity" (¶ 3). This does not, however, mean building heaven on earth.

One gathers that the Pope has no illusions about the difficulty of the task or the certainty of its success. "Amid changing historical circumstances, this movement [in defense of human dignity] has contributed to the building up of a more just society, or at least to the curbing of injustice" (¶ 3). The last part of that is important. Sometimes, indeed most of the time, we will fail in our efforts to establish what is worthy of being called a just society. We nonetheless strive toward a *more* just society, knowing that for most of us it will be work enough to curb injustice. For the Christian, taking care of business in a free economy is working for justice and for the curbing of injustice.

GOD LOVETH ADVERBS

Of course, there is taking care of business and then there is taking care of business. It depends not only on what we do but on how we do it. Joseph Hall, a seventeenth-century Puritan preacher, put it this way:

> The homeliest service that we doe in an honest calling, though it be but to plow, or digge, if done in obedience, and conscience of God's Commandment, is crowned with an ample reward; whereas the best workes for their kinde (preaching, praying, offering Evangelicall sacrifices) if without respect of God's injunction and glory, are loaded with curses. God loveth adverbs; and cares not how good, but how well.

God loveth adverbs. The implication is that we are to take care of business conscientiously, fairly, honestly, lovingly, and, yes, even prayerfully. To many in the business world that may seem impossibly idealistic. What do love and prayer have to do with sales reports, corporate takeovers, management studies, and reducing inventories? It would seem that Christians should have an answer to that question. One might suggest that the Church has a serious pastoral responsibility to help people answer that question, for occupations that are pursued "without respect of God's injunction and glory, are loaded with curses."

Let it be readily admitted: the churches have generally done a deplorable job of enabling people in business to work adverbially to the glory of God and love of neighbor. What is needed, it

seems, is a spirituality of economic enterprise. Consider the
Catholic case. In a provocative essay titled "American Catholicism and the Capitalist Ethic," George Weigel addresses himself
to a hypothetical chief executive officer of a major corporation.
This person is serious about the faith and generous in supporting the Church and other charitable activities. He is marginally
aware of priests and theologians who claim that his entire life's
work is a project of oppression directed against the poor, but he
doesn't believe it and doesn't let it bother him too much. Like
good laymen are supposed to be, he is content to pray, pay, and
try to obey. Isn't that enough? Weigel doesn't think so. He asks:

> But what about your daily activities? Do you hear or read anything
> from the formal religious leadership of the church that could be
> construed as a moral, theological, and spiritual legitimation of your
> efforts to create wealth? Your entrepreneurial energies have made
> jobs available to others. Your success has meant success—in invest-
> ments, in employment, in personal satisfaction—for thousands of
> your employees and shareholders. Through the tax system, and
> through your philanthropic activities, you are making a significant
> contribution to the common good. What does your Catholicism
> have to say about all that?

Weigel answers, "If the truth be told, it probably doesn't
have much to say at all. And, if a further truth be told, that
probably doesn't worry you very much." Weigel's point, and I
daresay John Paul's, is that this situation should be worrying. It
is spiritually eviscerating that what millions of men and women
do fifty or seventy hours of most every week is bracketed off
from their understanding of their faith. What do people mean
when they say they offer their lives to God if the most important
activity in those lives—next to the family or, all too often, even
more than the family—is not included in the offering? Of

course, they might say that the fruit of that activity is offered in the form of money. As spiritually important as the money offering is, it might be pointed out, the Sunday "collection" is no substitute for a life lived with "respect of God's injunction and glory." And economic enterprise that is not grounded in a sense of moral legitimacy and urgency will always be easy prey for the ideological attacks of the cultured despisers of business.

Especially since the 1950s, Catholics, once viewed as the unwashed immigrant hordes, have done extremely well in America. We are told that Irish Catholics in particular are next only to Jews in the ranking of economic success. It would appear that there was nothing in the popular spirituality of American Catholicism prior to the Second Vatican Council that got in the way of the quest for economic success. The Church's emphasis on education, the traditional family, and personal discipline, joined to a perhaps tribal eagerness to demonstrate that Catholics could beat Protestants at their own game, all seemed to have contributed powerfully to economic advance. While a spirituality of economic enterprise may not have been necessary for economic success, one might argue that economic success now makes a spirituality of economic enterprise necessary. The alternative may be the morally corrosive pattern of capitalism with a bad conscience.

A STORY OF CATHOLICS, AND OTHERS

What brought us to the present pass is illuminated by a little history. It is a Catholic story, to be sure, but others can readily identify with important parts of it. The Catholic story is in significant ways paradigmatic of the experience of millions of Americans who do not trace their line back to the original Protestant establishments of Massachusetts and Virginia. To be sure, the Catholic story began with a kind of establishment, however modest. In 1776 there were about thirty-five thousand Catholics in the newly proclaimed United States of America (0.8 percent of the population). They were mainly in Maryland, with Catholic enclaves in New York, Pennsylvania, and the French settlements west of the Alleghenies. If there was a Catholic establishment, it was the Carroll family of Maryland. John Carroll was the first Catholic bishop in America, and his cousin, Charles Carroll, was the last surviving signer of the Declaration of Independence. At his death, Charles was said to be the wealthiest individual in the entire country.

Archbishop John Carroll of Baltimore worked assiduously and spoke eloquently to advance the claim that Catholics both belonged and had a deep stake in the American experiment. Indeed, elements of his ringing endorsement of what the Founders viewed as "a new order for the ages" (the Great Seal's *novus ordo seclorum*) would a century later be shadowed by the Vatican censure of ideas associated with "Americanism." Carroll's voice, while newly relevant to Catholicism in America today, was soon to be drowned out. The Catholic establishment of Maryland, Weigel writes, was "quickly displaced by the waves of immigration that, beginning in the early nineteenth century, engulfed and transformed the American Catholic community."

The "wretched refuse" of the Old World that was Catholic, largely Irish, immigration was ill prepared for the rigors of an industrial revolution then in full swing. The remarkable success of the Church in helping the immigrants to adjust to the New World is a story that has yet to be told adequately. In dramatic contrast with the situation in Europe, the Church here did not lose what was then called the laboring classes. There are many theories why socialism did not gain a popular following in America. One obvious but often overlooked reason was immigrant identification with the Church. Already in the nineteenth century, the "working class" or the "proletariat" provided a kind of church, a primary community of "solidarity," for millions of people. American Catholics were different. They already had a church. Their allegiance to the Catholic Church and its Mass worked against their enlistment in the revolution of "the masses."

The ecclesiastical context, however, did not nurture a spirituality of capitalist enterprise. They were, after all, working people. Owners and managers might be preoccupied with the production of wealth; Catholic immigrants were concerned about "three squares a day" and the chance for their children to be a little better off. Moreover, the ways of capitalism, no matter how productive, were suspiciously Protestant. In the first part of the last century Catholics had fewer voices more articulate than that of Archbishop John ("Dagger John") Hughes of New York. In a lecture on the industrial revolution and the state of workers, he underscored the enormous gap between the rich and the poor. Weigel notes that the following observations were about England, but Hughes' fear was that America would repeat the English experience:

> These are results which puzzle political economists, but which never could have happened, if Political Economy had not been transferred from the Christian basis on which it was originally reared in that country, to the inadequate foundations of mere individual interest. I am willing, then, to ascribe to the Protestant religion the credit of England's wealth; but her poverty, and the destitution of her millions, must, I insist upon it, be charged to the same account.

Capitalism came at the too high price of abandoning the social and economic order of the Middle Ages, and required an embrace of the radical individualism associated with the Protestant heretics. Profit, many clerics contended, was the result of a morally reprehensible unbridling of greed and selfishness. Only a society grounded in Catholic teaching and piety could inculcate the duties of charity and direct human energies to the common good. Hughes' strictures against capitalism were temperate compared with the polemic of the influential convert Orestes

Brownson. One captures something of Brownson's disposition in an 1840 blast:

> The owner who is involved in the systematic exploitation of poor laborers is frequently one of our respectable citizens; perhaps he is praised in the newspapers for his liberal donations to some charitable institution. He passes among us as a pattern of morality, and is honored as a worthy Christian . . . It is for the interest of the trader to cheat—to buy under value and to sell over value; it is for the interest of the master to oppress the workman . . . Thus is the interest of one opposed to the interest of the other . . . Wages is a cunning device of the devil, for the benefit of tender consciences who would retain all the advantages of the slave system, without the experience, trouble, and odium of being slaveholders.

No spirituality of economic enterprise there. Hughes, Brownson, and others were no doubt motivated by passionate concern about the sorry plight of many workers. They, like many who were to follow them, attributed what was wrong to "capitalism." At the same time, however, they left no doubt capitalism was part and parcel of the deeper problem of the modern world. At the heart of modernity is what social scientists call the "differentiation" of societal functions. In *Centesimus Annus*, John Paul calls it, approvingly, the distinction between "spheres of sovereignty."

A MONISTIC PREFERENCE

In the first half of the nineteenth century, the Church was not ready to make peace with this aspect of modernity. Catholic thinkers looked back longingly to a world in which there was a more intimate bond between the Church, on the one hand, and the culture, economy, and polity, on the other. It was a more monistic vision of society or, as today's jargon has it, a holistic vision. They wanted a social order that could be understood, in which things held together, in which things made sense in a readily accessible way. Historically, a monistic preference has driven both antimodernism and socialism. A great attraction of Marxist socialism is that it promised both modernity and a communal solidarity that could satisfy humankind's monistic hungers.

Communal solidarity, for all but a few Catholic immigrants, was supplied by the Church. Communal solidarity was such that it posed no problem for major figures such as Archbishops John Ireland of St. Paul and James Gibbons of Baltimore to be on very friendly terms with rich capitalists, including a few Catholics who were beginning to get the knack of the Protestant game. But these prelates never forgot that their people were, after all, workers, and by the end of the nineteenth century workers were organizing for their rights. In the 1880s, some of the hierarchy, alarmed by labor violence, moved to have the Vatican condemn the Knights of Labor. Gibbons intervened with Rome and in 1887 prevented a condemnation, although the Holy Office's allowance that the Knights could be "tolerated" was accompanied by severe cautions against labor radicalism, underscoring the moral necessity of respecting "the right of private property."

Weigel writes: "Gibbons's intervention in the Knights of Labor controversy established a pattern of support between the American hierarchy and the American trade union movement that continues to this day—a pattern that, although not precluding the development of an ethic of wealth creation, mitigated against it because of a primary focus on issues of wealth distribution." The 1919 Bishops' Program for Social Reconstruction was condemned by the National Association of Manufacturers as "partisan, pro–labor union, socialistic propaganda." To the extent that the mainstream labor movement in America represented the left, the left became synonymous with social justice in official American Catholic thought.

The Bishops' Program was the brainchild of Monsignor John A. Ryan of Catholic University, who twenty years later would be celebrated as "The Right Reverend New Dealer." Ryan's close alliance with labor and the Democratic Party, joined to his emphasis on the distribution rather than the production of wealth, established a lasting tradition. It is very much alive today in the United States Catholic Conference and in the work of such a venerable stalwart as Monsignor George Higgins, a prominent commentator on Catholic social thought and one of the last in a line of "labor priests" who earned their medals in the battles of the American version of the class struggle between labor and management. The fact that the American struggle was, compared with those of most European countries, so temperate is due in no small part to the role played by the Catholic Church and priests such as Monsignor Higgins.

Meanwhile, official teaching from Rome was also evolving in accord with the development of social doctrine. While in *Rerum Novarum* Leo XIII called down a pox on the houses of both socialism and liberalism (i.e., capitalism), the more noxious pox was invoked on socialism. In 1931, Pius XI (*Quadragesimo Anno*) came out for "corporatism," which was taken to be a "third way" between capitalism and socialism, and bore an embarrassing similarity (embarrassing at least in retrospect) to aspects of Mussolini's Fascist order. The Second Vatican Council (notably in the 1965 "Pastoral Constitution on the Church in the Modern World") moved toward a differentiation of the social order. There one can find the seeds of democratic capitalism's distinctions between economy, culture, and politics, but the emphasis of the Council was still much more on wealth distribution than on wealth creation, and the problem of poverty was to be addressed chiefly, it appears, by the transfer of goods from the rich to the poor.

The last theme was dramatically reinforced by Paul VI's encyclical of 1968, *Populorum Progressio*. Paul did not say so explicitly, but the encyclical was thought by many to invite the conclusion that capitalism and the capitalist model of world development are inherently and irredeemably unjust and exploitative. Liberation theologians in Latin America and elsewhere, along with a good many Catholic intellectuals of a less activist bent, were quick to pick up on the perceived invitation.

At the end of this all-too-brief historical excursus on why Catholicism has not developed a vibrant spirituality of economic enterprise, we return to the conclusion drawn by George Weigel, written, be it noted, before *Centesimus Annus:*

> Still, there is more readiness for such an evolution [of an ethic of wealth creation] in contemporary American Catholicism than there has been at any time in our history. The immigrant church of the working class has been transformed into the suburban church of the middle and upper middle class. That transformation is not without its own difficulties and tensions; but it also creates the sociological conditions for the possibility of such an ethic. Whether that opportunity will be seized—for the benefit of the poor, as well as for the moral legitimation of the entrepreneur—is, of course, another question.

DOCTRINE RETHOUGHT

There is reason to believe that that opportunity has been seized by John Paul II, as witness *Centesimus Annus*. The argument of *Centesimus* came as something of a surprise, although there were intimations of it in the Pope's earlier statements, notably in the 1987 encyclical, *Sollicitudo Rei Socialis*. While the breakthrough to the development of a spirituality of economic enterprise did not come directly out of the American context, *Centesimus* demonstrates an unprecedented sensitivity to the dynamics of the American social order. The chief impetus for the encyclical came, of course, from the quite unpredictable events associated with the Revolution of 1989.

Those developments occasioned, even forced, a thorough re-thinking of Catholic social doctrine regarding the economy. From that rethinking came the unfolding of truths that were always there but not previously developed in the tradition, as well as insights that must be described as new. Observers also note, however, that because of the Vatican's concern for churches under Communist oppression, the more antisocialist aspects of Catholic teaching were frequently muted in public statements. After 1989, they say, the Church was free to say what was in the teaching all along. There is no doubt some merit to that observation.

The sociologically transformed circumstance of Catholicism in this country gives American Catholics a particular opportunity and obligation to cultivate the spirituality of enterprise set forth by John Paul II. This, too, is part of a "Catholic Moment" in which it would seem that Catholics can make a singular contribution to a society that is increasingly unable to define its common good, and is even lacking the language for debating such a definition. Sociological transformation, however, would also require spiritual transformation. In the Catholic context, that would seem to mean a fuller understanding of, and deeper allegiance to, the living tradition of the Church. In the next chapter we look at teaching authority in the Catholic Church, and at *Centesimus* in particular, asking what such a transformation might mean for Catholics, and what it could help Catholicism mean for America in a postsocialist world that must make the choice between "two capitalisms."

NOTES

Page 47. Paul Hollander, *Political Pilgrims*, Oxford University Press, 1986.

Pages 47–48. Tillich on the Christian necessity of being socialist is quoted in Michael Novak, *The Spirit of Democratic Capitalism*, Madison, 1991. On capitalism as demonic, see Paul Tillich, *Political Expectations*, Harper & Row, 1971.

Page 48. Keynes, *The End of Laissez Faire*, Hogarth Press (London), 1927.

Page 61. Joseph Hall is quoted in *Sources of the Self*, by Charles Taylor, Harvard, 1989.

Page 62. George Weigel, "American Catholicism and the Capitalist Ethic," in *The Capitalist Spirit: Toward a Religious Ethic of Wealth Creation*, edited by Peter L. Berger, Institute for Contemporary Studies (San Francisco), 1990.

Page 65. Weigel, op. cit.

Page 69. For an analysis of *Sollicitudo Rei Socialis* that illuminates some of the themes later developed in *Centesimus Annus*, see *Aspiring to Freedom*, edited by Kenneth A. Myers, Eerdmans, 1988.

Part Two

Chapter Three

. . .

LIVING THE
TRADITION

Among Catholics and non-Catholics alike, there is today wide-spread puzzlement about teaching authority in the Church, and especially about papal teaching authority. In this chapter and the next I do not pretend to offer a definitive treatment of the many and important questions raised by such teaching authority. The purpose, rather, is to suggest a way of thinking about a document such as *Centesimus Annus* and how it should be interpreted. In the second half of this book (Chapters Five through Ten), I make bold to set forth such an interpretation, sometimes with very specific reference to public policy disputes in our society. I emphasize—and critics will no doubt reinforce the point—that mine is *an* interpretation, not necessarily *the* interpretation. Before getting to that eminently disputable interpretation, however, we should try to understand what kind of document an encyclical is and how we should go about applying it to our own circumstances.

   An encyclical is, quite simply, a letter that is to be circulated. Paul's letters in the New Testament might be called encyclicals, since they were circulated among the churches. So also a pastoral letter issued by the bishops of the United States—such as the 1986 letter, *Economic Justice for All*—might be called an encyclical. As the term has been used since Benedict XIV in the eighteenth century, however, only popes write encyclicals. A papal encyclical carries more weight of authority than a pastoral letter or apostolic exhortation, but not as much weight as, say, an apostolic constitution. Encyclicals are intended to be taken seriously by anyone who takes the pope seriously. It used to be that encyclicals were addressed to the bishops and, often, to the Catholic faithful. About thirty years ago, John XXIII began, and subsequent popes have continued, the practice of addressing encyclicals also to "all people of goodwill."

An encyclical is by no means an "infallible" pronouncement. The last pope who officially spoke in the infallible mode was Pius XII when in 1950 he promulgated the dogma of the bodily assumption of the Virgin Mary. To say that an encyclical is not infallible, however, does not mean that it is no more than the pope's opinion. The Catholic Church teaches that the entire ministry of the papacy is attended by "the special assistance of the Holy Spirit." There is, therefore, a strong presumption of agreement with and obedience to papal pronouncements on matters of faith and morals. That is significantly more than simply saying that on matters of faith and morals, the pope should be given the benefit of the doubt. In 1950, Pius XII said, "In writing such letters the popes do not exercise the supreme power of their teaching authority." That language was adopted by Vatican Council II in the "Constitution on the Church." The Council pointedly did not adopt Pius' additional statement that when an encyclical takes a stand on a controverted subject, the subject "can no longer be regarded as a matter for free debate among theologians."

M ORE   THAN   A NOTHER   O PINION

The *effective* authority of encyclicals was weakened by the reaction to *Humanae Vitae*, which deals with human sexuality and was issued by Paul VI in 1968. Liberal or "progressive" Catholics—and that includes most of the theological establishment—vigorously and publicly protested that encyclical's teaching, especially on contraception. According to some students of Catholicism in America, the reaction to *Humanae Vitae* did more than any other one thing to undermine confidence in the teaching authority of the pope. *The Encyclopedic Dictionary of Religion*, published under Catholic auspices, blithely states, "The consensus today is that no generalization may be made about the teaching authority of encyclicals. Each must be judged on its individual merits." We may confidently assume that John Paul II was not consulted in the establishment of that consensus.

The fact remains, however, that even those Catholics who incline to the view that an encyclical is little more than the pope's opinion on this or that still quote papal pronouncements —sometimes very selectively—to show that the pope is "on our side." Likewise, some "traditionalist" Catholics who attribute near-infallibility to every papal utterance are, when faced with a disagreeable encyclical, skilled at explaining why the pope did not say what for all the world he appears to have said. Probably most Roman Catholics who read encyclicals at all try to accord them the respect due the chief teaching office in the Church. An encyclical is not the final word. It is not necessarily even the most felicitous word. But, in both theory and practical influence, it is far from being merely one opinion among others.

An additional factor is that this Pope, more than his predecessors, has employed encyclicals not so much to set forth authoritative teaching as to invite reflection. For example, *Redemptoris Mater*, a reflection on Mary's role in the Christian life, and *Dominum et Vivificantem*, a reflection on the work of the Holy Spirit, are for the most part theological-devotional exercises. They are more in the nature of spiritual writings than of pedagogical or juridical pronouncements. In almost all of his writings, and certainly in *Centesimus* as well, John Paul combines various literary genres, and it is important to keep these interweaving styles in mind. The person who reads John Paul in search simply of propositions and rules will encounter frequent frustration. He invites the reader, rather, to join him in entering into a process of disciplined reflection. The mode is typically more personal than juridical, keeping always in mind, of course, that the person speaking is also the bearer of a teaching office that is authoritative for the entire Catholic community.

Communities of consequence perdure through time. That is to say, they have histories or traditions. As the oldest and largest institution in the world, the Catholic Church has an unparalleled sense of historical continuity and development. As Francis Canavan, S.J., makes clear in "The Popes and the Economy," *Centesimus* must be understood within a tradition of social teaching that dates at least from the 1891 encyclical of Leo XIII, *Rerum Novarum*, which this encyclical intends to commemorate. A pope must be almost painfully conscious of the continuity of tradition in everything he writes or says, and that consciousness is fully evident in *Centesimus*. At the same time, John Paul does not hesitate to indicate the points at which he is advancing the tradition, just as Leo XIII and other popes advanced the tradition in their time. In the writing of encyclicals, too, the axiom applies: One must change in order to conserve.

The question of continuity and discontinuity in Christian teaching is as old and troubled as is the history of the Church itself. Among the first disputes over this question is found in Acts 15, when the apostles had to decide about the continuity of the Christian community with the ritual observances prescribed by Judaism. It was a question that had not been specifically addressed in the teaching they had received from Jesus. It was a question that did not have to be decided until it became obvious that the Christian movement was not going to remain a Jewish sect. About the decision that they made the apostles expressed their confidence that "it seemed good to the Holy Spirit and to us." Two thousand years later, new questions, or old questions in new forms, require decisions that, Christians hope, will seem good not only to them but also to the Holy Spirit.

TAKING TIME FOR TRADITION

The question of continuity and discontinuity arises also in connection with the present encyclical. The newness of John Paul's firm endorsement of the free economy poses a problem for some interpreters of Catholic social teaching who have, especially in the last few decades, taken the tradition in quite different directions. This, as we earlier noted, is the case with those who thought the Church's teaching favored socialism, tilted toward socialism, or proposed a third way between socialism and capitalism. *Centesimus* cannot help but be disorienting to such thinkers. It has to be painful to contemplate all the books, tracts, and educational materials on Catholic social teaching that have now been rendered obsolete in important respects. What, in light of this encyclical, would seem to have been misinterpretations of the tradition were frequently advanced in the best of faith. It should also be readily acknowledged that earlier papal statements did not prepare the way for the argument of *Centesimus* as clearly as many might have wished.

It appears that everybody—except, presumably, the Pope and those who worked with him in the writing of the encyclical —was at least somewhat surprised by the direction of *Centesimus*. This is as true of those who were vindicated in their understanding of Catholic social teaching as it is of those who received such a severe jolt. For the latter, it will no doubt take some time before this development is thoroughly internalized. That, one might suggest, should not trouble anyone excessively. Time is what tradition is about. Tradition, if it is a *living* tradition, is also about development.

A few days after the encyclical was issued, one writer vigorously challenged a published commentary suggesting that

Centesimus firmly endorsed democratic capitalism. He allowed that he had not yet had a chance to read the encyclical, but, he insisted, he knew what this Pope thought on these questions and therefore the commentary in question must be wrong. It is worth noting that some who seem to be most disoriented by the alleged discontinuities between this encyclical and earlier papal teaching are enthusiastic about other discontinuities. They are, for instance, frequently the same people who have for years celebrated what they claim is the sharp discontinuity between the Second Vatican Council and what they typically call "the pre–Vatican II Church." The Church proposes, however, that its tradition is of a piece, although not always smoothly or self-evidently so. That is why it must be authoritatively interpreted.

The Center of Concern, a leftward Catholic institute in Washington, D.C., that claims to represent "the justice community," was manifestly distressed both by *Centesimus* and by the way it was being interpreted by the dread "neoconservatives." The Center attempts to put a favorable reading on the text, asserting, for instance, that John Paul's mention of "a certain equality" among peoples is a call for "a new world order in which supranational agencies—some form of world government —will provide the social controls necessary" to bring about economic justice. For the most part, however, the Center of Concern concludes that *Centesimus* leaves "the justice community" with "some perplexing concerns for ongoing reflection."

According to the Center's analysis, John Paul does not pay sufficient attention to the inequalities of wealth in the world, and runs the risk of "cultural imperialism" by affirming the universal importance of private property, market economics, and democratic polity. The fact that the Catholic Church is not itself organized along democratic lines, says the Center, "undermines the credibility of its claim that the dignity of the individual demands some form of democratic polity." The Center apparently cannot make up its mind whether the neoconservatives are misinterpreting *Centesimus* or are simply explaining a document for which they are in part responsible. "Their advance preparation and high-level media access," says *Center Focus,* "have done damage to the teaching tradition and a disservice to the church and to the U.S. public." Presumably, they have seriously misrepresented the encyclical. Later, however, we are told that "the neoconservatives helped to shape its content in addition to pre-empting its interpretation for the public." It is hard to have it both ways.

There is an understandable tendency to adopt a thoroughly selective attitude toward the development of teaching, and toward specific documents touching upon that development. People are inclined to applaud what confirms their own views and to resist what they find disagreeable. That phenomenon is hardly limited to life in the Church. One form of resistance is simple denial. And one form of denial is to say that there has, in fact, been no significant development. In the months following the appearance of *Centesimus,* there were what appeared to be many instances of such denial. We earlier noted the way in which the encyclical was generally reported in the press, suggesting that it was but "another" papal criticism of capitalism, and of American capitalism in particular.

Also in some scholarly circles there were claims that *Centesimus* did not say much that is new, that it was entirely in tune with the conventional wisdom in the Catholic academe and with earlier statements issuing from various Church bureaucracies. Such resistance is not surprising. Certainly it serves no useful purpose to get distracted by polemics, and it is unacceptably tedious to spend time in detailing the ways in which *Centesimus* throws familiar interpretations of Catholic social teaching into question. The argument of the encyclical can be engaged on its own terms, and the resistance to that argument might simply dissolve in time.

MOTHER AND TEACHER

Another group of Catholics might also be disturbed by the proposed development of teaching in *Centesimus*. They believe that the eternal verities taught by the Church do not change. The distinction between change and development quite escapes them. Some developments are so gradual as to be almost imperceptible. Others seem rapid, even breathtaking. Whether something is a change or a development is not a question of speed but of substance. The question is whether we can recognize in the new statement an unfolding and making explicit of what was implicit before. In any event, there is a formal continuity in the authority of the voice that is speaking. An editorial in the conservative *National Review* warmly welcomed the new encyclical. It was titled "Mater et Magistra, After All." The title alluded to an editorial years earlier on John XXIII's encyclical *Mater et Magistra*. That editorial was memorably titled, "Mater Si! Magistra No!" This is lively journalism but does not sit well with Catholic theology. The official teaching insists that deciding when one will and when one will not recognize the Church as both mother and teacher was as unacceptable in 1961 as in 1991.

At the same time, tradition that does not develop is dead. There is a critical difference between tradition and tradition*alism*. Here the bon mot of Jaroslav Pelikan, a Lutheran historian, is regularly and usefully invoked: "Tradition is the living faith of the dead. Traditionalism is the dead faith of the living." In 1845 John Henry Cardinal Newman drafted his last major work before becoming a Roman Catholic, *An Essay on the Development of Christian Doctrine*. Newman's formative insights, as he refined them decades later, have become part of orthodox Catholic teaching. Some conservative Catholics may be unhappy with *Centesimus* because of its measured approval of aspects of modernity. None should be unhappy, however, because it represents a clear, even bold, development of social doctrine. The idea of dynamic orthodoxy does not oppose development but aims to guide it in the way of an ever-fuller apprehension of the truth.

Among the most baneful untruths burdening the modern mind is the false antithesis between tradition and creativity. Tradition, it is supposed, has to do with the dead past while creativity is about the living present. Whether in the arts, the sciences, or even in theology, the creative person, we are told, is the one who defies tradition. But every field of human endeavor is itself a tradition. Only those who have immersed themselves in the tradition can creatively extend and develop the tradition. Creativity requires humility, which is the discipline of apprenticing oneself to the creativity of the past. The creativity of the ignorant and unpracticed is nothing more than "self-expression," which is, regrettably, what many mean by creativity today. A bawling child is engaged in self-expression. Adults who demand attention for their self-expression assume, usually without warrant, that they have very interesting selves to express. Truly interesting people are people who understand themselves to be serving a tradition, and interesting traditions are traditions that aspire to a truth or a good beyond themselves.

John Paul writes that he is proposing a "rereading" of the tradition. "A rereading of this kind will not only confirm the permanent value of such teaching, but will also manifest the true meaning of the Church's tradition, which, being ever living and vital, builds upon the foundation laid by our fathers in the faith and particularly upon what 'the apostles passed down to the Church' in the name of Jesus Christ, who is her irreplaceable foundation." He takes his inspiration, he says, from the image of "the scribe who has been trained for the kingdom of heaven," whom Jesus compares to "a householder who brings out of his treasure what is new and what is old" (¶ 3). The Pope invites people to read the encyclical as a kind of "Aha experience." Aha, they may say, so this is what the tradition has been leading up to. And, of course, the development has not ended with *Centesimus*. The living tradition of the Church, it is understood, will develop until Christ returns in glory. Every stage of the tradition is to point to that hope of humanity's ultimate and complete apprehension of the truth.

DEMOCRACY AND DELIBERATION

Every church and every community of consequence has to deal with the question of transmitting and interpreting tradition. Tradition is sustained identity through time. The Catholic Church has a particular understanding of how tradition is authoritatively transmitted and interpreted. Catholics recognize that other ways have been adopted by other churches, and at least some Catholics find those ways attractive by comparison with the Catholic way. In American Protestantism, churches typically determine their teaching through committees and conventions. Unlike the Catholic Church, they have no "magisterium" or authoritative teaching office. In the view of some Catholics, the Protestant way has the merit of being more "democratic."

As in the Center of Concern analysis mentioned above, the complaint is heard that since Vatican Council II, the Church has been blatantly inconsistent, if not hypocritical, on the question of democracy. It has many kind things to say about democracy in the political order but is adamant about maintaining a nondemocratic and hierarchical structure for governing the internal life of the Church. Differences over the merits of democratizing the life of the Church represent different ways of thinking about the Church—or, in more technical language, different ecclesiologies. If a church is essentially a voluntary association created by people of similar conviction and purpose, how to organize the association is up to the members who created it, and there may, in that case, be much to be said for democracy.

If the Church, however, is a community established by Christ with a structure of continuing apostolic authority, if it is the "Mystical Body of Christ" and "People of God" through time, a quite different approach to ordering its internal life would seem to follow. The Catholic Church very deliberately sees itself as a unique institution that is a "contrast structure" to all the social orders in which it finds itself. A democratic polity would be incompatible with what it understands to be its Divine constitution. Democracy is not designed to determine the truth but to achieve politically viable agreements on the basis of compromise over different versions of the truth. As John Paul argues in *Centesimus*, the possibility of democracy *presupposes* certain truths. It even presupposes certain truths that the Church proclaims. But democracy is not in the business of *determining* the truth. To recognize no truth other than the truth determined by majority vote is to recognize no truth at all.

In 1990 there was a considerable flap when the editorial writer for the *Philadelphia Inquirer*, much agitated over "abortion rights," declared that the Catholic Church was "un-American." There was predictable and fully justified protest by many Catholics who were incensed by such language, reminiscent of an earlier era of know-nothingness. If democratic determination of the truth is taken to be the characteristic mark of the American Way, however, the Catholic Church is indeed "un-American."

By the same token, every church and synagogue that understands itself to be bound by authority not of its own creation may be deemed un-American. In that case, the Founders who declared that "we hold these truths" were un-American, for the truths in question were not democratically determined but were the "self-evident" presuppositions that made our political order possible. Obviously, there is something drastically wrong with the logic that leads to the conclusion that the Founders were un-American. The alternative is to recognize that the truth of democracy requires something more than the truth of democracy. The truths upon which democracy depends are maintained by the "contrast structures" that, by their very nature, cannot be ordered by the principles of democracy.

Yet it is true that most religious groups in America, unlike

Catholicism, are organized according to a "free church" tradition and claim to be more or less democratic in the way they deliberate about the truth. Those who have some familiarity with these churches, however, know that they are not nearly so democratic as their organizational charts suggest. As the "permanent government" of the state is the bureaucracy, so the permanent government of these churches is generally located in national and regional bureaucracies. Committees are "democratically" selected with political care, and every effort is made to orchestrate the outcome of convention action. When there are real disagreements on questions of enormous moment, there is often no effective appeal beyond a majority vote. The minority either goes along, organizes politically to change the vote the next time around, or leaves to form another church. The history of American Protestantism is littered with the resulting schisms.

Whatever its other merits or demerits, the "democratic" way determines not the truth but the viewpoint that can politically impose itself as the will of the majority. To be sure, it can happen and often does happen that on this issue or that, the will of the majority will coincide with the truth. Despite the absence of an effective teaching authority, most Protestant churches have retained a remarkably large measure of what is historically defined as orthodox Christianity. In theory decisions are made by a democratic process that tries to accommodate private judgments, each appealing to scriptural authority. In reality most churches draw upon the reservoir of tradition even when they insist that they reject the authority of tradition. The most hard-shell "Bible only" Baptist, for example, typically accepts the teaching of the early church councils on the two natures of Christ and the Holy Trinity, even though these dogmatic formulations are not explicitly taught in the Bible. So more democratic forms of church government do not preclude the guidance of the Holy Spirit. Catholics persistently point out, however, that Jesus promised the Spirit's guidance not through majority rule but through the apostles and their successors.

FREEDOM ORDERED TO TRUTH

Few Catholics would deny that there are serious problems with the way the teaching authority in the Catholic Church actually functions. It seems almost quaint that there are still people around who think of Catholicism as a monolithic structure in which everybody walks in lockstep with the official line. Many Catholics, too, look back to the days when it was possible to view the Church in that way—some looking back in nostalgia, others in dread. But the Catholic Church is a multifarious, some would say many-splendored, thing. A communion of nearly a billion people encompassing every language, race, and culture is bound to be multifarious in its expression of the faith. In this sense, too, the Church is "catholic" in a manner that confounds the pretension of anyone who might claim to have mastered the diversity of its expression. The magisterium strives unflaggingly, but not always successfully, to make sure that in all this diversity, it is the one faith that is being expressed.

The teaching authority of pope and bishops is understood to be ordered in continuity with, and accountability to, the apostolic tradition. It strikes both Catholics and non-Catholics as odd when it is claimed that there is more authentic freedom in the Catholic Church than in communions organized along more democratic lines. Yet that is the claim frequently made by Protestants who have become Catholics. There is more freedom, they say, because, as John Paul also repeatedly insists in *Centesimus*, "freedom is ordered to truth." There is authentic freedom for deliberation and debate because the appeal is to more than private judgment, or to the politically determined position of a religious institution, or to confessional documents of the Reformation era. The appeal, it is asserted, is to the Great Tradition of the Church through time, centered in God's self-revelation in Christ according to the apostolic witness. The magisterium understands itself to be not the master but the servant of that Great Tradition.

Put differently, Catholicism claims to possess a ministerial ordering of the *continuing conversation* that is apostolic Christianity's reflection on God's self-revelation in Jesus Christ. This conversation is ordered, in one of Joseph Cardinal Ratzinger's favored phrases, by the "structure of faith." Ratzinger, who as prefect of the Congregation for the Doctrine of the Faith is the monitor of theological orthodoxy, prefers that phrase to "hierarchy of truths," a formulation that has been much used since the last council. "Hierarchy of truths," it is argued, implies that the "lower" teachings can be ignored without damage to the "higher" teachings. "Structure of faith," on the other hand, suggests an internal coherence in which all teachings, no matter how seemingly peripheral, are related to the center, which is God's revelation in the Christ event.

In this view, the question is not, first of all, whether one has to believe this or that or submit to this or that official pronouncement. The question is one of entering ever more deeply into the structure of faith, at the center of which is the truth incarnate, Jesus Christ. At the beginning and at the end and all along the way, the conversation is Christocentric. The image of conversation is apt. In a coherent conversation not everybody speaks at the same time or in the same way or with the same authority. The alternative to coherent conversation, one may suggest, is babble, or endless political battle, which is much the same thing. There are few contexts more stifling and unfree than that in which everyone is free to say anything or everything and therefore nothing really matters. In such a context, one may seek to dominate the group with *my* truth or *our* truth, but all have despaired of *the* truth, and therefore nothing of ultimate consequence is at stake.

Against those Catholics who press for a more American and democratic mode of church governance, it is argued that the magisterium of bishops in union with the pope provides multiple sources of initiative for a conversation that is lively and yet keeps all participants within the sphere of responsive listening. Of course, it does not always work that way. Nothing that is human, one may observe, works perfectly. The Church, although confident that it is brought into being by God and guided by his Spirit, is nonetheless very human. There is almost universal agreement that the present functioning of the magisterium can certainly be improved. One may suggest that some proposals would be of doubtful benefit. For example, there is stiff resistance to the idea of theologians as some kind of "parallel magisterium," inevitably dominated as they are by the strictures of the academic guild, as well as to the idea of national churches organized on the model of democratic politics. Either of these alternative models of teaching authority, both of which have their vigorous proponents, would likely result, it is argued, in a narrower and more partisan discourse less directed to the question of truth.

THE CONVERSATIONAL CIRCLE

G. K. Chesterton remarked after becoming a Catholic that the Church is ever so much larger from the inside than from the outside. To the extent that is true, it is in no small part because teaching authority in the Church is ordered in a manner that holds it accountable to the living faith of the dead. It is thus able to resist the imperiousness of the present with its intellectual fashions designed to scratch transitory itches. Chesterton described tradition as the democracy of the dead, which is not a bad way of putting it. Peter, Paul, Ignatius of Antioch, Thomas Aquinas, Catherine of Siena, Robert Bellarmine, and John XXIII are all participants in the continuing conversation. And, however imperfect was their communion with the universal Church, so are Martin Luther, John Calvin, Roger Williams, and Reinhold Niebuhr.

As I have written at length elsewhere (see *The Catholic Moment*, 1987 and 1990), we modern folk have an extraordinarily difficult time distinguishing between the authoritarian and the authoritative. The difficulty becomes acute in connection with Church teaching. The radical "turn to the subject" in modern thought has produced what might be described as a severe crippling of the mind. The turn to the subject has come to mean not simply the self at the center apprehending reality but the self at the center creating reality. Truth that is not authenticated by the autonomous self, even *invented* by the autonomous self, is thought to be alien and therefore false. To the mind so crippled, the Church's teaching cannot help but seem authoritarian. However, those who acknowledge a truth external to themselves that is communally articulated through time can welcome authoritative points of reference in the continuing conversation. Being liberated from the iron cage of the autonomous self, they enter into the freedom of a communal conversation that ever aspires to a truth that will only be understood perfectly when we no longer see in a mirror, dimly, but face to face (I Corinthians 13).

For Catholic thinking about social responsibility, *Centesimus Annus* is such an authoritative reference. It is not definitive in the sense of being the last word on the subjects that it addresses. But it is defining in terms of the state of the Catholic conversation. The last word, it is understood, belongs to Christ when he returns in glory. The expectation is that there will be a large measure of continuity between the Church's penultimate words and his ultimate word, although one may doubt that Christ or his followers will be much interested in questions of social justice at that point. But a document such as *Centesimus* has an important part in defining the questions under discussion. For those to whom being part of the Catholic conversation matters, an encyclical helps to locate that conversation.

Precisely because they speak authoritatively, popes must take great care to limit the questions that they address with the full weight of their office. Papal authority is not to be squandered on every transient thought and contingent judgment that passes through the papal head. The Pope is bound to holding himself accountable to the tradition. He proposes in *Centesimus*, for instance, to develop the implications of the "structure of faith" for Christian responsibility in the right ordering of society. Catholics respond to that proposal not with passive receptivity but active engagement. The first obligation is not to think like the Pope but to think with the Pope.

Catholics insist that their primary allegiance is not to the Pope, which is an insistence that the Pope wholeheartedly seconds. To be a Catholic is to be committed to God in Christ, then to Christ's body the Church, then to the ordered ministry of the Church, then to the Petrine Ministry in the Church, which is the ministry exercised by the Pope. He is the *servus servorum Dei*—the servant of the servants of God. At the same time, however, these commitments are not conceived as being in sequential order, as though one can move from this to that and then to the other. Nor are they, as in a Tinkertoy set, separable pieces that can be taken apart and rearranged at will. Rather, they fit together in the structure of faith. They cohere. If the word "integral" had not been so spoiled in the past century by its association with certain abuses of Church authority, one might say that the pieces of Catholic commitment are integrally related.

According to this view of things, to say that the Pope speaks authoritatively does not mean that the Pope has spoken and therefore everybody else must shut up. Exactly the opposite is the case. The Pope has spoken in order to give a new impetus and direction to the conversation in which all participate. And again, he has spoken not only to Catholics but to the entire Christian community and, indeed, to all people of goodwill. In this ecumenical era, it might be agreed that anyone who cares about the Christian project in world history cannot afford to ignore the voice of the Bishop of Rome, although they might have very different ideas about the authoritative status of that voice.

ENGAGING ARGUMENTS

There are no doubt Catholics of goodwill who effectively ignore papal teaching by saying that they accept it without bothering to read it. Of course, all Catholics presumably approach an encyclical with an inner disposition of assenting to it. But, if we accept the image of a coherent conversation, the first duty to a document such as *Centesimus* is not to agree with it but to read it. Except in the sense of what is sometimes called "implicit faith," a person cannot agree with it unless he reads it, puts questions to it, argues with it, probes it, and makes it his own. This Pope more than most others does not simply make pronouncements to which the faithful are to submit. He makes arguments that he expects his readers to engage. In discussing how people are to approach authoritative teaching, a phrase frequently used is *sentire cum ecclesia*—to think with the Church. Thinking with the Church, one might suggest, begins with thinking.

Certainly not every Catholic is obliged to read every papal statement. Especially in this pontificate, many might find that duty altogether too burdensome. In 1991 alone the Pope issued two very challenging encyclicals—one on world mission (*Redemptoris Missio*), and *Centesimus*. These are in addition to dozens of other statements that count as major. In this pontificate, some have complained with considerable hyperbole, reading papal statements has become a full-time job. Some people are vocationally required, and others are for whatever reason so disposed, to read everything. (Well, almost everything.) But Catholics may be grateful that being a Catholic in good standing does not require that one be an expert on every nuance of papal teaching.

Those who presume to speak on Catholic social teaching, however, must read and carefully engage the argument of *Centesimus*. That may seem obvious, but the cacophony that has replaced coherent conversation in much of contemporary Catholicism is due in no small part to Catholic experts who, far from recognizing papal statements as authoritative, seem not quite sure that the Pope should be a full participant in the conversation. "But, Mrs. Luce, I *am* a Catholic," Pius XII is alleged to have said to Clare Boothe Luce, who was waxing enthusiastic about the wonders of the faith. Similarly, John Paul might protest that he, too, is a Catholic in a time when much discussion of Catholic teaching is conducted in a manner almost cavalierly indifferent to the authoritative references by which the community is defined. One very progressive theologian, when recently asked on television about a statement of the Pope, responded, "You mustn't confuse Catholic teaching with what the Pope says." The fullness of Catholic teaching is undoubtedly *more than* any pope might say, but what a pope says is not incidental to Catholic teaching. Were it otherwise, it seems the word "Catholic" would designate some community other than the community that is defined by communion with the Bishop of Rome.

In considering how to respond to *Centesimus*, another set of objections might at least be mentioned. They have been raised from several quarters, but Peter Steinfels puts them nicely in a little essay in the *New York Times*. He worries that John Paul's method of argument in the encyclical "may detract from the power of his insistence on the necessity of truth." *Centesimus*, for instance, depicts Leo XIII as being remarkably prescient on many scores. John Paul, says Steinfels, suggests that the amelioration of the evils of capitalism and achievements such as religious freedom are drawn from the teaching of Leo. He four times cites Leo's 1888 encyclical, *Libertas Praestantissimum*, in support of the proposition that the rights of human conscience must be grounded in devotion to truth.

What the Pope does not note, says Steinfels, is that the same encyclical by Leo declared the separation of church and state to be a "fatal theory" and viewed freedom of worship as a "degradation." In *Centesimus*, according to Steinfels, "one looks in vain for a hint that religion and its followers, including important Catholic groups, contributed anything to nationalism, militarism and even totalitarianism—or that atheists and, yes, socialists were often outstanding champions of human rights when believers were lagging behind." "For some," writes Steinfels (and one infers that he includes the Pope in that "some"), "being in the Vatican means never having to say you were mistaken."

DIFFERING MODES OF DISCOURSE

As mentioned earlier, in *Centesimus* John Paul says he is "rereading" Catholic social teaching. The quotation marks around "rereading" are in the text, and it has been suggested that the Pope was being just a little coy, signaling that his is a very *creative* rereading of the tradition. Mr. Steinfels and others worry whether the rereading of history is not in fact a rewriting of history, and whether rewriting history does not undermine what the encyclical says about devotion to truth. It is an important question. One might point out in response that John Paul is not writing as an academic historian. It is unlikely that he sees it as his task to give a historian's account of the development of ideas. He writes as chief pastor of the Church, and his task is to discern the Spirit-guided intention of a tradition. Steinfels says, "Just as the church that is jockeying over *Centesimus Annus* splits into camps over economic theories, it is also divided into those who want to acknowledge and analyze the reality of changes in the church's life and those who want to highlight only the continuity."

Mr. Steinfels may be confusing quite different modes of discourse. He privileges one mode of discourse by saying it deals with "the reality" while other modes of discourse presumably deal with something other than, and less than, reality. If the claims for Church teaching are accepted, the living tradition lives by faith-filled and Spirit-guided discernment, not simply by the scientifically determined "facts" that moderns call reality. Protestants and Catholics alike are familiar, for instance, with a style of historical-critical biblical scholarship that aims to get at "the facts" that are presumably to be discovered beneath and behind the biblical texts. Such scholarship can make a useful contribution, but it is hardly adequate by itself. The Bible is studied as something more than an antiquity of interest only to historians precisely because it is the sacred text of a continuing community of faith.

The *truth* of the biblical text is discerned in the community's continuing reflection on its relationship to *the* truth, namely, God's self-revelation in Christ. Similarly, the early fathers of the Church discerned all kinds of truths in the Hebrew Scriptures that modern historical studies might find quite fanciful. For instance, one would be hard put to demonstrate that the writer of Genesis 3:15 thought that God's statement to the serpent in the garden ("I will put enmity between you and the woman, and between your offspring and hers") referred to the Virgin Mary and her child. Yet, here and elsewhere, most Christians believe that the Church fathers—employing analogy, allegory, typology, and other modes of interpretation—illuminated the truth and the reality of the Hebrew Scriptures. Marcion (d. 160) would have prevailed with his argument that the Hebrew Scriptures should be rejected by the Church had not Christians "reread" those writings in the light of Jesus, whom they call the Christ.

Tradition, in this view, is an ongoing "Aha experience." Prior to their definition by the early councils, many Christians did not understand Christology or the Trinity in the terms that are now accepted as orthodox. To cite a more recent example, the Second Vatican Council's teaching on religious liberty is a clear development beyond what the Church had taught earlier, notably during the period of the Counter-Reformation that was launched in the sixteenth century. If one is so inclined, one can construe such development in terms of discontinuity with and contradiction of earlier teaching. If one is inclined to "think with the Church," however, one can discern that Vatican II was a developing, unfolding, and clarifying of the tradition in light of "new things." It was also, and very importantly, a *recovery* of earlier aspects of the tradition that had been obscured by the reaction to the Reformation and to the anti-Christian, and virulently anti-Catholic, face of modernity. Councils and popes are engaged in more than mere historical analysis. They understand their mode of discourse to be not just analysis but discernment and teaching as they lead the community's continuing reflection and conversation about the truth.

In Catholic thought and piety, a sharp distinction is sometimes made between the teachers and the taught. The pope and bishops, it is said, constitute "the teaching Church" while the faithful are "the learning Church." As valuable as that distinction may be, it is also proposed that the faithful who have internalized the teaching are to become teachers of others. In addition, there is a "sense of the faithful" *(sensus fidelium)* that is to be discerned and respected by "the teaching Church." Moreover, "the teaching Church" is always learning. In *Centesimus*, for example, the Pope does not disguise but displays in great detail what he has learned from the "new things" thrown up by history for the Church's consideration. This teacher, like all good teachers, wants it to be understood that he is also a student.

It would seem obvious that the Pope emphasizes continuity rather than discontinuity. His primary concern is supposed to be for the continuity and vitality of the tradition. Steinfels is surely right in saying that not everything the Pope has taken from the past is drawn exclusively from the Church's own treasury. The Church's story interacts with many other stories. One need not protest Steinfels' claim that development of teaching since Leo XIII "owes more to the American experience with church-state separation and to the Enlightenment and maybe even to a few atheists than to purely papal thinking." But it is perhaps not helpful to present this as an either/or proposition. Just as the Council of Nicaea (325) cannot be explained apart from imperial politics under Constantine, and just as the Council of Trent was a response to the Reformation, so the issues addressed by *Centesimus* were frequently raised most importantly by forces outside, and often hostile, to the Church. But the fact remains that the Church's response to such forces is itself part of what the Church claims as its own story.

DEVELOPING TOWARD ADEQUACY

In the Catholic view, there would seem to be no reason to hesitate to acknowledge that the Church's responses in the past were sometimes inadequate. If they were adequate, there would be no need for development; indeed there would be no need for a continuing office of authoritative teaching. As we have seen, a completely adequate understanding of the fullness of truth is an eschatological hope that awaits Christ's return in glory. Meanwhile, Christians trust the promise of Jesus: "I will not leave you orphaned. The Advocate, the Holy Spirit, whom the Father will send in my name, will teach you everything, and will bring to your remembrance all that I have said to you" (John 14). In ecumenical discussions among Christians, it is agreed that an instrument of that promised guidance is associated with Peter or, as it is called, the Petrine Ministry. Catholics are persuaded that that Petrine Ministry is exercised by the Bishop of Rome, whom they understand to be Peter's successor, and by those bishops in communion with him.

The word "remembrance" in Christ's promise underscores that the transmitting and interpreting of the tradition is always a process of retrieval and recapitulation. There are indeed "new things," but the understanding of the new things is incorporated into the continuing story. The pope's is the leading voice, the authoritative voice, the defining voice in the telling of the story. But all Christians are involved in the telling of the story. In an important sense, *they are the story*, for the story is about a Spirit-guided community interacting with new things. Catholics listen obediently to the pope's telling of the story—keeping in mind that "obedience" is from *oboedire*, which means to listen responsively. Obedience, in this view, is not passivity but engagement.

As the children of Israel in the wilderness no doubt gathered by their tents to recapitulate and reflect on what had happened to them and what it meant for the future, so Christians understand themselves to be on the way to the Kingdom and are in constant conversation about where they have been and where they are going. The Church's conversation is not an academic seminar. It is the urgent deliberation of a people on purpose, a people on pilgrimage. Christians readily concede that they have learned from those who are not of their company, and in fact from those who are their declared enemies. Were the Church an academic seminar, Christians might well talk about the "contribution" of Voltaire and Lenin to their understanding of the importance of religious freedom, for instance. But it does seem a little much to expect a pilgrim community to "give credit" to those who declared themselves to be the community's mortal enemies. Similarly, in everyday life people learn from affliction and failure, but they do not for that reason praise affliction and failure. We do not thank Hitler for teaching us the full evil of anti-Semitism, although it seems probable that we would not understand the depths of that evil were it not for Hitler.

Of course, not all those outside the community are the enemies of the community. The basic disposition of Christians to those outside the community is that they are potential members of the community. Nonetheless, the community does have enemies. When Christians say that Jesus Christ is Lord, they are saying that nobody else and nothing else is lord, and that is a good way to make enemies. In *Centesimus*, the Pope is not denying "the reality" of discontinuities in the Church's experience or the influence upon the Church of those outside the Church. The Pope is simply telling the Christian story in a way that makes it clear that he is on the community's side. That would appear to be the least that Christians might expect of him.

All that having been said, however, Peter Steinfels raises questions that future papal teaching might take into account. While the Pope is not leading an academic seminar, neither is he speaking to a sect. His argument is a *public* argument, directed to "people of goodwill" who participate in several worlds of discourse. To this audience, which includes many Catholics, the credibility and persuasiveness of the Church's telling the story of how it came to affirm democracy, religious freedom, and the free economy requires an acknowledgment of the extra-Catholic (and even anti-Christian) forces that prompted the Church to reconsider its earlier statements. A Church that is faithful to the truth has nothing to fear from the truth, including the elements of truth advanced by its enemies. Again, were the Church's teaching formulated in an entirely adequate way at any given point, there would be no need for a continuing teaching authority such as the magisterium led by the pope.

THE DOCILE AND THE ENGAGED

Catholics, then, are to listen responsively *(oboedire)* to what the pope says because to stay in communion with him is, among other things, to stay in conversation with him. To stay in communion with him, it is believed, is to be in communion with the institutional "centering" of the Christian community through time. And so Catholics contend that they are not submitting blindly to the authoritarian but responding appropriately to the authoritative. This response, they maintain, is not one of grudging acquiescence or dull conformity. It is not the abdication of personal responsibility. On the contrary, they say, it is accepting responsibility for what they perceive to be true. It is a matter of taking one's stand. In pledging allegiance to that which is greater than themselves, they believe that they become more than themselves. In other words, freedom is not being true to the self but is the self freed for the truth. As noted, it is an understanding of truth and freedom that does not sit well with dominant traditions of modernity and the autonomous self.

Non-Catholics typically have a hard time understanding a faithfully Catholic response to papal authority. It strikes them as

unthinking obsequiousness and servile tractability. In formal
Catholic teaching the faithful are exhorted to cultivate the virtue
of "docility." Docility means eager to be taught, very much as in
responsive listening. It is a lovely word, but it has been quite
spoiled, probably beyond rehabilitation. In American English,
docility suggests a disposition more appropriate for a donkey
than for a human being. The disposition that "docility" intends
to suggest is perhaps better described as one of thoughtful defer-
ence and eager receptivity. Catholics, or at least serious Catholics, earnestly want to think with the Church, and recognize that
the pope is singularly positioned and graced to express the mind
of the Church.

But what if a pope betrays his duty? Protestant Christians are
much, and understandably, worried about that risk. (A good
many Catholics worry about it as well.) Some Protestants can-
didly acknowledge that they depend upon Catholicism to provide a continuing center of historic Christianity, although they
cannot in conscience commit themselves to sustaining that center. Some Catholic apologists, on the other hand, turn the risk
anxiety entirely around. They positively exult in the number of
"bad popes" that there have been over the centuries. The fact
that the Church has survived so many wayward popes, they say,
is further evidence that theirs is indeed the Church of Christ.
While it no doubt highlights the recuperative powers of the
papacy, that is a little like saying that surviving numerous auto-
mobile accidents is evidence of being a safe driver.

Trust is not blind trust. Trust that is worthy of the name is
trust with eyes wide open. Faith is not the opposite of doubt but
a disposition that has taken doubt fully into account. This, one
might argue, is true in marriage, friendship, and every undertaking of great consequence. Things may turn out to be other than
we trust them to be. This is also true, at least some Catholics
would say, of the confidence that they place in papal teaching.
But not all Catholics by any means. A philosopher who wants to
be a *very* orthodox Catholic announced at a recent conference
that if the pope declared that two plus two equals five, he would

instantly believe it. An unimpeachably orthodox but more reflective Catholic theologian responded by recalling Wittgenstein's remark that if a person claims that two plus two equals five he is wrong, but if he says that two plus two equals forty-seven he just might be on to an interesting idea. "In fact," this theologian said, "if a pope said two plus two equals five or any number other than four, I would take it as my duty to hope that he is on to an interesting idea. If after careful examination, however, it turned out that he seemed to be saying nothing more than that two plus two equals five, I would publicly say, were I required to say anything, that I perhaps misunderstand the pope. I would privately pray for his speedy recovery."

In this view, one does the credibility of Catholicism no favors by depicting it in terms of blind submission to papal authority. The pope's is an authoritative voice, but it is not the only authoritative voice. There is the voice of Scripture, of the historic tradition, of reason, of experience, and of the "sense of the faithful." Papal authority is, by its own definition, in service to truth that is not exhaustively embodied in the office and person of the pope. Catholics can hypothetically conceive of the possibility that some pope might declare that there are not three but four persons in the Godhead, or that the bread and wine of the Eucharist is nothing more than bread and wine after all. That is *hypothetically* possible and, if it ever happened, the expectation is that such a pope would promptly be declared mad and be removed from office. But reasonable people, it is suggested, do not live on the basis of what is hypothetically possible. Paranoids and people congenitally incapable of commitment live by hypothesis.

A TENTATIVE AND TIMOROUS THING

Thinking with the Church begins with thinking. Short of the End Time, the community's understanding will always be partial. But along the way Christians believe that they are accompa-

nied by Christ, and by the Spirit promised to the apostles, and
—Catholics believe—by Peter, who is commissioned to
"strengthen the brethren" (Luke 22). Non-Catholics who recognize the scriptural foundation of the Petrine Ministry may
have reason to ask themselves where else that ministry might be
located other than in the Bishop of Rome and those bishops in
communion with Rome. *Hypothetically*, the biblical pattern of
Petrine leadership may have expired. *Hypothetically*, the Petrine
Ministry may have become simply an idea without institutional
expression. *Hypothetically*, historical developments could have located the Petrine leadership somewhere else. *Hypothetically*, another and more compelling form of Petrine leadership might be
devised some time in the future. But Christianity by hypothesis
tends to be a tentative and timorous thing.

In the Catholic perspective, the "structure of the faith" always begins and ends with Christ. The response to papal authority does not, as it were, stand on its own. There is an ordering of allegiances. The ultimate allegiance is to God in Christ.
The only Christ that can be known, it is then asserted, is the
head of the Church, which is his body. In the words of Vatican
II, "This Church, constituted and organized in the world as a
society, subsists in the Catholic Church, which is governed by
the successor of Peter and by the bishops in union with that
successor" *(Lumen Gentium)*. Here, Catholics believe, the
Church is most rightly and fully ordered; here the voice of Peter
is to be heard.

The same Catholic teaching asserts that wherever Christ is
preached and received by faith, there is Christ. And wherever
Christ is, there is the Church, for the head cannot be separated
from the body. The Second Vatican Council declares that all
who believe and are baptized "are brought into a certain, though
imperfect, communion with the Catholic Church" *(Unitatis
Redintegratio)*. The responsiveness of Catholics to papal authority is itself, Catholics would contend, an ecumenical contribution of the first order. In this way they understand themselves to

be advancing the hope of full communion among all those for whom Christ intended the gift of the Petrine Ministry.

At present, however, the Petrine office is seen as one of the chief obstacles to Christian unity. There are doctrinal and historical reasons for that, but many non-Catholics are suspicious of the Church's teaching office for practical and moral reasons. They fear it requires an abdication of personal responsibility, or provides a false certainty that precludes the risks of faith. For all of the insistence upon the distinction between the authoritarian and authoritative, they nonetheless view papal authority as a purely top-down process that evokes the either/or of submission or dissent. In this way, it is said, the teaching authority neither elevates the level of discourse nor serves the cause of unity even within Catholicism itself. These misgivings cannot be dismissed lightly. How the teaching authority is actually exercised has a strong bearing on whether others will find believable and attractive what Catholics claim for that authority.

Among Catholics, the exercise of teaching authority has been much discussed in the years since the Second Vatican Council. The discussion, however, is almost always about what the pope and the bishops do or should do. The complaints are typically about the need for greater consultation, a larger role for theologians, and a more democratic process of decision-making. Again, it is almost universally recognized that there are real problems at present, although there is slight agreement on how the problems are defined. The way the Church teaches has developed over the centuries. The relationships between councils, popes, curia, bishops, clergy, theologians, and laity have not always been what they are today. There will no doubt be further development in the future. That, one may assume, is in the nature of a living tradition.

A WIDER RESPONSIBILITY

In contemporary Catholicism, one encounters a widespread re-
luctance to accept responsibility for the exercise of the teaching
authority. That is to say, the discussion usually assumes that it is
up to popes and bishops to make that authority more convincing
and attractive both to Catholics and others. How popes and
bishops exercise their office can no doubt always be improved
upon. But no matter how well they fulfill their task, the *effective*
teaching mission of the Church would finally seem to depend
upon the Catholic people. They, in turn, it has repeatedly been
observed, need the sustained encouragement of theologians,
priests, and religious to let authoritative statements come alive
in the communal conversation.

Centesimus, touching as it does on so many aspects of everyday life, could be an extraordinary opportunity for letting that
happen. If other Christians saw a community gathered, engaged,
and strengthened by the argument of this encyclical, it could be
a powerful practical demonstration of what Catholics assert
about Peter in their midst. It would be in refreshing contrast to
the embittered disagreements, partisan politicking, and factional
ghettoization that characterize so much of contemporary church
life, both Protestant and Catholic.

This reflection on tradition, community, and teaching authority does not pretend to be a complete or systematic treatment of the subject. Far from it. We have done no more than
touch on some considerations that might help create a climate
for lively engagement with the argument of *Centesimus.* John
Paul takes the lead in an ever-developing communal conversation. The conversational circle includes not only Catholics but
other Christians and all people of goodwill. His effort will be of
little effect, however, unless people enter into the conversation.
Whatever one may believe or not believe about the charisms
attending his office, the Pope has little control over whether the
teaching of the Church informs and transforms the way we think
and live. He can only propose. A living tradition is the common

enterprise of all who live from that tradition. Although he was not speaking specifically about the tradition of which *Centesimus* is part, Johann Wolfgang von Goethe caught the challenge very nicely:

> What you have as heritage,
> Take now as task;
> For thus you will make it your own!

NOTES

Page 78. Francis Canavan, S.J., in *First Things*, October 1991. A suggestive overview of Catholic social doctrine is *That They May Be One: The Social Teaching of Papal Encyclicals 1740–1989* by Michael J. Schuck, Georgetown University, 1991. The author dates the beginning of the tradition before *Rerum Novarum* and, of course, does not include *Centesimus Annus*, which is the focus of this book. He also contends that the tradition is marked not only by development but also by substantive internal contradictions.

Page 80. The Center of Concern analysis is in *Center Focus*, August 1991.

Page 82. On the incorporation of Newman's insights into Catholic orthodoxy see the 1990 statement of the International Theological Commission, "On the Interpretation of Dogmas."

Page 85. *Philadelphia Inquirer* comment by editorial page editor David Boldt, July 1, 1990.

Pages 93–94. Peter Steinfels, "In Search of 20/20 Hindsight," *New York Times*, June 8, 1991.

Page 102. On the Church being coterminous with Christ, see Johan Cardinal Willebrands "Vatican II's Ecclesiology of Communion."

Chapter Four

. . .

A SOCIAL GOSPEL

Those who would make the tradition their own, then, must get on more intimate terms with it. *Centesimus* is an opportunity to do exactly that. It is not the entirety of the tradition, of course. But it provides the chance for a "learning moment" under the direction of a master teacher who is on intimate terms with the entire tradition. Those who would enter into conversation with this teacher must probe the text carefully and put their questions to the argument presented.

Catholics, oddly enough, may have a harder time doing that than other Christians. Or maybe it is not so odd. The more highly people think of a text, the more authority that it carries for them, the more they are inclined to "freeze" themselves into a passive mode of reading it. Many Christians have this problem in reading the Bible. Here, they say to themselves, is the very word of God. It is very intimidating. It makes it hard to read the Book of Joshua, say, as a ripping good story. It makes it hard to read Paul's letters as *letters* written of course to the churches of the time but also to people today. So keenly conscious are many

Christians that they are reading the *Holy Bible*. Intimidated by the authority of the text, they do not probe it, asking why it says this rather than that, why this conclusion follows from that premise, and whether, when you get down to it, it really makes sense to them. Such a close, probing, and even playful reading may seem to be irreverent.

Devout Catholics may have a similar problem in reading the words of the Pope. He is, after all, the Holy Father. Many people, including many Catholics today, are not comfortable in calling him the Holy Father. They think it fawning toward him and demeaning of themselves. If he is the father, then they are the children, and the modern mind-set is inclined to rebel against that. People want, as we incessantly say, to be treated as adults. The rebellion against the suggestion that we are children is, in fact, very much the way children behave. It may be that people are never so childish as when they stand on their dignity and demand that they be treated as adults, even as equals. Of course, sometimes the demand is legitimate, as when we do not acknowledge the authority of the one who talks to us as though he is something more than equal in the structure of the conversation.

It was a hard word when Jesus said that unless people become like little children, they cannot enter the Kingdom of God. The familiar distinction between child*like* and child*ish* helps a little, but only a little. After all, we spend our entire lives growing out of childhood, and it is no easy thing when it seems that we are being told to go back to it. Becoming childlike, however, may be understood as going forward, not backward. Paul Ricoeur, a noted Protestant thinker, talks about a "second naïveté" in the Christian life. When we were children, we were inclined to take things at face value. As we got older, we began to see that things were not quite as they seemed. We lost our naïveté. The second naïveté is the fully self-conscious and reflective rediscovery of the capacity to wonder and to believe. It is a grace. "Distrust simplicity," said the philosopher Alfred North

Whitehead, "except for the simplicity that is on the far side of complexity."

A RELATIONSHIP OF TRUST

In the simplicity that he believes to be on the far side of complexity, the Catholic expects to be instructed by the Holy Father. The student is not in the role of a dumb, acquiescent, passive, and unquestioning child. A close reading of the argument that the Pope sets forth requires students who are eager and alert. Catholics do papal teaching no favors by suggesting that it works better with the stupid and unthinking, although a good many Catholics seem to hold that view. Eager students have questions to put, objections to raise, and they do not hesitate to say when something is not clear to them. Such questioning, one may argue, is not disrespect but evidence of trust in the relationship. Of course, all such questioning assumes that they really do want to understand, they really do want to agree, they really do want to make the tradition their own.

For a great teacher, the issue is not whether students agree with him. His overriding concern is that they wrestle with the truth of which he is the servant. Indeed, he is gratified when his most faithful students go beyond him in discerning aspects of the truth. The pope is not, by virtue of being pope, the most brilliant thinker in the Church. John Paul is a philosopher and theologian of stature, but that is more the exception than the rule in the history of the papacy. The pope's task is not to outshine the intellectual superstars in the Church but to help them avoid becoming individual entrepreneurs by holding them accountable to the truth by which the Church is constituted.

John Paul encourages an "open search for truth," and holds up the example of young people. What he says about cultural traditions is also, mutatis mutandis, relevant to the conversation within the community of faith. "From this open search for truth," he writes, "which is renewed in every generation, the culture of a nation derives its character. Indeed, the heritage of values which has been received and handed down is always challenged by the young. To challenge does not necessarily mean to destroy or reject a priori, but above all to put these values to the test in one's own life and through this existential verification to make them more real, relevant, and personal, distinguishing the valid elements in the tradition from false and erroneous ones or from obsolete forms which can be usefully replaced by others more suited to the times" (¶ 50).

In *Centesimus*, the Pope is not only developing the Church's doctrine, he is also developing the very idea of social doctrine. He notes that with *Rerum Novarum* something new was started. Leo XIII created a "lasting paradigm" for what John Paul calls "social teaching" or "social magisterium" in which the Church "formulates a genuine doctrine" in response to social problems. This doctrine constitutes "a corpus which enables the Church to analyze social realities, to make judgments about them, and to indicate directions to be taken for the just resolution of the problems involved." John Paul recognizes that in Leo's time "such a concept of the Church's right and duty was far from being commonly admitted" (¶ 5). The concept is much more commonly admitted today, but a good many Catholics, not to mention other Christians, still have problems with it.

Few would doubt the Pope's authority to speak on doctrinal matters in the usual sense of "doctrinal"—on matters having to do with theology and the formulation of Christian faith. But a lot of people get their backs up when popes or bishops venture into fields where, as it is commonly put, "they don't know what they're talking about." Economics and politics, for example. In all the churches there is a deep-seated sentiment that "religion and politics don't mix." It cannot be denied that the ways in which theological indicatives and political imperatives have been mixed in some churches have resulted in great confusion—and great resentment about "using" religion to advance partisan agendas of social change. Such confusion and resentment have played a major part in the demoralization and decline of the mainline/oldline Protestant churches in this country. A similar uneasiness surfaced in some responses to social statements by the American Catholic bishops in recent years. Is Catholicism, it is asked, going the way of oldline Protestantism by "politicizing" the Church?

Not, one may suggest, if Catholics follow the directions indicated by this Pope. The new "paradigm" of social teaching created by Leo XIII is only a hundred years old. In this encyclical, John Paul intends to make clear that it is a lasting paradigm and that such social teaching is to be viewed as integral to the Church's teaching ministry. How the paradigm will be refined in practice over the years to come nobody can know, but in *Centesimus* the Pope offers precedents and principles that can preclude the "politicizing" of religion that plagues so much of Protestantism and, it must be admitted, so much of contemporary Catholicism. The "Social Gospel" movement that, beginning in the nineteenth century, dominated most of American Protestantism turned out to be fatally flawed on that score. But something like a Social Gospel seems to be required by the Christian project in history. This time Christians must hope that they get it right. It may be that the Catholic response to that felt Christian need will be yet another ecumenical contribution of "The Catholic Moment."

A QUESTION OF COMPETENCE

Yet many Catholics no doubt agree with Peter Berger when he argues that the Church risks its credibility when it moves beyond its specific competence—"competence" meaning both ability and legitimate authority. Reflecting on an earlier encyclical dealing with social doctrine, Berger wrote: "I wonder what is gained from these exercises. Very possibly they actually undermine the authority of the teaching mission that they are supposed to express. I'm reminded of the reply given by Samuel

Gompers to the question as to what the American labor movement wants: 'More!' he replied. I ask myself what I would want
from Rome in terms of its social doctrine. Respectfully, regret-
fully, but with increasing assurance, I find myself replying:
Less!"

We may say that social policy prescription is not what we
need from the Church. We may go further and invoke authoritative Church statements declaring that the sources of wisdom
for rightly ordering the earthly city are to be found in human
reason and prudential judgment, quite apart from the tutelage of
the Church. That having been said, however, the development
of something like a social doctrine, knowing full well the risks of
politicizing the faith, seems almost inevitable. Consider simply
the fact that the Church around the world has a vast network of
ministries and institutions devoted to serving human needs of a
maddening variety. These ministries and institutions are inescapably caught up in the public-policy disputes that shape the
politics of the societies in which they work. Decisions must be
made about whether to go this way or that. In the second half of
this book we examine some of the specific policy directions indicated by *Centesimus.* Such indications are part of a social doctrine and are necessary if the Church's ministries and institutions are to maintain their distinctiveness.

In addition, there is what might be called a psychological and
spiritual need. Christians in the public square participate in
many different communities of discourse. They belong to political parties, interest groups, corporations, and other associations.
Caught in the midst of the partisan conflicts of sundry factions,
they need to order their communal allegiances. For the serious
Catholic, the community of premier allegiance is the Church.
Surrounded by competing truth claims, here is the community
constituted by *the* truth. Resisting the temptation to become
merely one faction among others, the Church seeks to be a zone
of truth in a world of political mendacities. Its social doctrine is
not a political platform competing with other political plat-

forms, but an authoritatively guided conversation in which all such platforms are kept under critical judgment by reference to the truth of the Gospel. That at least is the ideal, and, like all ideals, it is very imperfectly realized. Human sinfulness virtually guarantees that there will always be parties in the Church who will try to capture its moral status in support of their political propensities.

The risk of that happening increases when the Church tries to become an institutional player in the politics of the earthly city. In that connection, the American bishops were much acclaimed (and also criticized) when they issued their pastoral letters of 1983 and 1986. The first, *The Challenge of Peace*, dealt with nuclear weaponry, and the second, *Economic Justice for All*, set forth a rather specific program of measures aimed at economic fairness. In issuing these statements, the bishops were obviously worried about the danger of politicizing the faith. In the 1983 statement they said: "In doing this we realize, and we want readers of this letter to recognize, that not all statements in this letter have the same moral authority. At times we state universally binding moral principles found in the teaching of the Church; at other times the pastoral letter makes specific applications, observations and recommendations which allow for diversity of opinion on the part of those who assess the factual data of situations differently. However, we expect Catholics to give our moral judgments serious consideration when they are forming their own views on specific problems" (ii).

In the 1986 statement on the economy, they write: "In our letter, we write as pastors, not public officials. We speak as moral teachers, not economic technicians. We seek not to make some political or ideological point but to lift up the human and ethical dimensions of economic life, aspects too often neglected in public discussion . . . We know that some of our specific recommendations are controversial. As bishops, we do not claim to make these prudential judgments with the same kind of authority that marks our declarations of principle. But, we feel obliged to teach by example how Christians can undertake concrete analysis and make specific judgments on economic issues" (vii, xii).

Partaking of the Sacred

As you might expect, not everybody is happy with the way the American bishops go about addressing social, economic, and political questions. But the statements above make clear that the bishops are very much aware of the problem of politicizing the Church, of using their teaching office to promote partisan agendas. Obviously, the process can and should be improved. In these and other statements, the bishops sometimes seem to suggest that they have a concern for the "human and ethical dimensions" of public policy that others do not share. Further, "principles" are sometimes framed in a tendentious way that already imply their "application," thus blurring the distinction between principle and policy. On crucial issues in public dispute, the recommendations in the pastoral letters on weapons and economics tended to be situated left of center on the political spectrum. That raised questions about credibility for those Catholics who do not think that it is self-evidently true that the Democratic Party is more attuned to "the human and ethical dimensions" than the Republican. Nonetheless, in their discussion of "levels of authority," the bishops wrestled with the distinction between social doctrine and partisan pleading, and their cautions can be helpful also in reading social encyclicals such as *Centesimus.*

An important protection in Catholic teaching against the politicizing of the faith is evident in John Paul's repeated affirmation of spheres of human activity that have their own sovereignty and integrity. They do not need to be "sacralized" by the Church because they already partake of the sacred. The Catholic spirit is one of respect for reason, nature, and the dynamics of the created order. It is freely acknowledged that as a result of human sinfulness, the world is indeed in very bad shape. But the Church's mission is not so much to save the world from itself as to call the world to itself. In the Catholic perspective, spheres of human activity such as politics, economics, science, and education do not need so much to be "Christianized" as they need the freedom to be what they most authentically are.

The Church, we are told, does not fear the independence of these spheres from the Church's tutelage or control. The Church's confidence is that when humanity is fully human, the Church's message will not be viewed as something imposed from the outside. As John Paul wrote in his 1991 encyclical *Redemptoris Missio,* "The Church imposes nothing; she only proposes." She proposes to human beings what they were meant to be, and therefore what they most truly are. This is often described as the thoroughgoing humanism of Catholic Christianity. That humanism is reflected in the chapter heading and the entire argument of the conclusion of *Centesimus:* "Man is the Way of the Church."

Following from that is a posture toward the world that is, at the same time, affirmative and critical. When the Church seems to be against the world, it is only against the world for the world. When the Church criticizes the way of humanity, it is not because humanity is being "all too human" but because it is not being human enough. The Church understands itself to be not something apart from humanity but the part of humanity that has found the authentically human way in Christ. Also in such "mundane" spheres as economics and politics, human nature is not to be defied but respected and nurtured. John Paul asserts that the wisdom of this theological insight is borne out by practical experience. "Not only is it wrong from the ethical point of view to disregard human nature, which is made for freedom," he writes, "but in practice it is impossible to do so. Where society is so organized as to reduce arbitrarily or even suppress the sphere in which freedom is legitimately exercised, the result is that the life of society becomes progressively disorganized and goes into decline" (¶ 25).

The Church also claims to recognize and respect the competence of those who have primary responsibility in the several spheres of human activity. We are told that while the power of grace "penetrates" the temporal order, it does not displace that order. "In this way the requirements of a society worthy of man are better perceived, deviations are corrected, the courage to work for what is good is reinforced. In union with all people of goodwill, Christians, especially the laity, are called to this task of imbuing human realities with the Gospel" (¶ 25). The Church does not, we are told, seek to control how Christian lay people perform their work but to alert them to the dignity and responsibility of the work that is authentically theirs. Individual persons and persons in community must freely and conscientiously discern what is to be done and how it is to be done. Even when they are not sure precisely what is to be done, they know it is to be done faithfully, remembering that "God loveth adverbs."

S ELF - D ENYING   O RDINANCES

In addition to respecting the integrity and autonomy of various spheres of human activity, the Pope explicitly puts limits on what the Church can legitimately say and do. The late Paul Ramsey of Princeton, an influential Methodist theologian, regularly pleaded with oldline Protestant leaders to accept "self-denying ordinances" with respect to their pronouncements on temporal matters. Religious leaders whose words are not taken seriously promiscuously pronounce on everything, thus ensuring that their words will not be taken seriously. Those who have real authority use it judiciously. Authority that is used sparingly is not spent but is, as it were, increased by compound interest. Karol Wojtyla is a theologian-philosopher with opinions on many things. When he speaks as Pope John Paul II, however, one can see him striving to observe what Ramsey called the self-denying ordinances. Readers will judge whether he is always successful in that observance.

The teaching of the Church is not to provide detailed directives but "inspiration for [Christian] involvement in the world." The Pope portrays himself as a concerned pastor offering his analysis and counsel in the hope that others will find it helpful. He expects others to pay close attention, and paying close attention includes making distinctions between purely contingent judgments and the authoritative teaching of principle. "Pastoral solicitude . . . prompts me to propose an analysis of some events of recent history . . . However, such an analysis is not meant to pass definitive judgments, since this does not fall per se within the Magisterium's specific domain" (¶ 3).

After the horror that was Communism, John Paul urges the cultivation of a robust skepticism toward grand schemes for the reordering of society, also when those schemes are presented as a "Christian" model of society. "The Church has no models to present," he writes. "Models that are real and truly effective can only arise within the framework of different historical situations through the efforts of all those who responsibly confront concrete problems . . ." (¶ 43). The Christian faith, he insists, is not an ideology; it is not a set of ideas in the service of advancing a sociopolitical program. "Since it is not an ideology, the Christian faith does not presume to imprison changing sociopolitical realities in a rigid schema, and it recognizes that human life is realized in history in conditions that are diverse and imperfect." There is also another reason why the Church is not setting forth an ideology. "In constantly reaffirming the transcendent dignity of the person, the Church's method is always that of respect for freedom" (¶ 46).

Those familiar with the history of the Catholic Church may question whether the Church's method is, or was, always that of respect for freedom. The verb in John Paul's statement might be understood as the idealistic present tense or the teleological perfect tense, as in the statement, "Man is a rational animal." The Pope leaves no doubt, however, that it is his intention that the Church's method always be that of respect for freedom. Human freedom, we are told, aspires to nothing less than full union with

God, and everything short of that, including *all* real or proposed social orders, must be relativized and kept under judgment by that transcendent destiny.

The Church points out needs to be met, she challenges the smug pretensions of all social orders, she proposes a moral "orientation" to temporal tasks, but she does not presume to tell societies how specific problems are to be solved. The Church does not do that, the Pope says, because the Church does not have the right to do that. The Church is not "entitled." "The Church respects the legitimate autonomy of the democratic order and is not entitled to express preferences for this or that institutional or constitutional solution. Her contribution to the political order is precisely her vision of the dignity of the person revealed in all its fullness in the mystery of the Incarnate Word" (¶ 47).

ENDS AND MEANS

To be sure, there is not always a clear line between moral orientation, on the one hand, and specific policy proposals, on the other. Abortion serves to illustrate the point. The Church, also in the present encyclical, insistently teaches that abortion is a great evil and that justice requires the most protective laws possible for the unborn. The Pope would seem to be asserting, however, that the Church is not entitled to say which is the right political solution for achieving such protection. Catholics, and bishops in particular, must relentlessly press politicians on what they are doing to secure legal protection for the unborn, the severely handicapped, the vulnerable aged, and others who are increasingly defined as being beyond the shelter of the law. Catholic politicians may favor different ways of achieving that goal. In the case of those who give every evidence of rejecting that goal and moral orientation, however, it would seem that the Church is not only entitled but obliged to make clear that they are in grave violation of Christian truth.

The practical application of the self-denying ordinance that the Church's teaching office places upon itself is by no means self-evident. The lines between eternal verity and contingent judgment, between moral principle and specific policy, are often blurred. These things must be worked out in concrete circumstances, as *Centesimus* says again and again. One way of discerning what the Church is or is not entitled to say authoritatively is to keep the focus on what the Church *must* say. John Paul writes in various ways about "the Church's specific and decisive contribution" to society. Specifically, decisively, and most distinctively "the Church renders [its] service to human society by preaching the truth" about creation, redemption, love of neighbor, and the hope of glory (¶ 51).

This is what some theologians call the *proper* mission of the Church, meaning that it is the utterly singular thing (the *propria*) that the Church is to do. Declaring the Christian message and sustaining the community gathered by that message is what no other institution can do. It is the single most important thing to be done, and, if the Church did not do it, it would not get done. What the Church has to say about social, political, and economic questions is authoritative to the degree that it is implicated in the revealed story of salvation. John Paul is keenly aware that Christian leaders, too, are tempted to overstep the bounds of their distinctive authority, acting as though they have some kind of revealed blueprint for the right ordering of society. He writes: "Nor does the Church close her eyes to the danger of fanaticism or fundamentalism among those who, in the name of an ideology that purports to be scientific or religious, claim the right to impose on others their own concept of what is true and good" (¶ 46).

Catholic social doctrine is directed against both utopianism and despair. The Church's distinctive contribution is not to remove all uncertainties but to sustain people in a world where, short of the Kingdom Come, uncertainty is a certainty. Christian faith is to enable them to act in the courage of their uncertainties, knowing that some problems are not amenable to solution. The Pope speaks of the "practical and experiential" dimension of the Church's social teaching that "is to be found at the crossroads where Christian life and conscience come into contact with the real world." At such crossroads, people often do not know what to do, and their best judgments frequently result in failure and suffering. "Faith not only helps people to find solutions; it makes even situations of suffering humanly bearable, so that in these situations people will not become lost or forget their dignity and vocation" (¶ 59).

Many critics, in the spirit of Nietzsche, deride Christianity as a religion for losers. It is a sop seized upon by those who do not dare to be more than human. Such derision, Christians would contend, is based upon the self-deception that we can escape the human condition that is bounded by death—and by the little deaths of our failures along the way to death. Christianity, and especially Catholic Christianity, is on friendly terms with the human condition, knowing full well that humanity "bears the wound of original sin" (¶ 25), and knowing, too, that the wound is hardly superficial. Human "dignity and vocation," it is believed, is not to be more than human but to be fully human. Andthe fullness of that humanity, it is further claimed, is revealed in the crucified and risen Christ. To know that, to know him, is to be freed from a life that is captive to the denial of failure and death. That core Christian claim is very much at the heart of John Paul's contention against both utopianism and despair.

"Therefore, in order that the demands of justice may be met and attempts to achieve this goal may succeed, what is needed is the gift of grace, a gift that comes from God." And then what may be one of the most graceful and suggestive affirmations in *Centesimus:* "Grace, in cooperation with human freedom, constitutes that mysterious presence of God in history that is providence" (¶ 59). That statement comes toward the end of the encyclical, and it evinces both the modesty and the faith that mark the Church's teaching on social responsibility. Human beings can act in the courage of their uncertainties because they are accompanied by the mysterious presence that is providence. T. S. Eliot writes in *East Coker*, "For us, there is only the trying. The rest is not our business." That could be understood as a statement of melancholic resignation. More accurately, it is an expression of inexpressible relief that we are not God. It is as though to say, "God is God, thank God." Helping humanity to trust that truth is what John Paul calls "the Church's specific and decisive contribution."

R E A L   D O C T R I N E

The powerful sense of possibility and limit that comes through in the teaching of this Pope may put the reader in mind of one of the better-known reflections of the great Protestant thinker Reinhold Niebuhr. In *The Irony of American History* (1952), Niebuhr wrote:

> Nothing worth doing is completed in our lifetime; therefore, we must be saved by hope. Nothing true or beautiful or good makes complete sense in any immediate context of history; therefore, we must be saved by faith. Nothing we do, however virtuous, can be accomplished alone; therefore, we are saved by love. No virtuous act is quite as virtuous from the standpoint of our friend or foe as from our standpoint. Therefore, we must be saved by the final form of love which is forgiveness.

As modestly and carefully defined as it is, Catholic social doctrine is nonetheless real doctrine; it is part of the official teaching of the Church. It is "a valid instrument of evangelization." If it is in any serious sense of the term a Social *Gospel*, it is related to the *evangel*, the good news of God's saving work in Christ. "As such, it proclaims God and his mystery of salvation in Christ to every human being and for that reason reveals man to himself. In this light, *and only in this light*, does it concern itself with everything else"—such as economics, family, the duties of the state, war and peace, and respect for life (¶ 54, emphasis added). Social teaching is derived from Christian anthropology, which is a "chapter of theology." How we are to conduct ourselves in the world (and here he cites his earlier encyclical, *Sollicitudo Rei Socialis*) "belongs to the field of theology and particularly of moral theology" (¶ 55).

We have noted the ways in which *Centesimus* is developing not only the content but also the function and status of social doctrine. John Paul takes pains to underscore that social doctrine is not, so to speak, freestanding. It must never be allowed to break from its moorings in "the mystery of salvation in Christ." It is *only* in the light of that mystery, of insights derived from that mystery, that the Church can speak authoritatively on social questions. Social teaching is closely disciplined by that maxim. If an authoritative social teaching cannot be clearly related to the mystery of salvation, so that it is seen to be an implication of that mystery, the assumption is that we have not understood it rightly. The relationship may not always be direct, it may be more than one step removed, but the relationship must be clear. John Paul seems eager to impress upon Catholics, and no doubt upon separated brothers and sisters, that in its social teaching the Catholic Church is not claiming an independent source of wisdom or authority other than the revelation of God in Christ.

The Church, moreover, is not in the business of burdening consciences unnecessarily. A Catholic is not morally obliged to agree with John Paul or any pope on what might be called contingent historical judgments. For instance, a Catholic may disagree with John Paul's assertion that Marxist socialism has been tried and found disastrous, or that such socialism is necessarily atheistic. We may think such a person obtuse and wrongheaded, but his dissent in no way incurs the judgment that he is in less than good standing with the Church. Similarly, a Catholic may agree with John Paul's strong affirmation of free trade while, at the same time, opposing a specific proposal for an economic community between, say, the United States and Mexico. These are contingent judgments regarding facts and prudential judgments regarding policies on which people may disagree without questioning the Pope's authority in matters of faith and morality. These judgments need not engage what Cardinal Ratzinger calls the "structure of faith." Such judgments are not salvific but instructive, not revealed but reflective.

Two cautions are in order, however. First, one cannot in good conscience endorse a social program that infringes upon the Catholic anthropology that John Paul calls a "chapter of theology." If, for example, a person believes that human freedom and "the subjectivity of society" are the enemies of a just social order, he would seem to have a serious *theological* disagreement with the Pope. Second, even in contingent and prudential judgments one should *want* to "think with the Church" as the mind of the Church is expressed—not exclusively, but always importantly—by the Pope. That is not because one has such great respect for the intellectual acumen of a particular pope. Such respect cannot be demanded if it is not warranted by the evidence. Rather, one wants in this way to think with the Church because of devotion to the Church, and because one is aware of the indispensable role of the Petrine Ministry in the Church. In short, we should want the papacy to exercise its teaching role effectively even when—maybe especially when—a particular pope may be an inept teacher.

As careful as John Paul is in his teaching, he will probably not satisfy all Catholics who worry about the dangers of politicizing the faith and burdening consciences. Nor will he satisfy many Protestants who protest what they view as a confusion of the Gospel. The worried Catholics perhaps can only trust and pray that popes and bishops will always observe the self-denying ordinance set forth and embraced by John Paul. The worried Protestants raise a somewhat more complicated objection. Most Protestants do tend to speak of "the Gospel" in a more narrow sense. By "Gospel" they mean the *kerygma*, the proclamation of God's saving acts, centered in the death and resurrection of Jesus.

THE LAW AND THE GOSPEL

In the classic Reformation phrase, the Gospel is the declaration of "justification by grace through faith because of Christ." And each of those—grace, faith, Christ—is accompanied by an "alone" (*sola*). It is grace alone, faith alone, Christ alone. Correctly understood—and this has been clarified in many theological dialogues with Catholics—the Reformation teaching does not intend to deny that grace engages human cooperation, nor that faith results in God-pleasing works, nor that Christ is always accompanied by his Church, including the saints of past and present. The Reformation proclamation is that when it comes to the ultimate question of how sinners are made righteous before God, people are to rely not on themselves but entirely on the grace of God in Christ that is received by faith. That proclamation is what traditional Protestants mean by "the Gospel."

Catholics, on the other hand, are accustomed to use the term "Gospel" in a more expansive way that includes the entirety of Christian teaching. In Catholic preaching and conversation, "the Gospel" typically extends to what is implicated in what Protestants mean by "the Gospel." For instance, a Catholic will say, "The Gospel demands that we love one another." That way of speaking poses a very big problem for many Protestants and perhaps most acutely for Lutherans. God's Gospel, they insist, *demands* nothing. It is God's Law that makes demands. The Gospel is the good news of what God has done for us. The Law is the news—and, it is often suggested, the bad news—of what God demands of us. This "Law/Gospel dialectic," as it is called, is at the heart of Reformation Christianity. The different ways in which Catholics and Protestants use these terms are entrenched in the linguistic habits of almost five centuries, and both Catholics and Protestants need to be aware of them today if they are to avoid confusing one another.

This is not the place to try to sort out the many confusions and conflicts between Rome and Reformation. Suffice it that the heirs of the Reformation need to be assured that Catholics do indeed rely for their salvation on the utterly gratuitous mercy of God in Jesus Christ. At the same time, Catholics will no doubt continue to talk about "the Gospel" in the more comprehensive and flexible way that Christians have talked about it from the New Testament and early Church fathers up to the present. While welcoming the valid and critically important Reformation insight regarding the grace of God *(sola gratia)*, it would seem a bit excessive to claim that ecumenical sensitivity requires Catholics to adopt the distinctive vocabulary of that limited part of Christian history called the Reformation.

Social teaching is intimately connected to the Gospel and is an "instrument of evangelization" because, in the logic of *Centesimus*, the new birth in Christ cannot be separated from the new life in Christ. Being "born again" is not simply, as some Protestant revivalists put it, a matter of "accepting Jesus as Lord and Savior." Catholics would not deny that it is that for sure. The "born-again experience," however, is not just a moment of intense spiritual illumination. It is less an experience of a lifetime than a lifetime of experience lived in obedience to Christ as Lord and Savior. In the Catholic understanding, people are born again, truly converted, when they are baptized, and the entirety of life is a living out of that baptismal grace. Whether one is baptized as an adult or as an infant, one is born out of sin and death and born into Christ. Moreover, to be born into Christ who is the head is to be born into his body, the Church. Thus Christians say with Saint Paul, "It is no longer I who live but Christ who lives in me" (Galatians 2). The new identity is constituted—and daily reconstituted—by embracing, in one act of faith, Christ and his Church. In this understanding, the Gospel necessarily entails the Church, and the Church is the communal living out of the Gospel. This is the context in which it becomes possible to think of the Social Gospel as really being *Gospel.*

NEW BIRTH, NEW LIFE

As human beings are by nature social beings, so the new life in Christ is emphatically social. Nobody baptizes himself. People are baptized by the society of the Church into the society of the Church. It would then seem to follow that the teaching of that society is social in character. It is teaching about how Christians are to live in the society that is the Church, but also about how they are to conduct themselves in the world outside that society. Recall the proposal that the Church makes its most important contribution by being a "contrast structure" to the other structures in which Christians live. In this sense, social doctrine or the Social Gospel is nothing new. The New Testament is filled with apostolic instruction about how Christians are to live both in the Church and the world. One might even suggest that it would seem very odd if the Church did *not* have a social doctrine, thus leaving those who had experienced the new birth without guidance on how to live the new life.

We can readily acknowledge that the New Testament does not propose a "social doctrine" along the lines initiated by *Rerum Novarum* and developed by *Centesimus Annus.* There are a number of reasons for that, not least among them being the obvious fact that Christians were not then in positions of public authority, and the infant Church was in no position to offer moral counsel on the right ordering of society. In addition, the Christians of the New Testament era lived in the expectation of Christ's imminent return in glory. They would have been amazed, and perhaps bewildered, by the suggestion that two thousand years later the Church would be reflecting on its social responsibilities in the third millennium.

A contemporary Methodist theologian, Stanley Hauerwas of

Duke University, has written provocatively on the theme that "the Church does not *have* a social ethic; the Church *is* a social ethic." In this view, how Christians live out their new obedience in the Church is itself the Church's great social contribution to the society. Those who share that understanding insist that ethics—no less than doctrine, ordered ministry, sacraments, and liturgy—is integral to the life of the Church. In an address in Washington, D.C., during his first visit to the United States in 1979, the Pope raised some ecumenical hackles by suggesting that theological dialogue with other Christians should include not only theology in the usual sense of that term but also Christian morality. He was proposing, as he again does in *Centesimus*, that ethics, in fact, is a "chapter of theology."

Some critics, and not only non-Catholics, thought the Pope was "raising the ecumenical ante" by suggesting that ecumenical dialogue include Christian morality. It might be more accurate to suggest that he intended to deepen and make more concrete the dialogue. If we maintain the distinction between theology and ethics, it would at least seem necessary to say that while theology informs ethics, ethics also informs and tests theology. One may be permitted to wonder, for instance, whether Christians who disagree about whether the unborn child is a God-given life that we are obliged to protect have the same meanings in mind when they talk about "God" and "life" in their theological dialogues.

In 1991, John Cardinal O'Connor of New York wrote to a pro-life delegate to the national assembly of the Evangelical Lutheran Church in America (ELCA). He expressed the strong hope that the ELCA would take a publicly unmistakable position in defense of protecting the unborn. Some delegates and bishops betrayed a fragile understanding of the mutual accountability that is ecumenism when they protested that the Cardinal was "interfering" in the internal affairs of the ELCA. One bishop was quoted as saying that he supported the Lutheran–Roman Catholic ecumenical dialogues, "but those dialogues are about theology, not about ethics." The problem with that, of course, is that the ethics of chief concern to churches is, presumably, *theological* ethics.

Nothing said here is intended to suggest for a moment that Protestants are less concerned about ethics than Catholics. The old Catholic canard that the Protestant teaching of "salvation by faith alone apart from works" is an invitation to moral licentiousness is well laid to rest. Those Protestants who hold themselves accountable to Scripture and the Reformation tradition are frequently much more serious about living the new life in Christ than are many Catholics. As communities of faith, however, they have acute problems in the absence of a churchly order for deliberating questions of great theological and moral moment. (Catholics, needless to say, have big problems as well, but, as we have seen, in the magisterium they have a theologically grounded framework in which the task can be addressed.) Gilbert Meilaender, a Lutheran who teaches at Oberlin College, writes insightfully on "How Churches Crack Up," examining in particular the painful disputes that divided the Lutheran Church —Missouri Synod in the 1970s.

A CASE IN POINT

That Lutheran body was held together for more than a century by shared immigrant experience, ethnicity, familial ties, and the imposing authority of seminary faculties. When those bonds were weakened, as they inevitably were by time and sociological change, there was no way to sustain communal deliberation. The old centers could not hold, and the community fragmented into contending factions of liberals versus conservatives, traditionalists versus moderates. The issues in controversy were moral and theological, and they drove to the very heart of the authority and interpretation of Scripture in the life of the church. As Meilaender notes, what happened in the Missouri Synod was emblematic of a much more general problem. "These are problems of enormous importance and difficulty for any church body that lacks a clearly defined magisterium, and they are no doubt accentuated by the democratic spirit of American Christianity."

Internal church conflicts, whether among Lutherans, Baptists, or anyone else, almost inevitably get defined along the lines of conflicts in the general culture. The problem is more acute when the media are enlisted, as they almost always are, and almost inevitably on the "progressive" side of the conflict in question. Meilaender writes, "If the issues involved—how to read the Bible and how to locate authority within the church—continue to trouble church bodies, we do well to consider carefully whether it can be of any benefit to tackle them via the news conference. In our time and place the media will almost always be on the side of those who claim conscientious freedom; they will seldom be able to understand sympathetically a church's need for a magisterial voice to articulate and sustain its public teaching. Almost never will helpful theological discussion be fostered in this way; almost always the church will be harmed."

Some Catholics may resist the idea that this is their problem because they do indeed have a magisterium that is more or less well defined. Flannery O'Connor is among those who have observed that the besetting sin of Catholics is smugness. Even the most sympathetic observer would not likely suggest that a thoughtful and vibrant process of communal deliberation is evident in contemporary Catholicism. The reality of factionalism, often exceedingly bitter factionalism, is rife within Catholicism, and not least in this country. Among some "progressives," there is an effort to distinguish sharply, if not to separate, the "infallible" and "ordinary" teaching of the magisterium. This would seem to reflect an unwillingness to attend to the entirety of the Church's teaching with the "responsive listening" to which Catholics are pledged.

To say that we are obliged only by infallible teaching is to effectively remove ourselves from the Catholic conversation. Pius XII was the last pope to speak formally in the infallible mode, and that was in 1950. Between then and now would be a

very long absence from the conversation. Infallibility is a limited
and essentially negative concept. The teaching of infallibility is
that under carefully defined circumstances, the pope speaks in a
manner that is protected from substantial error. Such a juridi-
cally cramped notion of authoritative teaching is far removed
from the vibrant conversation of Catholic faith and life. As is the
case with a loving father or a wise teacher or a cherished friend,
we do not listen to the pope only when he, as it were, pulls out
all the stops and invokes infallibility. As with such a father,
teacher, or friend, we are in a sustained state of attentiveness.
We are attentive not, or not first of all, because of our respect
for the person and office of the pope, but because of our devotion to the Church that he serves. Of course it helps considerably when the pope is as impressive a teacher as is John Paul II.

TRUSTING THE PRESENCE

There is no blinking the fact, however, that the ecclesial conversation is today often replaced by a factious cacophony, and not
least of all on questions of social doctrine. It is not uncommon
to find people on all sides of the Catholic barricades (the zigzag-
ging barricades have more than two sides) who confidently assert that their opponents are no longer in communion with the
Church. It is said by some traditionalists, for instance, that the
progressives have clearly gone into schism and apostasy, while
the same progressives assure us that their opponents are in communion with a "pre–Vatican II Church" that no longer exists.
"The attractive thing about Luther, Calvin, and that bunch,"
says one traditionalist, "is that they, unlike today's dissenters,
had the decency to leave the Church when they had left the
Church."

Such polemics aside, however, one is impressed that nobody
(the late Archbishop Lefebvre excepted) seems interested in
moving toward a formal break with the Petrine Ministry that is
Rome and the bishops in communion with Rome. Even those

most publicly defiant of the magisterium still seek the color of magisterial authority for their views. That may be deplored as hypocrisy or welcomed as a sign of a deep Catholic sensibility that whatever may be wrong in the Church, it is still the Church. Further, it is recognized that its being the Church, rather than simply a church, is intimately and inextricably tied to communion with Peter.

Catholics will no doubt continue to contend with one another. Sometimes contention will be transformed into conversation. But all families have contentious children and sometimes contentious parents, and Catholicism is a very big family. Not least among the tasks of the magisterium is to try and maintain communion in contention. And the magisterium is inescapably hinged on what is claimed for the Petrine Ministry. Catholics frequently express irritation when others describe them as the people who "believe in the pope." They protest, rightly, that there is much more to being a Catholic than believing in the pope and, anyway, they do not "believe in" the pope the way they believe in, for instance, God. All that is true enough, of course. But it is nonetheless the relationship to Rome, more than anything else, that distinguishes Catholic Christians from others. One may be Lutheran, Anglican, or Orthodox, for instance, and be committed to almost all that Catholics hold, except for this relationship to the one who claims to be Peter among us. And, of course, one cannot make that commitment unless one is persuaded that—however confused and tortured its development through the centuries—this form of apostolic leadership most fully approximates what Christ intended for his continuing community of discipleship.

Among the "new things" considered by John Paul in *Centesimus*, then, is the magisterium's development of a social doctrine aimed at helping those who know the new birth to live the new life. Those who expect this Social Gospel to answer all their questions about how they are to live or how the world is to be set right will be greatly disappointed. The doctrine intends to clarify and engage the questions, while providing a conceptual and institutional framework that makes it possible for those who disagree to remain in conversation with one another. Its purpose is to provide a disciplined way of bringing to remembrance the Great Tradition to which all Christians are more or less pledged, and thus it keeps Catholics in conversation also with separated brothers and sisters.

Moreover, if, as Christians claim, they are the people ahead of time, the people who have sighted in Christ the future of all humanity, this teaching requires that they be in conversation with all that is human. If that is the case, one may suggest that this Social Gospel really is what the word "gospel" means— good news. The "lasting paradigm" set forth by Leo XIII and advanced by this Pope may then be seen as an invitation to move confidently and together into the future, trusting the grace and freedom that constitute the "mysterious presence of God in history that is providence."

NOTES

Page 111. Peter Berger in *Aspiring to Freedom*, Eerdmans, 1989.

Pages 113–14. For a trenchant critique of the U.S. bishops' pastoral letter on nuclear weaponry, see George Weigel, *Tranquillitas Ordinis: The Present Failure and Future Challenge of American Catholic Thought on War and Peace*, Oxford, 1987. For a critical analysis of the bishops' letter on economics, see Michael Novak et al., *Toward the Future*, University Press of America, 1984, and *Liberty and Justice for All*, Notre Dame, 1986.

Pages 126–27. Among the many writings of Stanley Hauerwas, the theme of the Church as a social ethic and his basic project are perhaps best set forth in *A Community of Character: Toward a Constructive Christian Social Ethic*, Notre Dame, 1981.

Pages 128–29. Gilbert Meilaender in *First Things*, June/July 1991.

Pages 129–30. On the question of infallible and ordinary teaching, see "The Ecclesial Vocation of the Theologian," a 1990 instruction from the Congregation for the Doctrine of the Faith.

Interlude

Chapter Five

. . .

READING THE SIGNS
OF THE TIMES

*When it is evening, you say, "It will be fair
weather, for the sky is red." And in the
morning, "It will be stormy today, for the sky
is red and threatening." You know how to
interpret the appearance of the sky, but you
cannot interpret the signs of the times.*

—Matthew 16

Since the Second Vatican Council, the theme of "reading the
signs of the times" has been prominent in Catholic thinking.
That theme is also a salient feature in this Pope's writing and
speaking. While he pays close attention to history, John Paul is
by no means a "historicist." That is to say, he emphatically does
not believe that all social and cultural facts are determined by
impersonal historical forces. Nor does he accept the proposition
that there are no experiences, standards, or truths that transcend
particular historical circumstances. But he does insist that the
way of history is the way of the Church; indeed, history is the
way of God who entered history in the God-man Jesus Christ.
In understanding history, we are to be ever alert to the mysterious conjunction of divine grace and human freedom that is
providence.

The theme of reading the signs of the times has been taken
up with notable enthusiasm by the "political pilgrims" of recent
decades who have followed the "red skies" of socialist promise,
proclaiming again and again that they have discovered in these

revolutionary signs the future of humanity. But now we live in a time when, as the Pope observes, "ideologies are being increasingly discredited" (¶ 5). He repeatedly cautions us against replacing the misguided enthusiasms of the past with new enthusiasms in our reading the signs of the times.

Yet, while guarding against unbridled enthusiasms, we have no choice but to try to read the signs of the times. Our readings should be sober, circumspect, and must often be offered as tentative. We saw in the last chapter how John Paul attempts to be very careful in circumscribing the sphere in which the Church pronounces authoritatively. The authority of the magisterium is not to be squandered on mere speculation. Reading the signs of the times requires a delicate mix of trust and skepticism. We are to trust that God is indeed at work in history, but we are to be skeptical of unseemly claims to certitude in discerning precisely what he is up to.

In the teaching of this Pope there is unquestionably a heightened sense of historical expectation. As we have seen, this sense of expectation is pronounced in connection with the beginning of the third millennium that is nearly upon us. Leopold von Ranke, the nineteenth-century German historian, wrote that God is equally present to every moment in history. That is no doubt true. But it is perhaps the case that not every moment of history is equally present to God. Put differently, there are some times more than others when the meeting of divine grace and human freedom makes it possible to discern more clearly a providential purpose. John Paul invites us to entertain the prospect that ours is one of those times.

THE PACE QUICKENS

As a result, there is a quickening pace in the development of the Church's social doctrine. Among the many indicators of that sharpened pace is the way the Pope cites the tradition of social doctrine. In the footnotes to *Centesimus*, there are 143 citations of earlier papal statements. Forty-five of those refer to Leo XIII, whom this encyclical intends to honor. Of the remaining 98 citations, John Paul cites himself 61 times. The six pontificates between Leo and the present Pope (excluding John Paul I, who was pope only one month), covering a period of 75 years, receive a total of only 37 citations.

The three encyclicals that have dominated much of Catholic social thinking in the last three decades—John XXIII's *Mater et Magistra* and *Pacem in Terris*, and Paul VI's *Populorum Progressio* —receive a combined total of only seven references. The Pope is, as he says, "looking around" at the "new things." By placing his own imprint so strongly upon the tradition, he would seem to suggest both that he is looking in a different way and that new things are happening with increased rapidity. Vatican-watchers have opined that he also feels that he is under the pressure of time, not only by the approaching millennium but also by intimations of his own mortality in this the thirteenth year of his pontificate.

The Pope evinces a palpable sense of urgency that at the end of this century of horrors, we must learn the lessons of humanity's monstrous errors. "Never again!" is the cry of Jews and others who have internalized the unspeakable horror of the Holocaust. John Paul alludes specifically to that lesson in what happens when "human freedom is detached from obedience to the truth and consequently from the duty to respect the rights of others." "Here," he writes, "we recall the Jewish people in particular, whose terrible fate has become a symbol of the aberration of which man is capable when he turns against God" (¶ 17).

When, by the grace of God, great horrors have passed, we cannot simply heave a sigh of relief and put the matter from our minds. It is morally imperative that we try to understand *why* they happened. The entire human project is implicated in these events. They are not simply things that happened "out there" in an anonymous arena called history. In reading the signs of the times, we are reading about ourselves. As Aleksandr Solzhenitsyn has urged us again and again, we must discern the line of good and evil that runs through our own hearts. "Never again!" means that there must be remembrance and repentance. A more promising future lies on the far side of contrition, confession, forgiveness, and amendment of life. As John Paul writes, "Thus the first and most important task is accomplished within man's heart" (¶ 51).

The Third Reich, declaring itself to be the Thousand-Year Reich, lasted for twelve years. In its last four years of increasingly unbridled brutality and bloodletting, it was responsible for perhaps 50 million deaths, including all the casualties of World War II. The full ghastliness of this century is evident in the fact that when it comes to the statistics of mass murder, we deal in rough estimates, "giving or taking" a million or ten million, or more. The horror of Communism lasted more than seventy years, and in some large parts of the world, notably China, it is by no means past. Through wars, induced famines, purges, and ideologically driven mass killings, it is estimated that Communism is responsible for at least 100 million deaths in this century. Some scholars say 60 million, others 150 million. Take your pick. In this, presumably the most enlightened of centuries, the arithmetic of death is less than precise. This much is clear, however: the atrocities committed in the name of and for the sake of Communism constitute the most massive assault against humanity in all of history.

Little wonder that John Paul insists that we remember—that we try to understand what happened, why it happened, and how it might be prevented in the future. Especially for the people of Eastern and Central Europe, the memory is bitter and divisive. During the years of Communist domination, the Pope writes, "much hatred and ill will have accumulated." A passion for retribution and the evening-up of scores could lead to a situation in which resentments "will re-explode after the collapse of dictatorship." John Paul writes in an almost poignant vein: "It is to be hoped that hatred and violence will not triumph in people's hearts . . . and that people will grow in the spirit of peace and forgiveness" (¶ 27).

We in the democracies cannot easily appreciate the tangle of passions and resentments that mock the aspirations toward democracy in formerly Communist countries. True, during the cold war and going back to the Bolshevik takeover of 1917, there were sharp divisions among us, too. Whatever their intentions, many intellectuals in the West, and all too many church leaders, played the role of apologists for Communist oppression. Some simply downplayed the horrors. Others, more openly and contemptibly, urged the West to appreciate the "positive achievements" of Communism. Yet others defined the "liberation struggles" of Marxist-Leninism as "the right side of history," to which the democracies of the West were opposed and thereby doomed.

THE ANTI-ANTI-COMMUNISTS

It is painful for us to remember how widespread and respectable was this belittling of the Communist terror. Even in the face of immense and indisputable evidence, most intellectuals refused to say that they were anti-Communist. It was assumed that every decent person was anti-Nazi, as it surely should have been assumed. But those who accepted the designation "anti-Communist" were derided as "right-wingers," "ideologues," and "cold warriors." Indeed, even today, even in the light of everything that everybody should now know about Communism, it is still the case that in some circles any discussion of the subject, such as our present reflection, is dismissed as "anti-Communist" and therefore self-evidently beyond the pale of respectable discourse.

The opprobrium attached to anti-Communism is culturally entrenched and, in ironic ways, extends far beyond the West. After the failed coup of August 1991, Mikhail Gorbachev was widely criticized for having kept members of the old regime in power. In reaction, trying to hold on to the Communism in which he professed his belief, Gorbachev warned the Soviet parliament against "a wave of anti-Communist hysteria." One delegate responded, "Mikhail Sergeyevich, I'm a political worker, I'm a teacher, and you say there's a sort of anti-Communist hysteria. I know that anti-Communism emerges as a reaction to Communism, just as antifascism arises as a reaction to fascism . . . An organization such as the CPSU [Communist Party of the Soviet Union] was based on nonlegal principles, it was a party of state treachery." So why is it "hysteria," she was asking, to be strongly anti-Communist? In Russia as in America, it would sound very odd to hear someone accused of antifascist hysteria.

It is not the case, of course, that a great many people in the West were actually in favor of Communism; it is simply that they were extremely uncomfortable with anti-Communism. They were and are unequivocally anti-Nazi, but, at best, very equivocally anti-Communist. It is to be feared that those who were equivocally anti-Communist were doubtfully anti-Communist. Of course, a big difference is that after World War II, Nazism was an evil of the past, whereas Communism was and is an evil of the present. Communism during the cold war years was a present danger, whereas Nazism had been definitively dispatched by history.

Throughout the cold war there was a systematic and successful effort to depict anti-Communism as vulgar and déclassé. The excesses of Senator Joseph McCarthy provided a handy reference by which anti-Communism was made synonymous with "McCarthyism." Moreover, many of the "Old Left" were, in the Depression of the 1930s, understandably disillusioned with democracy and capitalism. They desperately embraced an alternative that claimed not only to explain the failures of the democracies but to provide a "scientific" path to a lastingly just world. Even so moderate a thinker as John Bennett of Union Seminary, New York, was more exercised about countering anti-Communism than about countering Communism. In the 1970 preface to his *Christianity and Communism Today*, Bennett cautioned against anti-Communist "myths," arguing that Communism had largely given way to nationalism, and that the appropriate response to Marxism was one of "dialogue" in which we in the West had much to learn about social justice. He warned against "a holy war against Communism."

> As we see revolutionary movements which have Communist inspiration or support in Asia or Africa or Latin America, we should not conjure up the old fear of a Communist monolith behind these developments and we should not seek to keep an American counter-revolutionary lid on them . . . Revolutionary Communism of the Cuban type may succeed in establishing itself in some of these situations and this may be better for them than other actual alternatives . . . The world is and will continue to be disturbed for as long as we can see ahead, and in the United States we have our own need of radical change, in our cities and in the plight of our black citizens, with no sign of a comprehensive program to meet that need.

The last point, that we in the West had our own unsolved problems, was used as a frequent clincher in discussions about the evils of Communism. Whatever may be wrong with Communism, it was said, we are in no moral position to cast stones. Communism may impose a police state, deny religious freedom, and sentence millions to slave labor and death in the gulag, but remember that there are people in America who go to bed hungry, that we have not yet rid ourselves of racism, and thousands of homes still do not have indoor plumbing. This, too, was part of the argument for "moral equivalence" between "two unjust systems," and it was an effective inhibition against the voicing of anti-Communist sentiment in respectable circles—not least of all in the higher councils of many American churches. During the long night of the cold war, Christians in "the captive nations" pleaded for attention and help from the churches in the West, but few responded. The plight of Christians under Communism was viewed as a parochial concern of certain "right wing" ethnic groups in exile, and talk about "captive nations" was deemed to be both in bad taste and dangerously belligerent.

SORTING OUT CULPABILITIES

In partial explanation, if not exculpation, of those who minimized the evil of Communism, it should be noted that many were motivated by a fear and an expectation. The *fear* was that hostility to Communism would increase the chances of nuclear war. In their view, nothing, absolutely nothing, could be given precedence over physical survival—their own and, according to some scenarios, that of the planet Earth. That was aptly called survivalism. The *expectation* was that Communism was here to stay and quite possibly on the ascendancy, so we had better make our peace with it. That was called peaceful coexistence. Yet others hoped for some kind of long-term "convergence" between tyranny and freedom.

For years to come, honest people in the West will be trying to sort out their responses to the monstrous evil of Communism. But that task should be relatively easy compared with the "moral reconstruction" that John Paul calls for in post-Communist Europe. In a recent conversation, a devout Christian and leader of the democracy movement in Romania put it this way: "It is either forgiveness or retribution. Retribution means national suicide in a civil war that would have no end, because the crimes were without end. How do you allocate guilt when almost everyone was a collaborator? And how can there be forgiveness when those who have the power to absolve were the criminals?" He was speaking, of course, about the notorious alliance between the hierarchy of the Orthodox Church and the dictatorship of Nicolae Ceausescu.

The dilemmas of remembrance and forgiveness are at the heart of the Pope's hope for "moral reconstruction." The situation is not entirely unlike that of the fourth century when the Church had to deal with the *traditores* among priests and bishops. The *traditores* were those who surrendered the Scriptures when, under the persecution by the Emperor Diocletian, possessing the Bible was forbidden. After the persecution had passed, the Donatists, as they were called, refused to recognize the ministries of the *traditores* and those whom they had ordained. On behalf of what was recognized as the Catholic position, Saint Augustine made the argument that the unworthiness of the minister does not affect the validity of sacraments, since the true minister of the sacraments is Christ. In much of Central and Eastern Europe, that argument has to be made again today.

In most countries, the Catholic Church was not as severely compromised under Communism as was Orthodoxy. Indeed, Catholic bishops, clergy, and faithful were frequently heroic in bearing witness to the faith under persecution. John Paul rightly calls attention to that heroism in *Centesimus*. This does not necessarily demonstrate the moral superiority of Catholicism. When the frozen burial grounds of the gulag archipelago give up their dead, millions of Orthodox martyrs will swell the company of the saints who forever praise the Lamb who was slain (Revelation 13). Yet Orthodoxy and Catholicism have had a very different historical experience of church-state relations. What is pejoratively called the Caesaropapism of Orthodoxy, in which the patriarch is subordinated to the emperor, goes back to ancient Byzantium and provided a justifying precedent, even when the emperor in question was Joseph Stalin. Moreover, Catholics under Communism were greatly strengthened by the fact that their symbolic and institutional leadership, centered in the Pope, was in the free world. (Western intellectuals could afford to refer to "the free world" in the ironic mode. Those who lived and died under Communism could not and did not.)

Patriarch Alexy II of the Russian Orthodox Church wrestles with the same set of problems addressed by John Paul. In a recent statement he noted that the end of Communism means "that a new page in history has been turned." The new page forces attention on the questions of remembrance and forgiveness. "History is now passing judgment. Each of us has a claim to make against the party formerly in power and against the state government for the many unparalleled sufferings which have been our lot or that of our neighbors throughout the past 73 years. But do not let this judgment allow the devilish seeds of malice and bitterness take root in our hearts."

Alexy recognizes that the suffering and moral corruption were pervasive, but the experience of the Church was singular:

Of course, other social groupings, such as the peasants, the intelligentsia, scientists, those working in culture, or the army, suffered repression; but the regime was not intent on their mass destruction. As far as the Church was concerned, however, the policy was to annihilate totally millions of believers, and almost all of the Orthodox clergy perished . . . By God's mercy and the power of his grace the Russian Church survived, kept the faith pure, and attracted millions of members among new generations, who now constitute its flock and clergy. At the same time we recognize with humility that not all of the Church's ministers were equal to the task of their vocation in those trying years. Our Lord and Righteous Judge will reward each according to his merits. We need to purify and renew our Church, and in so doing we should be guided by a conciliar mind, by canonical order, and by each person's responsibility in conscience before God and before the people of God.

The Communist regime had for decades put "reliable" priests and bishops into positions of church authority, many of them being directly controlled by the KGB. Priests who dared to dissent from this corrupt arrangement, such as Father Gleb Yakunin, were censured and isolated by church authorities under orders from the party. The politically reliable clergy were those who participated in the programs of the World Council of Churches, as well as various Christian-Marxist dialogues and "peace movements." As things turned out, these are the clergy who, no matter how morally compromised, had some exposure to Western democracy and ecumenical interaction with Roman Catholics and Protestants. Historically, Russian Orthodoxy has had slight experience with, or sympathy for, either democracy or ecumenism. Thus the tangled web of memory and forgiveness becomes more tangled when we consider that the priests and hierarchs who most slavishly served their Communist masters may have an invaluable contribution to make in the post-Communist era.

Alexy himself was, on the anniversary of his election as patriarch, confronted by *Izvestia* with the fact that he had been listed in secret state documents as among the most pliable of the senior hierarchs. He replied with a candor that most would describe as a confession:

Defending one thing, it was necessary to give somewhere else. Were there any other organizations, or any other people among those who had to carry responsibility not only for themselves but for thousands of other fates, who in those years in the Soviet Union were not compelled to act likewise? Before those people, however, to whom the compromises, silence, forced passivity or expressions of loyalty permitted by leaders of the church in those years caused pain, before those people, and not only before God, I ask forgiveness, understanding and prayer.

A S   F O R   T H E   C A T H O L I C S   .   .   .

The Catholic situation is significantly different. In some places, and nowhere more dramatically than in Poland, the Catholic Church was what John Paul says the Church must be everywhere, "the sign and safeguard of freedom." The 1978 election of a Pope from that place at that time was, in the view of almost all Eastern Europeans, surely no coincidence. People who do not read the signs of the times so as to see the mysterious presence and purpose of providence in this pontificate are suspected of being entirely bereft of faith or discernment. And yet in some countries, and perhaps also even in Poland, there were *traditores.* Not all bishops and priests were steadfast; some went along, some actively collaborated. There are many ways of offering just a pinch of incense to Caesar. We who have not been through their ordeal and have not faced their temptations must be slow to judge. But the reality is not pretty, and it is that reality that impels the urgency of this Pope's appeal for moral reconstruction.

In addition to having the distinct disadvantage of being a heresy, the Donatist response to this reality could only lead to the explosion of the accumulated hatred and ill will that the Pope worries about. The morally "pure" Church cannot separate itself from the compromised. The "horizon of the Church," John Paul writes, "is man in his concrete reality as sinful and righteous" (¶ 53). (One notes the similarity to Martin Luther's understanding of man as *simul iustus et peccator*—at the same time righteous and sinful.)

If the Donatist option is precluded, what is left? Collective amnesia, perhaps. "Forgive and forget"—meaning that everybody should forget that there is anything to forgive. But a society determined to pretend that the difference between good and evil is of little consequence is a society eviscerated of moral content. The earnest plea of this encyclical is that we should remember. Above all, this successor to Peter would "bring to remembrance" Christ's teaching about forgiveness and a transcendent destiny that frees us from captivity to the past. At the heart of the darkness of Communism was the denial of the truth. Only by facing the truth about ourselves and our past are we opened to the truth that makes us free (John 8). In other words, the remedy for the damage done by Communism cannot be the denial practiced by Communism. It cannot be collective amnesia or indifference to moral truth. Nor can it be Donatist sectarianism or retribution. The only way is the way of contrition and forgiveness, in the assurance of God's love for a humanity that is both sinful and righteous.

In his visit to Poland after the imposition of martial law in December 1981, John Paul spoke of standing with a people "beneath the cross of Christ." Timothy Garton Ash, who chronicled the events leading up to 1989 perhaps better than anyone in the West, comments: "As much Western news coverage has amply demonstrated, it is impossible to translate into foreign newsprint what he had to say. It is impossible because he speaks to the Poles through a tapestry of symbols and allusions—historical, literary, philosophical, Mariological—each of which requires at least a paragraph of explanation. It is impossible because so much depends on a theatrical delivery that John Gielgud once called 'perfect.' It is impossible because poetry is what gets lost in translation."

Impossible or not, Ash conveys something of the spirit of the Pope's presence and message:

> His theme was victory. Out of this political defeat, he told them, they are called to win a moral victory. In part this must be an internal, spiritual victory: "Man is called to victory over himself," the victory of martyrdom, the victory of the cross. "It is the saints and the beatified," he declared in Kraków, "who show us the path to the victory that God achieves in human history." As the individual, so also the nation is called to the moral victory. This moral victory, however, is not to be won merely by patient suffering in

faith. No, it demands "living in truth." "It means," as he explained at Jasna Gora, "that I make an effort to be a person with a conscience . . . I call good and evil by name . . . It means: love of neighbor; it means: fundamental *solidarity* between human beings." . . . Effortlessly recapturing the word *renewal (odnowa)* from the communist dictionary, he preached the imperative of "moral and social renewal." The nation must bear witness to the truth as it did in August 1980, "that witness which amazed the whole world, when the Polish worker stood up for himself with the gospel in his hand and a prayer on his lips." Today, too, the Poles must not cease to stand up for certain fundamental human and civil rights.

BE NOT AFRAID

From the very beginning of his pontificate, John Paul spoke to those under the Communist yoke in terms not of survivalism nor of coexistence but of victory. The motto on his episcopal crest is *Totus tuus* ("All yours"), reflecting his devotion to the Blessed Virgin, but his motto might also be *Nolite timere*, "Be not afraid!" the words Jesus spoke to the disciples during the storm on the Sea of Galilee. On October 22, 1978, in the sermon at his installation as bishop of Rome, he three times cried out, "Be not afraid!" The French journalist André Frossard comments:

That October day when he appeared for the first time on the steps of St. Peter's, with a big crucifix planted in front of him like a two-handed sword, and his first words [in Italian], *Non abbiate paura!* (Be not afraid!) echoed over the square, everyone realized then and there that something had happened in heaven: after the man of good will who had opened the Council, after the deeply spiritual man who had closed it, and after an interlude as gentle and fleeting as the flight of the dove, God was sending a witness.

In *Centesimus* John Paul looks back on the events of 1989 that he was so instrumental in bringing about, and asks about the lessons to be learned. If we are to get to the heart of what went so monstrously wrong, John Paul urges, we must look to the ideas that gave birth to the wrong. The poison was in the seed of the idea called socialism. He writes, "Pope Leo foresaw the negative consequences—political, social, and economic—of the social order proposed by 'socialism,' which at that time was still only a social philosophy and not yet a fully structured movement." The problems of the working class were indeed severe, but John Paul says that Leo recognized that the "simple and radical solution" proposed by socialism would result in a "remedy that would prove worse than the sickness" (¶ 12). In the judgment of this Pope, Leo XIII has been monumentally vindicated in his analysis of what was wrong with the idea of socialism.

The practice of "real socialism" followed from the philosophy of socialism. In underscoring the prescience of Leo, the Pope leaves no doubt that "real socialism" is not an aberration but a realization of the socialist idea. If *Centesimus* is right, there would seem to be nothing that is rescuable from the socialist idea, even when it is dressed up as an "ideal." There is enormous, and perhaps understandable, resistance to this conclusion. There are those who would urge, for example, that in this encyclical the Pope is recommending more socialism for the West and more capitalism for the formerly Communist countries. But that construal has no basis in the text of *Centesimus*. The entire argument of the encyclical makes such an interpretation implausible.

John Paul does press many recommendations upon the West. The principles of solidarity and subsidiarity, for instance.

A stronger public role for morality and religion, and a deeper commitment to help the poor, for other instances. Nowhere, however, does he say or imply that the problems of the West might be remedied by a measure of socialism. Precisely and explicitly to the contrary, he could hardly be clearer in declaring that socialism is irrefragably wrongheaded. He endorses Leo's condemnation of the idea that the "poor man's envy" should be turned into a principle of justice by which wealth is coercively redistributed, taking it from the rich in order to make it, supposedly, "the common property of all." Were the contentions of the socialists put into effect, Leo wrote, "the working man himself would be among the first to suffer." Then he added for good measure that socialist proposals "are moreover emphatically unjust, for they would rob the lawful possessor, distort the functions of the state, and create utter confusion in the community." Lest anyone not understand his purpose in quoting Leo at such length, John Paul comments that the evils of real socialism "could not be better expressed" (¶ 12).

Some impossibly obdurate souls will no doubt continue to urge the socialist "solution." Socialism is the name of their dream. It is a chimera, an infinitely malleable and unfalsifiable fantasy. Every socialism that turns out to be what Leo and John Paul say socialism must turn out to be they lightly dismiss as an aberration of "true socialism." Such theorists must be left to their tired and tattered dreams. At least for Catholic social teaching, *Centesimus* indicates that the discussion has moved on, and it invites us to move on with it.

MAKING DEMOCRACY MORE DEMOCRATIC

The challenge before us now is how to make what John Paul calls "the new capitalism" or "the business economy" or, most simply, "the free economy" work better, especially for the poor and marginalized. In other words, the challenge is to make democratic capitalism more genuinely democratic. That is challenge enough for several lifetimes. Perhaps not much is to be done about those who will persist in claiming that a more democratic capitalism is really democratic socialism, except to give them time. Their attachment to the term "democratic socialism" betrays a certain fondness for the oxymoronic, and a desire to cling to a familiar dispute that *Centesimus* has left behind.

In helping us to understand what went so radically wrong in the past and how it might be prevented in the future, John Paul underscores that "the fundamental error of socialism is anthropological in nature." The first anthropological error is reductionism. The individual is reduced to being no more than an element in the social organism. While John Paul is highly critical of individual*ism*, he is a champion of the individual person as a moral agent. And that touches on the second anthropological error of socialism, namely, that "the good of the individual can be realized without reference to his free choice." Here we recall the Pope's emphasis upon "the subjectivity of society." When the individual is no longer a subject but, rather, an object of anonymous social planning, he is deprived of his freedom and, therefore, of his human dignity (¶ 13).

A person deprived of freedom cannot do work that is truly his, nor can he enjoy the benefits of that work. "A person who is deprived of something he can call 'his own' and of the possibility of earning a living through his own initiative comes to depend on the social machine and on those who control it" (¶ 13). Two insights of note are raised here. In the American context, discussions of recent years have focused on the problem of "welfare dependency." Policies intended to help the poor tend to create what are called "perverse incentives" for remaining poor. As we shall see, John Paul's reflections on subsidiarity and what he views as the excesses of the welfare state point us to new and more promising directions in responding to the needs of those who are marginalized from the free economy.

The second insight is in the words "those who control it." Here and elsewhere, the Pope wants to personalize the exercise of power and responsibility. As we have seen, socialist theory and habits of speech have a powerful depersonalizing effect. It is said that "Society" is doing this or that, or that a policy is adopted by "collective" decision-making. John Paul always calls us back to the fact that real people, people with names and interests and goals, are making decisions and exercising control. Social programs of all sorts, also in our society, tend to hide this reality behind the anonymity of "Society."

Among the baneful effects of the patterns criticized by the Pope is the demoralization of those who work in such programs. In the American setting, we are diminished by the fact that for many, if not most, Americans the term "social worker" more readily suggests "bureaucrat" than "helper." This has come about not simply because of conservative attacks on the welfare state. Rather, the experience of those in these social programs has led them to the suspicion that the programs are motored at least as much by the interests of those who provide services as by the needs of those who receive them. Even more demoralizing is the suspicion that such programs perpetuate and exacerbate the problems that they were designed to remedy. Also in the West, we need to explore the policy implications of the subjectivity of society, recognizing that "the social nature of man" is chiefly fulfilled in "intermediary groups" that are independent from the state (¶ 13).

The "first cause" of the disaster that is real socialism, however, goes much deeper. It is atheism (¶ 13). Many thinkers over the years have held that atheism was incidental to, and therefore detachable from, socialism. The component of atheism was frequently attributed to Marx's personal fixations about religion or to the fact that reactionary churches had opposed socialism's program of justice. The Pope argues, however, that if a person is no more than what Marx called "an ensemble of social relationships" and if those in control presume to embody the direction of Society, then atheism *necessarily* follows. The "collective subject" of the socialist society cannot tolerate other subjects who insist upon the freedom to exercise their "transcendent dignity"

(¶ 13). Those who testify that Christ is Lord are saying that the state (or the party, or the proletariat, or the revolution) is not lord. Their testimony, perhaps even their existence, cannot be tolerated by the totalitarian regime.

THE INTOLERABLE CHURCH

The formula for totalitarianism was first proposed by Benito Mussolini: "Everything within the state, nothing against the state, nothing outside the state." This helps to explain why the hostility of real socialism to the Church is not incidental but necessary. The Pope writes, "The state or the party that claims to be able to lead history toward perfect goodness and that sets itself above all values cannot tolerate the affirmation of an objective criterion of good and evil beyond the will of those in power, since such a criterion could be used to judge their actions. This explains why totalitarianism attempts to destroy the Church or at least to reduce her to submission, making her an instrument of its own ideological apparatus" (¶ 45).

By equating itself with society the state seeks immunity from external judgment. The very idea of limited government, of the state as servant rather than master of society, requires such external judgment. In our society, too, religious communities are the primary institutional bearers of witness to sources of transcendent judgment. To say, as we do in the Pledge of Allegiance, that ours is a nation "under God" is to say that not only the state but the entire social order is under judgment. Universities, the press, and myriad other institutions also have a critical role to play in providing "an objective criterion of good and evil beyond the will of those in power." But the popularly legitimated institutions that provide that *ultimate* judgment are the communities of religious commitment.

The atheism that is inherent in the logic of socialism, John Paul writes, also owes something to "the rationalism of the Enlightenment, which views human and social reality in a mechanistic way" (¶ 13). The Pope is not arguing that we can or should repeal the Enlightenment or go back to a period before the eighteenth century. As many scholars note, there was not just one Enlightenment but several Enlightenments. The Scottish Enlightenment that so influenced the American Founders, for example, had an ample appreciation of the purposes of "Nature and Nature's God." It was not the rationalistic, mechanistic, reductionistic, and therefore atheistic Enlightenment criticized by John Paul. Moreover, the achievements of democratic thought and practice affirmed by the Pope are attributable in large part to Enlightenment insights refracted through the English and American experience. In the European mind, and also in Vatican documents of the past, 1789 in France has loomed much larger than 1776 in America. That has contributed to a certain coolness, to put it gently, toward the Enlightenment and its political offspring.

The subject of the Enlightenment touches on an objection that has been raised to Catholic social teaching. It is frequently said that Leo XIII, in order to co-opt some of the compelling rhetoric of the opposition, uncritically adopted an Enlightenment notion of individual rights. From *Rerum Novarum* up through an encyclical such as *Populorum Progressio*, Catholic social teaching fairly bristles with "rights language." This, it is said, has reinforced the obsession with rights in the public moral discourse of Western democracies. As political philosopher Ronald Dworkin confidently asserts, "Rights are trumps." Many seem to think that rights are, in fact, not only trumps but the only cards in the deck. The problem with rights language as the dominant mode of public discourse is that, historically and at present, it is associated with a radical individualism. It tends to picture a social order composed only of the state and the autonomous individual, with the latter having certain "entitlements" or "claims" or "rights" that the former must respect.

That is not the understanding of the social order found in *Centesimus*. The subjectivity of society assumes a multiplicity of actors, of which the state is only one and by no means the dominant actor. While he champions the individual, the Pope is sharply critical of individualism. The individual expresses and fulfills himself communally through myriad associations and allegiances freely chosen and adhered to. The stress is not on individual rights but on communal obligations that do not compromise freedom but order freedom to moral truth. Communities of memory, mutual aid, and moral formation hold center stage in the social choreography of *Centesimus*. The constantly recurring language is not about rights but about community, dignity, values, responsibility, truth, and solidarity.

RIGHTS AND RESPONSIBILITIES

The words "right" and "rights" in this encyclical occur, by my count, 71 times. Nearly half of those occurrences are in connection with John Paul's description of the teaching of Leo XIII. Leo, it must be admitted, did tend to be somewhat promiscuous in multiplying rights. There are the rights of workers, the right to private property, the right to private association, the right to limited working hours, the right to a just wage, and much more. John Paul does not deny, indeed he explicitly affirms, the values that Leo wanted to protect, but he typically does so in language and logic other than that of rights. With exceptions, he uses rights language in a more generic sense, as in "human rights" and the "rights of conscience." Rights language necessarily occurs in John Paul's reiteration of the Vatican's long-standing devotion to the United Nations and international covenants, the latter being fraught with references to rights.

The Pope does employ the vocabulary of rights by insisting upon the "right to life" of the unborn, but even that is framed in terms of our obligation to the weakest among us. Otherwise, in making his own argument—as distinct from his discussions of Leo and international covenants—he tends to use language other than that of "rights talk." It is noteworthy that in the concluding chapter ("Man Is the Way of the Church"), where he summarizes the entire argument of the encyclical, rights language has no part. So the complaint that Catholic social teaching has uncritically adopted the Enlightenment concept of individual rights finds very limited support in *Centesimus*. In the lively American debate between thinkers who see individual rights as *the* paradigm for the rightly ordered society and those who are commonly called "communitarians," it would seem that John Paul is much more on the side of the latter. At the same time, however, the complaint is not without some justification. The tradition of Catholic social teaching has not to date given a careful account of the source and status of the "rights" that became such a prominent feature in the writings of Leo XIII.

The relative absence of an accent on rights is closely related to another and most conspicuous absence. In both the structure of the argument and in the actual language used, the idea of equality simply plays no part in this encyclical. Many claim that the idea of equality is the single most important concept in the development of democratic governance. It appears that John Paul does not agree. *Liberté! Égalité! Fraternité!* was the slogan adopted by the French Revolution in 1793. In this encyclical, *liberté* is critically important, understood as freedom based in humanity's orientation to transcendent truth. *Fraternité*, understood as moral solidarity, is resoundingly affirmed. *Égalité*, however, is simply not to be found.

The absence of equality is the more remarkable when one considers that the focus of the encyclical is economics. Through large swaths of Western intellectual life, it has been assumed that equality is *the* question of economic justice. Inequality is thought to be the moral offense for which the remedy is equality, or at least more equality. On the shelf across the room from me is an influential book on economic ethics that is titled quite simply *More Equality*. In numerous church statements, both Catholic and other, the rhetoric and substance uncritically reflect the assumption that inequality equals injustice. John Paul turns our attention to the more classic understanding of justice, in which justice means giving everybody what is due them.

The concept of equality has played such an important part in American political culture that it is hardly avoidable for us. After all, the proposition that all men are created equal is enshrined in our founding creed. Among Americans, there has long been a contentious, and usually confused, debate between the proponents of "equality of result" and the proponents of "equality of opportunity." In different forms, that debate will certainly continue, and probably must continue. John Paul is not an American and is therefore not obliged to join that debate. One could make the case, however, that his argument for economic participation, and especially for the inclusion of the marginalized, is what in the American context is meant by "equality of opportunity."

In *Centesimus*, equality, understood as equality of condition, does not have the status of a moral imperative nor even of an ideal. The moral offense is not that some people have much more than other people. The offense is that many, many people do not have enough to live in a manner appropriate to the dignity of children of God. The proposed solution is not to redistribute the wealth from the rich to the poor but to include the poor in "the circle of exchange" that produces wealth. The absence of *égalité*, then, is closely connected to the Pope's caution with respect to the language of rights, and, as we shall discuss in the following pages, it has everything to do with his understanding of the free economy. In a Sherlock Holmes detective story the decisive clue is the dog that did not bark. So also, in trying to understand *Centesimus* it is useful to think of *Égalité* as the name of the dog that does not bark.

CLASS WAR AND WARS

Continuing to read the signs of the times, John Paul discerns a connection between the socialist version of class struggle and the development of the practice of "total warfare." If a state or party knows for certain, as a matter of "scientific" analysis, that it is the instrument of the unstoppable force of history, it will not allow itself to be "restrained by ethical or juridical considerations or by respect for the dignity of others." The Pope connects that lethal *hubris* with the doctrine of total war associated with "the militarism and imperialism of that time." "Therefore," he writes, "class struggle in the Marxist sense and militarism have the same root, namely, atheism and contempt for the human person, which place the principle of force above that of reason and law" (¶ 14).

Bringing the reading up to World War II and its aftermath, John Paul has no truck with the "revisionist" historians who claim that the West was equally or chiefly responsible for the origins of the cold war. His reading of the matter is straightforward: "Half of the continent [of Europe] fell under the domination of a Communist dictatorship, while the other half organized itself in defense against this threat." He describes the Communist dictatorship as an empire and leaves no doubt that it was an evil empire. There was, he says, an "insane arms race," reflecting a world thrown into mad disarray by an antagonist who employed "an ideology, a perversion of authentic philosophy . . . to provide doctrinal justification for the new war" (¶ 18).

In the course of this assault and the responses to it by the democracies, "Third World countries were systematically aggravated and exploited in order to create difficulties for the adversary" (¶ 18). It is not said, but we may infer, that he believes the West was also culpable in the events of the cold war, notably in some of its dealings with Third World countries. Nobody should protest that. The Pope is certainly not, however, proposing a moral equivalence between totalitarianism and the democracies. It is said very clearly that the genesis of the conflict was in the linkage of Marxist class struggle and militarism, and in the aggression of the Communist dictatorship. Nonetheless, he is by no means uncritical of the role played by the West.

John Paul brings a strong Polish sensibility to bear upon his reading of World War II. Poland has for centuries been perilously poised between, and brutally abused by, Germany and

Russia. Although those nations are not mentioned by name, they appear in the text by clear implication. The author is critical of the West for the way World War II was ended. "The war, which should have reestablished freedom and restored the rights of nations, ended without having attained these goals" (¶ 19). "Many peoples lost the ability to control their own destiny and were enclosed within the suffocating boundaries of an empire in which efforts were made to destroy their historical memory and the centuries-old roots of their culture" (¶ 18).

Who was responsible? Of course, the Communist dictatorship. But, John Paul notes, the situation prevailing after World War II was "sanctioned by the Yalta agreements" (¶ 23). To have "sanctioned" the subjugation of nations by the Communist empire is moral culpability of a large order. Although they are grateful for the resolve of the West during the cold war, many in Central and Eastern Europe feel that they were betrayed by America in particular. They believe that World War II did not have to end the way it did. Americans may protest that at Yalta they did not "sanction" the Communist empire, that the blame for what happened lies with Stalin, who broke the agreements made at Yalta.

The European victims of Yalta respond to that by saying the Americans, meaning Roosevelt, were culpably naive. It would appear that Karol Wojtyla shares that view. Some observers claim that this explains, at least in part, his seeming distrust of America's role in world affairs, a distrust that was evident in his vigorous protest against the actions of the American-led coalition in the Gulf War of 1991. It is fine to talk about America as the guarantor of freedom, but such talk may be less than convincing to someone who holds America largely responsible for his country's having suffered more than forty years under Communist tyranny.

In surveying the aftermath of World War II, the Holy Father notes that some countries, "following the destruction caused by the war," successfully worked "to rebuild a democratic society inspired by social justice." Here and elsewhere in the encyclical, one may infer a favorable reference to what was, until the recent reunification, West Germany. Other countries, trying to resist the Communist onslaught, set themselves up as "national security" states. "By emphasizing and increasing the power of the state, they wish to protect their people from Communism, but in doing so they run the grave risk of destroying the freedom and values of the person, the very things for whose sake it is necessary to oppose Communism." Yet another response to Communism is "the affluent society or consumer society" that is as materialistic as Marxism in "excluding spiritual values" and "reducing man to the sphere of economics and the satisfaction of material needs" (¶ 19).

These, then, are the three types of responses to the Communist threat. Are they only theoretical types or does the Pope have particular countries in mind as representatives of each? He does not say. In any event, it is unseemly for Americans to be excessively defensive. The maxim applies: "If the shoe fits . . ." The United States is large enough and various enough, and its record is mixed enough, to supply evidence in support of almost any indictment. We do well, also, to remember that the Pope is writing to the universal Church and about the entire world. It is a little presumptuous to think that he has America always on his mind. The description of the national security state sounds much like South Korea of, say, ten years ago, and some Latin American dictatorships of the recent past. The widely held stereotype of Japan might well fit what is meant by the consumer society. But no matter. To the extent that the Pope's reproaches are pertinent to the United States, Americans might accept them with good grace and try to mend their ways.

EQUIPPED WITH TRUTH AND JUSTICE

The chapter on "The Year 1989" is impassioned and moving. John Paul writes that the fall of the "empire was accomplished almost everywhere by means of peaceful protest, using only the weapons of truth and justice" (¶ 23). It might be complained that this analysis ignores the crucial role played by NATO and other military measures that contained Communist aggression and sapped the strength of the Soviet Union over the years. In response to that complaint, one notes that the Pope earlier acknowledges the role of Western defense. Moreover, the focus of this chapter of the encyclical is on what happened internally among the victims of Communist oppression. Finally, both here and elsewhere John Paul is accenting the possibilities of the peaceful resolution of conflicts, readily recognizing, as he does, that the world has not yet developed adequate alternatives to the use of military force. Against other analyses of 1989 that are almost totally preoccupied with military, economic, and geopolitical factors, the Pope stresses the fall of the Communist empire as a triumph of the spirit—and of the Spirit. As Timothy Garton Ash underscored, from the first days of his pontificate this Pope's message has been that of *moral* victory.

Of course, economic and other factors were *also* important. In John Paul's reading, the economic inefficiency of socialism was not merely a "technical problem" that could have been solved by fiddling with the system. Rather, the economic failure of socialism was "a consequence of the violation of the human rights to private initiative, to ownership of property, and to freedom in the economic sector." Even more important, it resulted from a denial of cultural identity that created a "spiritual void." "At the heart of every culture," he writes, "lies the attitude man takes to the greatest mystery: the mystery of God." And then one of the most striking and suggestive statements of the entire document: "Different cultures are basically different ways of facing the question of the meaning of personal existence" (¶ 24).

The Pope returns to the argument that human nature must be respected. Any social system, socialist or otherwise, that disregards human nature is both unethical and doomed to fail. Human nature includes self-interest, rightly understood. While human beings bear within themselves "the wound of original sin," it is not sinful to act in self-interest, especially when self-interest includes the interests of one's family and others for whom one is most immediately responsible. Self-interest, rightly understood, is not to be condemned as selfishness and pitted against the common good. "The social order will be all the more stable, the more it takes this fact into account and does not place in opposition personal interest and the interests of society as a whole, but rather seeks ways to bring them into fruitful harmony" (¶ 25).

From his reading of the signs of the times John Paul derives what he calls "a new and authentic theory and praxis of liberation." He understands how others, sincerely desiring to be on the side of the oppressed, read the signs differently in the past. But it should now be obvious to everyone that it was a grave error to seek "an impossible compromise between Marxism and Christianity" (¶ 26). Those who embrace the new theory and practice of liberation that he proposes must brace themselves for a very long-term effort "to rebuild morally and economically the countries that have abandoned Communism" (¶ 27). That effort needs the assistance of others, especially those countries of Europe responsible for the war and its aftermath. Such assistance is "a debt in justice." In the context, it would seem that he has Germany very particularly in mind (¶ 28).

A P O N T I F I C A T E   O F   F R E E D O M

As exhilarating as the Revolution of 1989 is, the apparent collapse of Communism is hardly the end of the world's problems. The "old forms of totalitarianism and authoritarianism are not yet completely vanquished; indeed there is a risk that they will regain their strength." In addition, and as in his 1991 encyclical on world missions, *Redemptoris Missio*, the Pope again focuses attention on the challenge of Islam, without mentioning Islam by name. Societies that close in upon themselves, seeking to impose a monistic order that stifles cultural freedom, are a threat to world peace and development. "No authentic progress is possible without respect for the natural and fundamental right to know the truth and live according to that truth" (¶ 29).

Freedom is the leitmotiv of the entire pontificate of John Paul. Freedom is the litmus test of every society and every design for world order. Where freedom is not secured, nothing else is secure. Moreover, the source and safeguard of every other freedom is religious freedom, the imperative that people be free to order their lives in relation to transcendent truth. When the Second Vatican Council approved the "Declaration on Religious Freedom," many thought it was an instance of an authoritarian Church finally and grudgingly coming to terms with the modern world. Twenty-five years later it appears that the Catholic Church, the oldest and largest institution in the world, is the paramount champion of human freedom in the world.

This is a development both astonishing and heartening. Few would have predicted it. The historical route was circuitous and filled with conflicts and apparent contradictions. Yet it now appears that the Spirit whom Christ promised would guide the Church into all truth has guided her to the understanding that truth and freedom, far from being enemies, are indissolubly conjoined. Even in the most oppressive of circumstances, those who know the truth can respond to the call, *Nolite timere,* "Be not afraid!" That is the truth drawn by this Pope from his reading of the signs of the times. And that is the reason why *Centesimus* adds to the likelihood that this Pope will be inscribed in history as the Pope of Human Freedom.

NOTES

Page 140. Delegate's response to Mikhail Gorbachev reported in the *New York Times,* August 24, 1991.

Page 141. John Bennett in *Christianity and Communism Today,* Association Press, first published 1948.

Page 144. Alexy II in "Turning Point in History and for the Church," *Catholic International,* October 1991. Throughout the cold war, one of the most reliable sources of information about the churches behind the iron curtain was *Religion in Communist Dominated Areas*, edited by Blaho and Olga Hruby. *RCDA* is a treasure of information on Communist control and penetration of the churches.

Page 145. Alexy's confession reported in the *New York Times*, November 9, 1991.

Pages 147–48. Timothy Garton Ash, *The Uses of Adversity: Essays on the Fate of Central Europe*, Random House, 1983.

Pages 148–49. For *Nolite timere* as a papal motto and for the Frossard quote, see George Weigel, "The Wojtyla Difference" in *The Final Revolution*, Oxford, 1992.

Page 154. For two very different accounts of the role of rights in modern political theory and practice, see Ronald Dworkin, *Taking Rights Seriously*, Harvard, 1977, and Mary Ann Glendon, *Rights Talk: The Impoverishment of Political Discourse*, Free Press, 1991.

=Part Three=

Part Three

Chapter Six

• • •

HUMAN FREEDOM
AND THE FREE
ECONOMY

We come now to John Paul's positive proposals for the right ordering of society, with specific reference to economics. Again, we remember that the Pope is writing to the entire Church in the entire world. It is only natural, therefore, that some of what he says applies to Zaire in ways that it does not apply to, say, Hungary, and vice versa. Yet he does propose concepts, dispositions, and principles that are universal in character. People in different societies, and not least in the Western democracies, can ask what these general truths might mean for changing attitudes and policies in their situation. As we have seen, John Paul strives to be a great respecter of the particularities of each concrete circumstance.

The message of *Centesimus* and the tradition that it develops is, I believe, best described as reformist. Some may think it radically reformist. What we find uncomfortable we are inclined to call radical. *Centesimus* does not fit comfortably into our too-familiar categories of social and political thought. As difficult as it may be, we are invited to make an effort to distance ourselves from our own snug assumptions in order to come to terms with the "new things" that John Paul asks us to consider. As he notes early on in the document, Catholic social teaching from *Rerum Novarum* onward "criticizes two social and economic systems: socialism and liberalism" (¶ 10).

We have discussed the Pope's analysis of the incorrigible wrongheadedness of socialist analysis and practice. He uses "liberalism," on the other hand, in the way that most Europeans use the term. In that context, "liberalism" does not have the left-of-center connotations that it has in American usage. Liberalism, rather, is what we here usually call libertarianism. There are, of course, varieties of libertarianism, ranging from the "philosophy" propounded by the late Ayn *(Atlas Shrugged)* Rand to confused minglings of market economics and what is today called "paleoconservatism." Some libertarians think of themselves as being on the right, while others say they are on the left. It is commonly observed that libertarianism is so far right that it is left, and so far left that it is right.

Those sectarian squabbles need not delay us here. Suffice it for our purposes that Catholic social teaching opposes the kind of liberalism that would leave everything to the dynamics of the market. Elsewhere in the encyclical, John Paul refers to that approach as "radical capitalism," and he thinks it very misguided indeed. Libertarians may protest that the Pope is attacking a straw man, that there are in fact few if any libertarians who fit the Pope's description of what might more accurately be called libertinism. Once again, the maxim would seem to apply: "If the shoe fits . . ."

FREEDOM FOR LOVE

The Pope addresses affirmatively the "new capitalism," the "business economy," or, most simply, the "free economy." That the economy should be free is one key to his entire argument. That a free economy is not enough for the right ordering of society is the other key. Those who persist in pushing socialist or libertarian ideology will likely have little or nothing to contribute in meeting the challenge that John Paul poses. That reformist challenge is to think through and act upon the ways in which the free economy should be related to culture, morality, and politics in the rightly ordered society. Professor Rocco Buttiglione, who has worked closely with John Paul for many years, puts it this way: "This corresponds to a general principle that underlies not only this encyclical but also the whole teaching of this Pope: Nothing good can be done without freedom, but freedom is not the highest value in itself. Freedom is given to man in order to make possible the free obedience to truth and free gift of oneself in love."

There cannot be reform without change. As much as it may distress certain kinds of conservatives, this Pope and the entirety of Catholic social teaching are decidedly on the side of social change. It is, however, social change that is very different from what is proposed by many folk who are most fond of the phrase "social change." As we said, John Paul's argument does not fit, and in fact throws into question, familiar categories of social and political thought. He forces his readers to decide whether they care more about clinging to their familiar categories or engaging the new thing that is John Paul's reading of the "new things."

Some may wonder why it is necessary to have reform, especially reform that is as far-reaching as John Paul proposes. His answer is that everywhere in the world—in post-Communist societies, in the poor nations, and in affluent societies with an efficient free market—societies are not working in a way that is worthy of the dignity of human beings created in the image of God. To be sure, he knows that no social order will be perfect short of the Kingdom Come. But the Pope is not talking merely about inevitable imperfections in a world wounded by sin. With an insistence that reaches out to take people by the shoulders and shake them into sharing his sense of urgency, the Pope is saying that the status quo is not to be tolerated. It is not to be tolerated, first and foremost, because the existing social and economic order is not working for billions of people who are left out. The challenge, he makes emphatically clear, is not to replace the free economy but to make it more free so that it works for everybody. In coming chapters we will discuss how this teaching calls for dramatic changes in our attitudes not only to the poor of the Third World but also to the endemically poor in otherwise affluent societies such as our own.

"Today the Church's social doctrine focuses especially on man as he is involved in a complex network of relationships within modern societies" (¶ 54). With such expressions, the Pope brushes aside the cobwebs of vestigial Christian romanticisms about returning to some premodern era. Favorite candidates of Christian romantics are the thirteenth century, the so-called "age of faith," and, most commonly, the New Testament era itself. The Church has by no means embraced modernity in an uncritical way. It simply acknowledges the fact that with all its problems, modernity is the historical context in which the Christian mission must be advanced. As the Pope says, "Man is the Way of the Church," and man's way is through modernity. As this writer has described elsewhere, in theology and philosophy the Church is proposing an agenda that might also be described as "postmodern." That is to say, the Church presents its teaching as being on the far side of modernity, ahead of modernity. Whether it is called modern or postmodern, however, John Paul's approach begins with and builds upon contemporary circumstances. When it comes to understanding economics and moral responsibility, the social doctrine presented by *Centesimus* focuses on the "complex network of relationships within modern societies."

Already a hundred years ago, Leo recognized that "a traditional society was passing away and another was beginning to be formed—one that brought the hope of new freedoms, but also the threat of new forms of injustice and servitude" (¶ 4). The Church's purpose, then and now, is not to resist change but to do what it can to maximize the promise and minimize the threat. Chronologically, the entire world lives in what we call the modern era but, experientially, large parts of the world have not yet entered upon modernity. That reality is, as we shall see, very important to the Pope's understanding of the plight of the poor who live in precapitalist or "primitive capitalist" economies. His point is that those who do live in modern economies, however, must accept responsibility for coming up with moral directions that are appropriate to their own situation.

That means, among other things, that they cannot be content simply to cite Bible passages that have to do with poverty and wealth. In our political culture both the right and left are practiced at invoking what Nelson Rockefeller called "that damn Christian ethic"—the left, it should be noted, more than the right, which helps explain why Mr. Rockefeller so disliked what he took to be the Christian ethic. The Bible, both Old Testament and New, has a great deal to say about wealth and poverty. Riches are depicted both as a sign of God's favor and as a source of fatal temptation.

A PLASTIC BIBLE?

The biblical story can be told in terms of God's siding with the poor against the rich. And it can be told, in the fashion of earlier Calvinists, as the story of God's vindicating the righteous with, among other blessings, earthly prosperity. Christians can point to the story of the young man who declined to follow Jesus "because he was very rich," and make a case against wealth. Or they can invoke the parable of the wise steward whom Jesus commends for his economic enterprise. So Christians can lob Bible passages at one another in the battle between economic prejudices. They not only can, they typically do. The practice would seem to prove little, although it does debase a sense of biblical authority in the life of the community. Those who watch such intramural battles from the sidelines may feel invited to draw the conclusion that the Bible is exceedingly plastic and can be made to say whatever people want it to say.

The biblical witness is rich in diversity and can legitimately be cited in favor of self-denial and asceticism. The poverty that attends self-denial and asceticism may be seen as a great Christian virtue. There is nothing in the biblical witness, however, that recommends the involuntary poverty that is imposed by circumstance. Rather, the Bible supports what common sense tells most people, that it is generally better to be prosperous than destitute. (That, no doubt, is why the destitute are so often promised that they will be prosperous, either in this life or the next.) If that is true, there would seem to be no reason to object to the fellow who said that he had been rich and he had been poor and he concluded that, all in all, it was better to be rich. Although the passage is often misquoted, it is not money but the *love of money* that is condemned as the root of all evil in I Timothy 6. The New Testament in particular is rich in warnings about those who trust in their money for security and status. Everything the Bible says about covetousness, envy, the lust for gain, and the obligations of generosity that attend prosperity would seem to be in full force today, and for as long as human beings are prone to sin. What the Bible does not provide is an economic model appropriate to what John Paul calls the "complex network of relationships within modern societies."

The essentially nomadic and agricultural economies of biblical times knew little about the *production* of wealth. Wealth was a zero-sum phenomenon—what one party had was at the price of depriving another party. Resources were a matter of finding and claiming what was there, not of creating what had not been there before. (In later centuries alchemists would try, but nobody *produced* gold.) It follows that the admonition of the rich in the Bible typically took the form of what we call *distributive* justice. The relationship between rich and poor was of necessity conflictual. What justice strives for today was then hardly conceivable. John Paul writes, "It is not possible to enjoy [peace and prosperity] in a proper and lasting way if they are achieved and maintained at the cost of other peoples and nations by violating their rights or excluding them from the sources of well-being"

(¶ 27). In a zero-sum world, peace was achieved by smashing the other fellow before he smashed you, and prosperity was precisely a matter of excluding others from the sources of wealth.

Facing up to modernity, then, would seem to require a recognition of the great differences between our world and the traditional societies of the past. One great difference is in the way we think of the social order itself. Our institutions and practices assume, along with *Centesimus*, crucially important distinctions (not separations!) between the economic, the political, and the cultural. At least in that sense, pluralism is integral to modernity. As the social scientists put it, modernity requires a "differentiated" social order. Things are not all of a piece, and it is no accident that, in Yeats' famous words, "the center does not hold." From a sociological viewpoint, it is hard, if not impossible, to say even where the center is.

By sharpest contrast, the social order of biblical times was conceived not in pluralistic but in thoroughly monistic terms. In that sense, it was what Islam, for the most part, is today. Islam—the very word means "submission" to Allah in all things—has such a hard time facing up to modernity because the very idea of differentiation, of distinct "spheres of sovereignty," is blatant heresy. Allah is sovereign and every reality is to be ordered according to his revealed law. The complete submission of everything to divine rule is not, as in Christianity, an eschatological promise but is the present political imperative. Moreover, in Islam there is, at least in theory, no development of doctrine, and therefore religion tends to be tied to a premodern social order and the zero-sum economics of the past. In these and other ways, Islam is very different from Christianity.

But some Christians, too, get very nervous when they hear it said that biblical statements must be historically "contextualized," or that the Bible is "culturally conditioned" and therefore not entirely pertinent to the present. The nervousness is perfectly understandable. For at least two hundred years varieties of theological liberalism have tended to undermine biblical authority. Today the erosion of biblical authority is pronounced in areas such as marriage, sexuality, and the protection of the help-less. Christians are told that the Church must update its teach-ing and get in tune with the way the modern world actually functions. Such expressions fall trippingly from the tongues of those whom many other Christians suspect of wanting to jetti-son the tradition, Bible and all.

THE TRUTH FOR THE TIME

Here we come up against a question of means and ends. The social teaching of *Centesimus*, it is argued, addresses the contem-porary means that best advance the ends enjoined by biblical faith—namely, concern for the common good and especially for the poor. The proponents of a "new sexual ethic," by way of contrast, would seem to be replacing biblical ends with ends more in keeping with the cultural climate, such as the satisfac-tion and fulfillment of the imperial Self. In other words, if the proponents of adultery, fornication, homosexuality, euthanasia, and abortion want to make the case that these are means by which to advance biblical imperatives of marital fidelity, chastity, the conceiving and rearing of children, and the care for the most vulnerable among us, it might be an interesting argument to listen to. But, of course, they do not usually attempt to make that argument. It is the biblical imperatives that they claim are culturally conditioned and therefore irrelevant. They are worse than irrelevant, they say. They are oppressive and must there-fore be jettisoned in order to make room for the flowering of creative souls who have thrown off the shackles of dead tradi-tion.

That way of thinking is utterly alien to the present argument that the economic structures of the biblical era are dramatically different from those that prevail in the modern world. There is a political analogy. Most Christians agree that they should be obe-dient to Paul's teaching in Romans 13 that Christians are to help secure civil peace and justice. How they go about doing that in a modern constitutional democracy, however, is very different from what the early Christians understood by the responsibilities of citizenship in the Roman Empire. The goals of maintaining civil order and seeing that justice is done remain the same, but in a modern democracy the means to securing those goals are not adequately taken into account by the simple injunction to "obey the powers that be."

In terms of the details of how a modern economy should work, the Bible has as much to say as it has to say about engineering airplanes. (Although I knew a cleric who claimed that things in the sky should go fast because Luke's nativity account says that "suddenly" there was with the angel a multitude of the heavenly host.) The Bible has everything to say, however, about the ends and goals of an economic order. And the actual working of the economy can at every point be subjected to the scrutiny of biblical teaching and of the entire Christian tradition. That is what John Paul intends to be doing in *Centesimus*.

At this point it is useful to ask, What does the Pope really want in a social and economic order? What does he have in mind? At several places in the encyclical he offers summary statements in response to those questions. Setting out a vision does not mean it can be realized any time soon, and it will certainly never be realized perfectly. Christians hope for a just society; Christians have the responsibility to work for "a more just society, or at least [for] the curbing of injustice" (¶ 3). Some thinkers claim that the very concept of a just society is misbegotten. Persons, they say, can be just or unjust in their dealings with one another. Society is not a person and is therefore not capable of either justice or injustice. John Paul's idea of the subjectivity of society is sympathetic to that argument. At the same time, he suggests that social structures can be ordered in such a way that either encourages or discourages people in acting justly. Societies structured in a way that encourages behaving justly is what this Pope appears to mean by a "more just society."

Clearly, what the Pope wants is something different from and better than almost all that he sees in the world today. As

noted earlier, existent capitalism is not "the only model of economic organization" (¶ 35). The goal is the "new capitalism" of
a more comprehensively free economy. He wants a social order
that is built upon "the principle of solidarity." Such a vision is in
continuity with what Leo XIII called a society of friendship, Pius
XI called social charity, and Paul VI called a civilization of love
(¶ 10). The reader may think that such phrases are altogether
too lofty. One might conclude that papal teaching merely calls
for a much nicer world. So who doesn't want that? But
Centesimus is much more concrete than that.

GETTING TO PARTICULARS

Specifics abound. Justice requires "a sufficient wage for the support of the family, social insurance for old age and unemployment, and adequate protection for the conditions of employment." These elementary conditions, he says, "constitute a goal
yet to be reached" in some Third World countries (¶ 34). States
have a significant role in reaching these goals, and labor unions,
if they are not dominated by Marxist ideology and are truly free
associations, can also play an important part. In discussing how
these goals were reached in developed countries, he focuses attention on "an open process by which society organized itself
through the establishment of effective instruments of solidarity
that were capable of sustaining an economic growth more respectful of the values of the person" (¶ 16). This idea of society
organizing itself is of course closely related to the concept of the
subjectivity of society. It is not that "Society" does this or that,
but that the *acting subjects who constitute society* rightly order their
life together. Similarly, John Paul underscores the subjectivity of
institutions within society, such as industrial enterprises. "While
cooperating with others, and under the direction of others,
[workers] can in a certain sense 'work for themselves' through
the exercise of their intelligence and freedom" (¶ 43).

In the section affirming capitalism, or the free economy, as the way the world should go, we find some of the marks of a "more just order." The capitalism affirmed is "an economic system that recognizes the fundamental and positive role of business, the market, private property, and the resulting responsibility for the means of production as well as free human creativity in the economic sector." The meaning of that affirmation is illuminated by contrast with the kind of capitalism that is definitely not affirmed. It is an order "in which freedom in the economic sector is not circumscribed within a strong juridical framework that places it at the service of human freedom in its totality and that sees it as a particular aspect of that freedom, the core of which is ethical and religious" (¶ 42).

Again, Professor Buttiglione is helpful in clarifying a distinction between capitalisms that may sound strange to American ears. He points out that the same word, "capitalism," may seem to have contradictory meanings.

> In the Anglo-Saxon countries, the free market economy experienced an organic growth. On the European continent, however, the industrial revolution was often the result of the activity of small groups, organized and led by banking rather than by industrial entrepreneurs, and possessing the decisive support of the state. This means that freedom of enterprise was restricted to a privileged social group and capitalism, from the beginning, was a *monopoly* capitalism. Even worse was the situation in many Third World countries, where control over all the resources of the country was concentrated in the hands of foreign companies and of corrupted local power elites.

In taking a much more favorable view of the Anglo-Saxon experience of capitalism, says Buttiglione, *Centesimus* is "a much needed step forward in the dialogue between the Catholic Church and the American spirit."

The Pope criticizes all systems, including those that call themselves capitalist, that deny or inhibit "the free and personal nature of human work." In criticizing such systems, "what is being proposed as an alternative is not the socialist system, which in fact turns out to be state capitalism, but rather a society of free work, of enterprise, and of participation" (¶ 35). The state capitalism that socialism fostered is simply a much more brutal form of the monopoly capitalism that Catholic teaching since Leo has so sharply censured. John Paul's mention of "state capitalism" may trouble some readers. After all, that was a term used by some Marxists to describe the Soviet system in order to dissociate that system from their versions of "authentic socialism." It was a rhetorical ploy designed to blame everything bad, including Soviet-style socialism, on capitalism. It may be that John Paul used the term to indicate his familiarity with the tangled twists and turns of intra-Marxist disputes. In any case, the one allusion to state capitalism should not distract us from following the gravamen of the Pope's argument.

Free work, enterprise, and participation—those three terms get at the heart of what the Pope wants and what he invites his readers to envision on a global scale. By free work, enterprise, and participation, the human being, who is the subject, "utilizes the things of this world as objects and instruments and makes them his own." "Man fulfills himself by using his intelligence and freedom" to enter into the circle of economic exchange and productivity that has the potential of unlimited growth as it leads to "a progressively expanding chain of solidarity" (¶ 43). That, then, is the goal.

HUMAN BEINGS, NOT WOLVES

That goal presupposes a number of understandings about human beings and the way they behave. The Pope rejects a Hobbesian worldview in which it is assumed that society is a war of all against all. This vision of humanity as *homo lupus*, as little better than a wolf, defies both Christian anthropology and our experience of the human potential for collaboration, he says. There is no room in John Paul's vision for the "rugged individualism" that was often associated with "primitive capitalism." The social Darwinism that described life in terms of "the survival of the fittest" must also be rejected. Those earlier and widespread rationales for free enterprise deprived capitalism of moral legitimacy in the judgment of many, and John Paul agrees with that judgment. To be fair, we note that some of the most important early proponents of capitalism rejected egotism and the survival of the fittest in terms every bit as emphatic as John Paul's. Adam Smith—to take the most notable example—was first of all a moral philosopher, and he insisted adamantly that the free economy depends upon the cultivation of virtue and the "moral sentiments" of a free people.

Leo XII spoke out, John Paul says, "in the face of a conflict that set man against man, almost as if they were 'wolves,' a conflict between the extremes of mere physical survival on the one side and opulence on the other" (¶ 5). Conflict, as we have seen, is inevitable in human relations. But a zero-sum understanding of wealth and poverty makes human relationships inherently and unrelievedly conflictual in nature. Some early capitalists joined Marxists in subscribing to that dismal view of human nature, which led to turning the class struggle into "total war" (¶ 14). As Lenin said, every economic, social, and political question comes down to "Who Whom"—who does what to whom. That view is by no means limited to the field of economics. In the West today, variants of that doleful Marxist doctrine are found in literary criticism, radical feminism, and racial politics, where it is confidently declared that all human behavior is explained by the quest for power. Those who deny that are blithely dismissed as naive souls who are suffering from "false consciousness."

John Paul excoriates the "realism" that does not acknowledge the human capacity for cooperation, for seeking a common good, and even for altruism. Those who are today working for the free economy and democracy in Eastern Europe regularly deplore the pervasiveness of popular distrust and suspicion shown toward people who, by their own enterprise, do well. The populations of formerly Communist societies were indoctrinated for so many years to believe that anybody who does well is doing so at the expense of others. Distrust and suspicion are at the heart of the socialist construction of reality. As Leo saw early on, "the socialists encourage the poor man's envy of the rich" (¶ 12).

John Paul writes, "A great effort is needed to rebuild morally and economically the countries that have abandoned Communism. For a long time the most elementary economic relationships were distorted and basic virtues of economic life such as truthfulness, trustworthiness, and hard work were denigrated" (¶ 27). In the moral ruins left by socialism, the idea that one might be doing good for others by doing well is ridiculed as preposterous and self-serving deception. And, of course, such ridicule is not limited to societies that have been subjected to the brutal distortions of Communism.

"We pretend to work and they pretend to pay us." That was the bitter jest heard almost everywhere in Eastern Europe prior to the Revolution of 1989. (A few years later, in the confusion that followed the Communist collapse, a variant of that gained popularity: "They pretend to rule, and we don't even pretend to obey.") Under Communism, to work hard and conscientiously was sure proof of being a sucker. Moreover, it was deeply resented by the slothful, for effective work invited a further hike in the "work quota" imposed by the state on other workers. As grateful as people are for the passing of Communism, however, the new leaders of these societies face problems of popular unrest over the loss of securities that were once guaranteed quite apart from whether or not people worked.

This, too, is part of the moral rebuilding on which this Pope is embarked. He earnestly wants to get across a sense of the dignity of work and of the worker. "Work thus belongs to the vocation of every person; indeed, man expresses and fulfills himself by working" (¶ 6). Those who cannot work—the aged, the ill, and the severely handicapped, for instance—possess a dignity simply as persons (¶ 11). So work is not the only source of human dignity. But work gives expression to that dignity. What is meant by "work," of course, is not limited to those directly involved in the market economy but includes, for example, those who rear children and take care of homes, as well as people involved in artistic enterprise that is only tenuously related to market values.

WORK ADVERBIALLY DIRECTED

These themes of the dignity of work and workers were developed earlier in John Paul's first encyclical, *Laborem Exercens* (1981). That encyclical met with considerable puzzlement, especially in the West. It seemed to be pitched at a highly abstract and philosophical level, and some critics thought it tended to romanticize and inflate the significance of work in the life of most people. All work, no matter how skilled, important, and "adverbially directed" to the glory of God, is attended by a large measure of vexation. Rearing children to the glory of God is one thing, cleaning up the bathroom after them is another. Expanding the wondrous circle of productivity and exchange is one thing, taking factory inventory and filling out tax forms is another. At a parish study group on *Laborem Exercens*, the manager of a local food store remarked, perhaps a mite irreverently, "I'm sure work is everything he says it is, if your job happens to be being pope." In other words: Nice work, if you can get it.

But, of course, John Paul's reflection was significantly shaped by his own experience of work under the Communist system. As a young worker, as an actor in amateur theater, as an aspiring philosopher, and as a priest and bishop, Karol Wojtyla reasonably assumed that he would spend the rest of his life in an oppressive socialist order. A student of Edmund Husserl and Max Scheler, Wojtyla embraced "phenomenology," a philosophy that is determined to attend not so much to grand principles as to the structures and patterns of behavior by which people think and act. This phenomenological thrust regularly recurs in his writing, and not least in *Centesimus:* "We are not dealing here with man in the 'abstract,' but with the real, 'concrete,' 'historical' man. We are dealing with each individual . . . The horizon of the Church's whole wealth of doctrine is man in his concrete reality as sinful and righteous" (¶ 53). If *Laborem Exercens* was too abstract and "philosophical," it hardly comported with the author's own philosophy.

In 1969, when he was archbishop of Kraków, Wojtyla laid out his understanding of "the acting person." This concept was directed at the socialist mind-set in which the person was not a source of initiative but simply a cipher in what Marx called "the ensemble of social relations." That mind-set had the most practical implications for work. In a top-down, command economy, work was totally absorbed in the mere production of things, the piling up of objects to meet imposed quotas. The "subjectivity" of the worker was completely disregarded, as no worker had responsibility or interest in seeing anything through. The worker was "alienated" from his work in that he had no connection with the "history" of the product.

In an efficient economy, a product is first conceived, then executed, then delivered to the seller, and finally put to satisfying use. The worker, as an "acting person," knows that he has, so to speak, a piece of the action. In the socialist disorder, the emphasis was on central planning and coordination, the action was "collectively owned." The responsibility belonged to everybody, and therefore to nobody. The collective "we" became in fact the bureaucratic "they." Little wonder that workers pretended to work and the state pretended to pay them.

These are the elements that contributed to the development of Karol Wojtyla's thought, including the encyclicals of this pontificate. Those who were surprised by the ringing affirmation of the free economy in *Centesimus* may have failed to pay due attention to signals of where this Pope was moving. In the

1987 encyclical, *Sollicitudo Rei Socialis*, for instance, there was this: "The right of economic initiative is a right that is important not only for the individual but for the common good. Experience shows us that the denial of this right, or its limitation in the name of an alleged 'equality' of everyone in society, diminishes, or in practice absolutely destroys the spirit of initiative, that is to say, *the creative subjectivity of the citizen*. As a consequence, there arises, not so much a true equality as a 'leveling down.' In the place of creative initiative there appear passivity, dependence, and submission to the bureaucratic apparatus." In 1987 that may have read like pretty tame stuff in Kansas City, but in Kraków it was understood as a manifesto for the Revolution of 1989.

The work of the acting person, then, is not romanticized or inflated into being the sole source of human dignity. In *Centesimus*, John Paul writes that "beyond the rights that man acquires by his own work, there exist rights that do not correspond to any work he performs but that flow from his essential dignity as a person." Obviously, if the most basic and generic of rights depended upon work, a case could hardly be made for, say, the unborn child's "right to life." Whether in Kraków or Kansas City, "the guiding principle of . . . all of the Church's social doctrine is a correct view of the human person and of his unique value." Here and at several other points, John Paul cites the statement of Vatican II *(Gaudium et Spes)* that "man is the only creature on earth whom God willed for himself" (¶ 11).

AN OPPORTUNITY FOR GLORY

The meaning of work is found in human creativity. Whether other people think a particular line of work is "creative" or not really does not matter. Work, even in its routine and irksome aspects, participates in the creative activity of God, who did not just create the world once and then sit back to watch it perk along on its own. References to God the Creator are not merely in the past tense. God the Creator continues to create. The work of the acting person, according to John Paul, is an opportunity "for human freedom to cooperate with the merciful plan of God, who acts within history" (¶ 26). The free economy does not guarantee that people are going to work in tandem with the work of God. The free economy does provide the opportunity for that to happen.

The clear conclusion would seem to be that capitalism is the economic corollary of the Christian understanding of human nature and destiny. That is, admittedly, an assertion of rather comprehensive significance. Needless to say, by "capitalism" we mean what the Pope means by the capitalism that he strongly endorses, namely, the new capitalism of the business economy, the market economy, or the free economy. To say that the free economy is a "corollary" means that it naturally follows from, it is clearly implied by, a Christian understanding of human nature and destiny.

In disputes over the interpretation of *Centesimus*, most readers might agree that the Pope's interpretation of his own document should be granted a privileged status. In the event that the argument was not clear enough in the text itself, John Paul held a general audience on May 1, 1991, to introduce the encyclical. He explained its message this way: "Economic freedom is an aspect of human freedom, which cannot be separated from its other aspects and which must contribute to the full realization of people in order to construct an authentic human community." Lest anyone still miss the point, he repeated that the economic teaching of *Centesimus*, which is "ideal and real at the same time, is rooted in *human nature itself*" (emphasis his). In sum, the free economy is the economic corollary of a Christian understanding of human nature and destiny.

This should not be taken to mean that a person could not be a Catholic and a socialist at the same time. Unless such a person is working with an eccentric definition of socialism, however, he would seem to be in clear disagreement with the Pope, which is no little matter for a serious Catholic. As discussed earlier, social teaching on economics is not an "article of faith" touching on salvation. If John Paul is right, one who endorses the theory and practice of socialism, as that word has any reference to the real world of human experience, is certainly an inconsistent Catholic. The point of disagreement with such a person should not be joined, first of all, in debating the relative merits of socialism and the free economy. The more basic point of disagreement would seem to be over human nature and destiny. When Christians are straight on that question, according to the argument of John Paul, the necessity of the free economy should become obvious in due course.

That much would seem to be settled, at least for the purposes of Catholic social teaching. It would be a great error, however, to think that this conclusion is aimed at making the friends of capitalism feel comfortable. This conclusion is hardly the end of the matter. It is a preparatory conclusion aimed at clearing away the ideological brush in order to move on to the formidable challenges posed by this reformist Pope. Having pinned down the necessity of the free economy, we are prepared to think more clearly about our responsibilities for property, enterprise, and the plight of the poor. We are now prepared to address those responsibilities in the chapters that follow.

NOTES

Page 169. Rocco Buttiglione in "Behind *Centesimus Annus,*" *Crisis,* July-August 1991.

Page 170. The meanings of modernity and postmodernity are developed in the author's *The Catholic Moment.* HarperCollins, 1987.

Page 181. The earliest examination of John Paul's developing thought on these questions in English, and still in some respects the best, is by George H. Williams, *The Mind of John Paul II,* Seabury, 1981. This discussion is indebted also to an unpublished manuscript by Michael Novak, "Capitalism Rightly Understood: The View of Christian Humanism."

Page 184. John Paul's news conference introducing the encyclical reported in *L'Osservatore Romano,* May 6, 1991.

Chapter Seven

· · ·

PROPERTY AND
CREATIVITY

In 1840 the socialist-anarchist Pierre-Joseph Proudhon wrote *Qu'est-ce que la Propriété?* His answer to the question of what is property was unambiguous: "Property is theft!" For a century and a half that answer has possessed the ring of truth for many, firing resentment and anger in the hearts of the propertyless and striking guilt and fear in the hearts of the propertied.

Leo XIII intended to meet the challenge of Proudhon's question head-on. "By defining the nature of the socialism of his day as the suppression of private property," writes John Paul, "Leo arrived at the crux of the problem." If Proudhon was right, then the socialist remedy would seem logically to follow. That many were to follow that remedy is now a fact of history. As John Paul ruefully remarks, "The remedy would prove worse than the sickness" (¶ 12). *chg ¶*

Private property is not entirely private. That is, it is not something to be grasped entirely for itself, or for oneself. Ownership can be *legally* free and clear, but it is not *morally* free and clear. There is always, so to speak, a social entailment that

comes with property. Commenting on *Rerum Novarum,* John
Paul writes, "The amount of space devoted to [private property]
in the encyclical shows the importance attached to it. The Pope
is well aware that private property is not an absolute value nor
does he fail to proclaim the necessary complementary principles
such as the universal destination of the earth's goods" (¶ 6).

The Psalmist declares, "The earth is the Lord's and the fullness thereof, the world, and those who dwell therein" (Psalm
24). If everything belongs to the Lord, it is obvious that our
ownership of anything cannot be absolute. John Paul observes
that the freedom to say that something is "my own" is necessary
to personal identity. But it identifies a person less as an owner
than as an acting person who is an administrator. And that, of
course, brings us back to the familiar biblical concept of being a
steward or caretaker.

The "universal destination of goods" means that the fullness
of the earth is to benefit all God's children. In the Christian
view of things, that will one day be the case. There is, as it were,
an eschatological proviso attached to all private property. But
the "universal destination" is not just a matter of future promise.
There is a present imperative to seek the ways in which the
fullness of the earth can best benefit all. On this there would
seem to be no big difference between socialists and the proponents of the free economy. It is just that "the simple and radical
solution" of socialism has been tried and found wanting. We
have seen the socialist future, and, to put it very gently, it does
not work. A better way is needed.

The better way, according to John Paul, is found by reading
the signs of the times thrown up by the historical experience of
freedom and creativity. "The type of private property that Leo
XIII mainly considers is land ownership," he writes (¶ 6). In
many parts of the world, the ownership of land and natural resources is still the main form of property. But today, John Paul
argues, property must be understood not in static but in dynamic terms. Property is not so much a matter of what happens
to be there and who claims it first. Property is the product of

work and creativity. The "origin of material goods" is, finally, in the continuing creativity of God.

"The original source of all that is good is the very act of God, who created both the earth and man, and who gave the earth to man so that he might have dominion over it by his work and enjoy its fruits . . . This is the foundation of the universal destination of the earth's goods." So both the originating foundation and the eschatological destination are in place. What is needed in between is "the human response to God's gift." Through work, a person "makes part of the earth his own" and this is "the origin of individual property." The response to God's gift is blessed by God, and with that blessing comes also the obligation "not to hinder others from having their own part of God's gift." More than not hindering others, we are to "cooperate with others so that together all can dominate the earth" (¶ 31). This, then, is John Paul's proposal for a dynamic and creative understanding of property. In this view, private property is not the enemy of the common good but an essential instrument for realizing that common good.

DESIRES RIGHT AND WRONG

Without work there will be no economic creativity, and without incentives there will be no work. One would like to think that the incentive to work exists because people recognize that work is a part of their dignity as acting persons who contribute to the common good, and all this to the glory of God. Although they may express it in a confused and inarticulate manner, perhaps that really is the reason why most people work most of the time. Witness the resistance of so many people to the prospect of retirement, and the resentment of the "indignity" of unemployment, even when material needs are secured. At the same time, however, incentives to work certainly include the desire for material gain. As we have seen, John Paul does not despise that desire, but generously affirms self-interest as natural and good.

In that connection, he affirms the role of profit in business enterprise. If they allow themselves to be influenced by John Paul's teaching, it will be more difficult in the future for religious activists to style themselves as "prophets against profits." He writes, "The Church acknowledges the legitimate role of profit as an indication that a business is functioning well." That may seem a little odd. Most people think of profit less as an "indicator" than as a good in itself. The Pope's formulation puts one in mind of the Texas billionaire who, when asked why he still wanted to make more money, answered, "It's a way of keeping score."

But John Paul is not unaware of the usual reason for profit. His concern is to underscore the intimate connection between profits and people. "It is possible," he writes, "for the financial accounts to be in order, and yet for the people—who make up the firm's most valuable asset—to be humiliated and their dignity offended." In thinking about "goods" to be valued, people come first. This is not simply an idealistic or rhetorical flourish. The Pope is not asking people to run their businesses on the basis of disinterested altruism. His point is that the "human and moral factors . . . are at least equally important for the life of a business" (¶ 35).

So it is also for the sake of business itself—it is in the self-interest of business—that the "human and moral factors" must be taken very seriously. Once again, John Paul highlights the sometimes curious ways in which "how the world works" can work to the benefit of all. If one believes that the origin of all goods and creativity is in the conjunction of divine grace and human freedom, it should not come as a surprise that there is a benign pattern in how the world works. The Church, he seems to be saying, is on friendly terms with how the world works—except when human sin and stupidity get in the way of its working.

The possession of property can be and should be put to a moral testing. The test is whether it expands the circle of exchange and productivity. Does it contribute to the vibrancy of an economy of "free work, of enterprise, and of participation"? Does it progressively expand the "chain of solidarity"? John Paul lays down the following rule: "Ownership of the means of production, whether in industry or agriculture, is just and legitimate if it serves useful work. It becomes illegitimate, however, when it is not utilized or when it serves to impede the work of others in an effort to gain a profit that is not the result of the overall expansion of work and the wealth of society, but rather is the result of curbing them or of illicit exploitation, speculation or the breaking of solidarity among working people. Ownership of this kind has no justification and represents an abuse in the sight of God and man" (¶ 43). The most fervent advocate of the market economy should have no argument with that. The non-utilization of resources and the exclusion of others from the circle of exchange and productivity are dumb ways of conducting business. Exclusionary and protectionist measures may sometimes seem to be in the short-term interests of the advantaged, but they end up by undercutting the very system by which such advantage was gained.

WHEN GAIN IS ILLICIT

At the beginning of the section where he offers that rule about the ownership of property, the Pope observes that "the Church has no models to present." What the rule means in application has to be worked out "through the efforts of all those who responsibly confront concrete problems in all their social, economic, political, and cultural aspects as these interact with one another." A question to be answered, for example, is what is meant by the criticism of "illicit speculation." At another point (¶ 48), he refers to the corrupting influence of "purely speculative activities." Since he repeatedly affirms the importance of capital and exchange, he obviously is not criticizing the trade in stocks, bonds, and other securities. Perhaps "illicit speculation" refers, in the East European context, to black-market exchanges or old-guard bureaucrats who made speculative gains on the basis of their positions in the party.

Coming closer to home, however, language about "illicit speculation" and "purely speculative activities" is not uncommon in American business and finance. One thinks, for example, of the controversy over the trade in "junk bonds" in the 1980s. Junk bonds are high-risk corporate bonds that, quite predictably, attracted high fliers on the financial markets. In financial circles there is lively dispute over whether junk bonds constitute "illicit speculation" or are an important contribution to economic vitality. Widely condemned in the 1980s, junk bonds seem to be making a comeback in the 1990s. The defenders of the trade in high-risk bonds claim that they make available billions of dollars to capitalize entrepreneurial ventures that would otherwise languish. While many criticize the corporate takeovers financed by junk bonds, others contend that such takeovers typically improve management and make corporations more accountable to stockholders. The public view of such high-risk activity as "illicit speculation" has been greatly influenced by the rather astonishing sums of money made by some who engage in the trade.

The most infamous, or famous, of dealers was a young man named Michael Milken. Later successfully prosecuted for technical violations of trading rules, Milken was reputed to have made more than $500 million in personal income in one year. The newspapers were full of it at the time, and one of them interviewed prominent financial figures to find out what they thought. Donald Trump, a New York financier who was riding high then, allowed that he had read about it and was somewhat puzzled. You don't need $500 million a year, he opined, in order to be happy. Mr. Trump was reportedly getting by on $50 million a year.

Americans have conflicting feelings about such financial goings-on. Some are morally outraged, others wish the super-rich well and hope that they or their children will get a crack at the same opportunities. Most people seem not to care very much.

Despite the conventional talk about America being an incorrigibly materialistic society, surveys over the years tend to confirm that Americans are relatively devoid of envy and not terribly interested in being rich. A bookkeeper making $30,000 per year would undoubtedly like to make $20,000 more, but the prospect of $500 million does not keep him awake at night. The Robin Hood stratagem of robbing the rich to give to the poor has seldom had great appeal in the American political culture. Most people seem to feel that it might ruin the economic game by which they and their children stand to gain.

The more ideologically-minded, however, have no doubt that a Michael Milken is engaged in "illicit speculation." His "earnings," they readily judge, are "unjust" and "obscene." The latter would seem to be more an aesthetic judgment than a moral one, but perhaps the line between the two is not as clear as one might suppose. In any case, comparable indignation is not usually expressed about sports figures, rock and movie stars, and others in entertainment who take in millions of dollars per year. A discussion of whether Michael Jackson or Madonna receives "a just wage" could make for an interesting seminar. When the Mets sign a player for a guaranteed $4 million per year, people mumble about its "ruining the game," and they may be right. But it is hard to know what is the *right* amount to pay, say, Dwight Gooden.

The idea that there is a right amount or a "just" amount always runs up against the question, Compared to what? The conventional answer is that one pays what the market demands, or what the market will bear. From Athens to Elizabethan England to the Great Terror of the French Revolution, societies have experimented with "sumptuary laws" setting limits on people's income and expenditures. The experiments have never worked out very well, the obvious reason being that it is almost impossible to agree on standards. Few egalitarians, even among the well-to-do, propose a top income limit that is less than what they themselves receive. At the same time, the average middle-class man or woman in America is living in incredible opulence compared with the majority of humankind. Yet they, who are already rich, are likely to think that "being rich" means making twice or three times what they do at present. It is all very confusing.

WHOSE POVERTY? WHOSE RICHES?

Since people think of poverty and riches in comparison with their own life situation, clergy are inclined to hold a peculiar view of what constitutes great, even "obscene," wealth. Clergy are among the lowest-paid professionals, and Catholic priests and religious are devoted to poverty or simplicity of life. A priest who receives $15,000 a year, plus room and board, might understandably have a keen eye for the obscene wealth that surrounds him. But again, it is difficult to say what is obscene or unjust. Unless, of course, we have available to us some moral principle mandating equality. *Égalité*, it will be recalled, is the name of the dog that does not bark in *Centesimus*. And, in fact, there is almost nobody who thinks absolute equality of income or wealth is a good idea. Yet innumerable religious statements on economic justice are haunted by the suspicion that there should be something like equality, more or less, and that somebody should be in charge of seeing to it.

Centesimus, like earlier papal statements, does speak about a "just wage" (¶¶ 8, 15). In the Catholic tradition this is frequently referred to as a "family wage," meaning that it is enough for a man to support his family in dignity. (The assumption that it is the husband and father who will be the "breadwinner" is implicit also in *Centesimus*.) Many free-market economists scorn the idea that there is such a thing as a just wage. Wages are determined by the market, and whatever wage the market sets is, if one insists upon using the term, just. One may, however, suggest that at least at the bottom end of the scale, it is meaningful to speak of a just wage. If an employer pays below what his business can afford and what would not disrupt the market, one might say that he is behaving unjustly. If workers are unnecessarily kept at a mere subsistence level of income, it would seem to be a clear case of what John Paul means by offending the dignity of the person.

We need not be entirely speculative, however, about the abuses criticized by John Paul. The daily financial pages supply ample instances of gross injustices in which people exploit the free market. It is no secret that some champions of capitalism are much more effective in undermining the ethos of the free market than are its declared enemies. For example, corporate executives give themselves millions of dollars in benefits while forcing a company into bankruptcy. Such behavior both deprives people of jobs and cheats the stockholders, while contributing absolutely nothing to economic productivity.

One need not believe that capitalism is driven by nothing more than greed in order to recognize the ugly dynamics of greed that both drive and corrupt the free economy. To recognize such wrong is not the same thing as having a remedy for it. *Centesimus* underscores in many ways the danger of remedies for the abuse of freedom that turn out to destroy the free economy itself. Contrary to libertarian ideology, John Paul knows that the market is not always self-correcting. The answer to abuses of the free market is not always to be found in the economic system, he says, but is finally moral and spiritual. Those who want a technical or legal fix for human sinfulness will find that answer unsatisfactory. In important respects, they are right. The moral and spiritual ethos required for the free economy will never be satisfactorily secured. That is why guidance, admonition, and encouragement such as that provided by *Centesimus* will always be necessary.

In making moral discernments we are always returned to specific circumstances of concrete cases. For instance, the statement that workers should not unnecessarily be kept at a wage below what is required for a life of dignity depends upon contingent judgments about business and market realities that determine what is and is not "necessary." At the upper end of the income scale, moral discernment is still more difficult. The Church, it would seem, has a serious obligation to warn the super-rich about the moral perils of great wealth, and to remind them of the duties of philanthropy and charity (on which more in due course). But should a Michael Milken make $500 million a year? Is what such people do an instance of "illicit speculation"? It would appear that the only answer *in principle* proposed by John Paul is that property and economic activity "is just and legitimate if it serves useful work."

Perhaps that is the only answer that can be given. Whether, in fact, trading in junk bonds and similar activities do contribute to expanding economic opportunity for all is, the Pope would seem to suggest, a question best left to "those who responsibly confront concrete problems" in the economic arena. John Paul does not pretend to be an expert on the operations of Wall Street. Were he to know about, for example, the discussion of junk bonds, he might well share the moral uneasiness generated by a case such as Milken's. The Church has effective ways of giving expression to that uneasiness. A good many of those who deal with these "concrete problems" in the market are in parish pews on a regular basis. Certainly there is a pastoral requirement to press them on their moral responsibilities.

THE INESCAPABLE QUESTION

Equally, there is a pastoral requirement to listen and to learn. The "self-denying ordinances" observed by John Paul caution against squandering Christian moral authority by indulging in ignorant judgments or, worse, self-righteous posturing. The Church has many searching, even painful, questions to ask of everybody. The more important questions have to do with the ordering of loves and allegiances to the truth revealed in Christ. Few of those questions are substantively affected by whether one is rich or poor. Our loves and allegiances, however, emphatically do encompass, for rich and poor alike, the world of work. Nobody can escape the question of whether his work enhances or impedes, expands or contracts, the human circle of freedom characterized by those key words in *Centesimus*—enterprise, exchange, productivity, participation, and solidarity.

Among the new developments in John Paul's examination of "new things," few are more striking than what he has to say about the "sources of wealth." Here Catholic teaching moves dramatically ahead of former attachments to assumptions that were appropriate to traditional societies and zero-sum economics. Section 32 of the encyclical in particular richly repays our careful attention. When we speak of property and ownership, John Paul says, we must give our attention to "the possession of know-how, technology, and skill." And then this: "The wealth of the industrialized nations is based much more on this kind of ownership than on natural resources."

Fans of Adam Smith are no doubt warranted in drawing some satisfaction from the implied reference in that sentence to *The Wealth of Nations*. (It seems unlikely that it is an accident.) At the very time the American Founders were launching this experiment in political and cultural freedom, Smith was laying out the rationale for a free economy that could benefit all. As becomes evident in John Paul's treatment of global poverty, his hope, like Smith's, is that "the wealth of the industrialized nations" will indeed become, through expanding the circle of exchange and productivity, the wealth of all nations.

The origins of the word "capital" are in a traditional economy, when *capita* referred to heads of cattle as a measure of wealth. As Michael Novak is fond of urging, however, the same word suggests *caput*, meaning the human head. The thinking, responsive human being is the source of the creativity and initiative that the Pope calls "creative subjectivity." This is the source of what he calls "know-how, technology, and skill," and therefore of wealth. The process involving "initiative and entrepreneurial ability," John Paul says, is one that "Christianity has constantly affirmed [and] should be viewed carefully and favorably." Land and what is in the earth are indeed resources, but "man's principal resource is man himself." That insight, as we shall see, has everything to do also with the Pope's understanding of "the potential of the poor."

Most of us assume that we know the difference between rich nations and poor nations, and which nations today are which. That knowledge has about it a taken-for-granted character. Japan is rich, Bangladesh is poor. Taiwan is rich, China is poor. And so forth. *Centesimus* invites us to consider *why* some nations are rich and others are not. It is not "natural." Something happened, and what happened didn't "just happen." There are studies beyond number on the causes of poverty, both domestically and globally. Some are no doubt useful, but one may be permitted to be mildly skeptical. If somebody came up with *the* definitive study on what causes poverty, what would we do with it? Nobody in his right mind wants to cause poverty. The Pope focuses our attention on the much more interesting and promising question of what ends poverty, of what produces wealth.

Some of the richest nations in the world today are not rich in what we ordinarily call natural resources. Were natural resources the only or even the most important key to prosperity, Japan would be a very poor country and most of the countries of Latin America would be rich. Peter Berger has brilliantly analyzed the factors that make for development in *The Capitalist Revolution: Fifty Propositions About Prosperity, Equality, and Liberty*. Berger certainly agrees with John Paul's judgment that "on the level of individual nations and of international relations the free market is the most efficient instrument for utilizing resources and effectively responding to needs" (¶ 34). But he would even more strongly underscore the Pope's focusing of attention on "concrete problems in all their social, economic, political, and cultural aspects as these interact with one another" (¶ 43).

Berger has given currency to the concept of "economic culture"—the attitudes, dispositions, institutions, patterns of behavior, and ways of being-in-the-world that make for development. It is in the possibility of influencing the economic culture that the Catholic Church can play such a powerful role. Stalin, who fancied himself a realist, foolishly asked how many divisions the pope has. So some equally foolish souls today might derisively ask how many billions of dollars the Church has for Third World development work. If that is the right question, the Catholic Church is almost entirely irrelevant to world development. The relatively modest operation of the Vatican itself runs an annual deficit of many millions. But that way of evaluating the role of the Church quite thoroughly misses the point about economic culture.

THE WEALTH OF THE CHURCH

This may be the place to address briefly the perennial canard that the Church is wealthy and, if it were really serious about poverty, it would sell its immense holdings and give the proceeds to the poor. The Holy See and probably every diocese in the worldwide Church regularly run a deficit. In 1991 the Holy See had to call upon the bishops, mainly those in America and Western Europe, to make up a shortfall of more than 100 million dollars. Would the sale of the art treasures of, for instance, the Vatican Museum and Sistine Chapel bring in billions of dollars? Almost certainly. Would the world be better off were those treasures privately owned by billionaires in Zurich or Tokyo? Certainly not. Being a careful steward of the artistic patrimony of the West is a service that the Vatican renders to the entire world. Selling off the holdings of the Metropolitan Museum would no doubt produce revenue enough to support the entire government of New York City for several years. There is no end to the good uses to which the money could be put, especially for the poor. To our knowledge, however, nobody has suggested that selling the art and turning the Metropolitan into, say, a vocational high school for the underprivileged would be a just and wise course of action.

But some critics point to the Church's huge investment in buildings—churches, rectories, convents, hospitals, and so forth

—in almost all our major cities. In fact, such buildings generally represent liabilities more than assets. They house service-giving, not profit-making, institutions. Churches, for instance, are entirely dependent upon free-will offerings by those whom they serve. Further, even were they sold, they are often worth very little. In recent years in Detroit and Chicago, more than fifty churches have been closed because they were no longer effectively serving their inner-city communities. In many cases churches that would cost millions of dollars to build today were sold to other denominations, such as black Baptist or Pentecostal groups, and sometimes for as little as a token payment of one dollar. The claim that the Catholic Church—or, for that matter, most other churches—has great economic wealth is a fantasy that has demonstrated remarkable endurance. The Church's contribution to the poor is not in distributing its physical property but in creating a moral and spiritual ethos in which the poor can benefit more fully from "the new meaning of property." The distinctive task of the Church in this connection is cultural.

At the heart of culture, we again recall, is religion, and with *Centesimus* the Church's influence is decisively thrown on the side of the economics of freedom and productivity. In large parts of the world, notably in Latin America, the attitudes and disciplines of entrepreneurship have in recent years been generated by evangelical Protestants, usually in conscious opposition to the cultural influence of Catholicism. Not tomorrow and probably not in the next year or two, but the teaching of *Centesimus* could significantly change that situation over time. In conventionally distorted views of reality, something like the economic influence of the Church is thought to be a "soft" factor, while, say, a change in the interest rates by the Federal Reserve Board is taken to be a "hard" factor. It is further assumed that hard factors have more impact than soft. This is almost certainly a great mistake. What is naturally complex we tend to call soft, and what we artificially simplify we tend to call hard. In a more nuanced understanding of how the world works, the religiocultural transformation proposed by *Centesimus* could turn out to be the greatest economic development of the next century.

OVERTHROWING MATTER

Old and familiar ideas about wealth and resources, then, are no longer helpful. Technology, know-how, and the things that make for economic culture have come to the fore. In short, "man's principal resource is man himself." The acting, thinking, creating person-in-community has become, far and away, the chief source of wealth. George Gilder, the author of *Wealth and Poverty* and a sometimes controversial seer who peeks around corners that most people don't even know are coming up, calls this new understanding of wealth and resources "the overthrow of matter." "The overthrow of matter reached its climax in the physical sciences when quantum theory capsized the rules that once governed and identified all solid objects. Physicists now agree that matter derives from waves, fields, and probabilities. To comprehend nature, we have to stop thinking of the world as basically material and begin imagining it as a manifestation of consciousness." According to Gilder, the computer is at the heart of this revolution. "By collapsing the computer to invisibility and imbedding it in the matter of everyday life, man may impregnate the world with his mind and waken it to the sound of its master's voice."

Gilder is an enthusiast, and it may be objected that others made similarly grandiose projections from the invention of, for example, the wheel, the printing press, and electricity. But that is not much of an objection, since those and other events were in fact revolutionary in their impact. The theologian might raise the more serious objection that "the overthrow of matter" is a problematic expression, since Christianity is rather firmly attached to matter, beginning with the Genesis account where God pronounces it good and centered in "God became man." But Gilder's essential point is an elaboration of John Paul's insight that "man's principal resource is man himself." In other words, the resources for the production of wealth to meet human needs are only as limited as are human imagination, initiative, and creativity. Which is to say, we live in a world of unlimited resources.

Resources are not simply given by nature. Resources are themselves the product of human ingenuity. To take an obvious example, oil was nothing but gunk in the ground until "know-how, technology, and skill" turned it into a valuable resource. Even more dramatic is the revolution of the microchip. Next to oxygen, silicon is the most abundant item in the earth's crust. There is so much of it that it is not even worth pennies per ton. Barring the end of the world, the supply is inexhaustible. Yet the development of the semiconductor has produced wealth that beggars by comparison all the wealth produced from "valuable" resources such as gold, diamonds, and copper. Natural resources are, by virtue of human ingenuity and enterprise, as inexhaustible as the Sahara or Gobi deserts. The useless sand that once covered what became, by ingenuity and enterprise, the natural resource of oil is now much more important than the oil it covered.

Moreover, *Centesimus* underscores the fact that *business itself* is a source of wealth. "A person who produces something other than for his own use generally does so in order that others may use it after they have paid a just price mutually agreed upon through free bargaining. It is precisely the ability to foresee both the needs of others and the combinations of productive factors most adapted to satisfying those needs that constitutes another important source of wealth in modern society" (¶ 32). This insight is crucial to John Paul's argument. It is not the case that creativity is limited to geniuses who make great inventive breakthroughs. There is a genius to knowing what to do with those breakthroughs. It requires the "ability to foresee" how they can be brought to the market in order to meet human needs and desires. Business people who, like Anatole France's juggler, are embarrassed by the modesty of their talent not only give pleasure to Our Lady but participate in the continuing creativity of God himself. It does, one might observe, give new meaning to taking care of business.

WEALTH AND WHIMSY

Business that is itself a source of wealth does not only require know-how, technology, and skills. It also requires *virtues*, disciplined habits of perception and behavior. The Pope writes: "Important virtues are involved in this process, such as diligence, industriousness, prudence in undertaking reasonable risks, reliability and fidelity in interpersonal relationships, as well as courage in carrying out decisions that are difficult and painful, but necessary both for the overall working of a business and in meeting possible setbacks" (¶ 32). He might have added that it takes a sense of humor, an appreciation of *homo ludens*—man as a player of games. There is undoubtedly a gamelike quality to economic enterprise, and a closer connection between wealth and whimsy than is ordinarily thought.

This author was recently in conversation with an entrepreneur in post-Communist Czechoslovakia who has made a stunning success of things. He started with a travel agency, expanded it into several, and then moved into computers, office equipment, and brokering loans for other entrepreneurs. One thing seemed to follow naturally from another. A devout Catholic, he explains what he has done in terms of promoting free enterprise, building democracy, providing useful work, supporting his family, and so forth. Then he pauses, and says with just a touch of embarrassment, "The one thing that has really surprised me is that doing business is so much fun."

True, *Centesimus* does not explicitly refer to the fun of the thing, but one expects that John Paul would approve. Of course, there are always people for whom their work is not fun. Sometimes because the work is onerous, backbreaking, degrading, and miserably paid. But all too often because they have not perceived the dignity and worth of what they are doing. There are drones who drag themselves to work at a brokerage house or retail business, just as there are drones writing books, directing graduate studies, and preaching sermons. The fault, in most cases, is not in our work but in ourselves. "God loveth adverbs; and cares not how good, but how well." A job that cannot be done adverbially to the glory of God and benefit his children should, in all likelihood, not be done at all.

There is frequently loose talk in our political culture about "meaningless and dead-end" jobs. All too often such talk reflects a class-based snobbery. Because we and "our kind" would not want to do a particular job, we say it is meaningless. As to dead-end employment, in the case of younger and basically competent workers, no job is dead-end in a free economy. Especially for the poor in the urban underclass, the challenge is not to move directly into the middle class but to move into any employment. Once that entry-level job is secured, the cultivation of the habits of reliability and initiative will, with a regularity that makes it almost inevitable, lead to other employment opportunities. To say this is not to subscribe to the much-derided Horatio Alger myth of limitless opportunity. It is simply to agree with social experts who point out that the great difference today is not between dead-end and open-ended jobs but between those who do and those who do not develop the habits appropriate to steady work.

Once again, however, the market, in and of itself, is hardly the answer to all our problems. The creativity that makes the market a source of wealth is also to be employed in making the market work better for everyone. As people are economically creative, so they have a capacity for political creativity. Some of the reforms of primitive capitalism, John Paul notes, "were carried out by states" through political means. The labor movement was and still can be a creative instrument of reform. Then he focuses on reforms brought about by "an open process by which society organized itself through the establishment of effective instruments of solidarity that were capable of sustaining an economic growth more respectful of the values of the person" (¶ 16).

INVITING OTHERS INTO THE CIRCLE

Creativity that is fully human is not captive to the market. Precisely as a resource, the market is an instrument. Things can be done that have yet to be imagined in order to make it a more effective instrument. But people will never do the creative things that might be done with the market unless they clearly assert who is in charge—human beings. The market was made for human beings, not human beings for the market. That means recognizing the limits of the market, and indeed of economics itself. As the Pope says, "There are many human needs that find no place on the market" (¶ 34). Part of the answer to that is to make the market work better, which means more inclusively.

The goal is to help "needy people to acquire expertise, to enter the circle of exchange, and to develop their skills in order to make the best use of their capacities and resources" (¶ 34). But there are also needs and goods that while they can find a place in the market, they *should not* be in the market. Here John Paul mentions drugs and pornography as examples (¶ 36). The list could be extended to include prostitution, the marketing of dead fetuses and human body parts, the renting of the wombs of poor women in surrogate motherhood, and so forth. John Paul is not pitting the market and morality against one another. His attention fixes on the *acting person*. The same creativity, initiative, and enterprise that make the market work can help direct the workings of the market to worthy ends, knowing full well that it will also and always be used for unworthy ends.

The generativity of the market may be beyond comprehension and seem almost magic at times, but the real mystery is in the human mind and spirit. An economic system in itself, the Pope says, "does not possess criteria" for determining what is worthy of human beings (¶ 36). The risk in becoming too impressed with the semimagical qualities of the market is that human beings abdicate their own responsibility for choices made. "The market made me do it" becomes another version of "The devil made me do it." When, for instance, John Paul criticizes the "consumerism" of developed societies, he is not criticizing the market, *he is criticizing us.* "The economy in fact is only one aspect and one dimension of the whole of human activity." Consumerism is like Marxism in that it constitutes a surrender of the human to economic determinism. The reason for the social decadence of the consumer society "is to be found not so much in the economic system itself as in the fact that the entire sociocultural system, by ignoring the ethical and religious dimension, has been weakened" (¶ 39).

Whether we clean streets, teach school, trade stocks, or sell computer software, the business that we are each given to take care of is but a small part of the whole. At the same time, we are not *wholly* defined by the business that is ours. Each of us is, above all, an acting person capable of and responsible for decisions. For those in business, says the Pope, "even the decision to invest in one place rather than another, in one productive sector rather than another, is always a moral and cultural choice" (¶ 39). The "business logic" of the decision is not the only determinant. It may, in the long run, be good business to "do the right thing" morally, just as we saw John Paul argue earlier that pitting profits against people turns out to be bad for business.

To that, many business people might respond with the very cynical Lord Keynes, "In the long run we're all dead." So John Paul offers another reason for doing the right thing. Making the moral decision, he writes, "is also determined by an attitude of human sympathy and trust in providence, which reveals the human quality of the person making such decisions" (¶ 36). The virtues required for business, including "courage in carrying out decisions that are difficult and painful," are only virtues if people accept responsibility for the decisions they make. The suggestion is that it is seldom true that we have no choice; those who say they have no choice are often saying that they have no imagination or courage.

In the Courage of Our Uncertainties

Of course, we may be more certain about the outcome of one decision than another. But courage is only courage in the face of uncertainty. At the core of this question is the Pope's adamant insistence upon the acting person. We are not ciphers but free moral agents. Having dispensed with socialist oppression, John Paul is not prepared to accept capitalist pusillanimity. Surrender of personal responsibility to the laws of the market can be as much a denial of freedom as surrender to the myth of collective ownership of the means of production. Between the socialist lickspittle to economic determinism and the capitalist lickspittle to economic determinism, there is little difference, except the latter has less excuse.

Toward the end of *Rerum Novarum* Leo declared, "Everyone should put his hand to the work that falls to his share, and that at once and straightaway, lest the evil that is already so great become through delay absolutely beyond remedy." In a similar vein, toward the end of *Centesimus* John Paul asks everybody to take care of the business that they discern to be theirs. Throughout Christian history, people have had different vocations or callings. He refers to the early Christians who distributed their goods to the poor, and to those in religious vocations over the centuries who "devoted themselves to the needy and to those on the margins of society, convinced as they were that Christ's words 'as you did it to one of the least of these my brethren, you did it to me' were not intended to remain a pious wish, but were meant to become a concrete life commitment."

Centesimus proposes that every acting person, whatever his or her vocation, is called to a concrete life commitment. On the last day, the judgment will be adverbial, less attention being paid to what people did than how they did it. Christians hope so to live that they will hear the words of the Lord, "Well done thou good and faithful servant" (Matthew 25). It is on that note of concrete life commitment that we turn to John Paul's argument about the moral challenge to the free economy posed by "the potential of the poor."

NOTES

Page 192. For a blistering popular treatment of junk bonds and other high-risk speculation, see *Den of Thieves* by James B. Stewart, Simon and Schuster, 1991. Although debunked by many financial experts, the book was for many weeks at the top of the *New York Times* bestseller list.

Pages 192–93. Data on most Americans not caring very much about being rich are from the Gallup Organization, *Emerging Trends*, Vol. 12, No. 9, February 1991. For further comment on this phenomenon, see "Numbers and the Numinous," *First Things*, April 1991.

Page 201. George Gilder, *Microcosm: The Quantum Revolution in Economics and Technology*, Simon and Schuster, 1989.

Page 204. On "dead-end" employment see, for instance, Lawrence M. Mead, *Beyond Entitlement: The Social Obligations of Citizenship*, Free Press, 1985. In thinking about unemployment, Mead urges, the relevant distinction today is between the "competent" and the "incompetent" unemployed. It is the latter, together with those who have voluntarily quit a job in order to look for a better one, who make up the great majority of people counted as unemployed in America today.

Chapter Eight

. . .

THE POTENTIAL
OF THE POOR

May choirs of angels welcome you
and lead you to the bosom of Abraham,
and there where Lazarus is poor no more
may you find eternal rest
—The Commendation of the Dead

In the Christian scheme of things, we enter the Kingdom of God by the permission of the poor. There Lazarus, who sat at the rich man's gate where the dogs licked his sores, is poor no more. Now he stands, surrounded by choirs of angels, at the gates of Paradise. He is the representative of all those embraced by a Lord who had not a place to lay his head and was put to death on a dunghill, abandoned by friends and abandoned by God. Christians are cautioned to live their lives in the knowledge that they will meet the poor again.

"The Church's love for the poor, which is essential for her and a part of her constant tradition, impels her to give attention to a world in which poverty is threatening to assume massive proportions in spite of technological and economic progress," writes John Paul (¶ 57). In unpacking that brief sentence we discover several themes that are key to understanding the Pope's mind on the subject of the poor. First, Christian concern for the poor, a concern that some may think is obsessive, is essential, it is integral to the Gospel of the Kingdom. Were it not to confuse the meaning of an expression that has become entrenched in the tradition—"preferential option for the poor"—we might say that love for the poor is not optional. Second, such concern is permanent, it is part of the "constant tradition" and cannot be changed. Third, the problem of massive poverty is "in spite of," not because of, the technological and economic progress of the modern world.

It is important to understand who John Paul is talking about when he refers to "the poor." Our concept of poverty has everything to do with what we think should be done about poverty. Early on in *Centesimus*, he discusses the increasing instances of poverty in the world. The exact formulation is worthy of note. We are faced, he says, by "the increasing instances of poverty or, more precisely, of hindrances to private ownership in many parts of the world" (¶ 6). Poverty, in other words, is exclusion from the sources of wealth produced by the free economy. As we shall see, poverty may result from *being excluded* by others or from *self-exclusion*, or from a mixture of both. Another word for exclusion is marginalization.

"The fact is that many people, perhaps the majority today, do not have the means that would enable them to take their place in an effective and humanly dignified way within a productive system in which work is truly central. They have no possibility of acquiring the basic knowledge that would enable them to express their creativity and develop their potential. They have no way of entering the network of knowledge and intercommunication that would enable them to see their qualities appreciated and utilized. Thus, if not actually exploited, they are to a great extent marginalized; economic development takes place over their heads, so to speak" (¶ 33).

POVERTY EQUALS MARGINALIZATION

The analysis of a problem gives birth to proposed solutions. In Marxist analysis, the word "exploitation" is crucial to understanding poverty. The poor are those who are, in myriad ways, exploited by the capitalist system. John Paul has a keen eye for the reality of exploitation in today's world. People are still exploited, he makes clear, in precapitalist traditional societies and in societies that operate by the monopoly rules of primitive capitalism. In the Pope's analysis, however, in all these instances the poor are best understood as those who are marginalized from the benefits of the free economy. The gravamen of what *Centesimus* says with such compelling urgency about the poor is that poverty and marginalization are synonymous.

"There was a rich man who was dressed in purple and fine linen and who feasted sumptuously every day. And at his gate lay a poor man named Lazarus, covered with sores, who longed to satisfy his hunger with what fell from the rich man's table." Lazarus was marginalized, as later, in the new order of the Kingdom, Dives the rich man would be forever marginalized. Abraham says to Dives, "between you and us a great chasm has been fixed" (Luke 16). Now, in this world, there is a great chasm between those living in precapitalist societies and those emerging from socialist oppression, on the one hand, and the beneficiaries of the free economy, on the other. The entirety of John Paul's analysis and of his frankly moral appeal is that that chasm must not be forever. It must not be tolerated now. The task of those on both sides of the chasm is to move billions of people into the circle of exchange and productivity that is the modern economy.

The phrase "preferential option for the poor" first gained currency in the 1960s with the emergence of a "liberation theology" that promoted a "theory and praxis" of liberation derived from "Marxist analysis." The practical excesses and theoretical errors of liberation theology were addressed in two notable "instructions" from the Vatican's Congregation for the Doctrine of the Faith in the 1980s. The phrase "preferential option for the poor" was accepted but given a substantively different turn toward what was called "an authentic theory and praxis of liberation." In the present encyclical (¶ 11), John Paul cites the definition of preferential option that he proposed in *Sollicitudo Rei Socialis*. The option means, he wrote then, a "special form of primacy in the exercise of Christian charity."

The concern of the Vatican in the earlier instructions and the concern of John Paul now is to definitively dissociate the "preferential option" from Marxist theories of class struggle— theories that this Pope contends are responsible not only for the economic and human disasters of socialism but also for the idea of "total war" in international conflicts. Lest there be any misunderstanding on this score, John Paul writes that the preferential option "is never exclusive or discriminatory toward other groups." It is both simplistic and exceedingly dangerous to reduce the question of poverty to a conflict between the rich and the poor. "This option is not limited to material poverty, since it is well known that there are many other forms of poverty, especially in modern society—not only economic, but cultural and spiritual poverty as well." (¶ 57)

The cooperation of the materially privileged is essential if the marginalized are ever to cross the chasm. The "principle of solidarity" requires that rich and poor understand that economic development is for the common good and in their common interest. The surest guarantee that Dives will more firmly shut the gate to Lazarus is for Dives to be convinced that Lazarus poses a lethal threat to his own well-being. If we follow John Paul's argument, the friends of the poor who advance a "class analysis" of the problem and propose revolutionary scenarios for its remedy are in fact the worst enemies of the poor.

If the poor have been tragically misled by the paradigm of class struggle, the prosperous have been equally misled into viewing the marginalized as the enemy. There are styles of conservatism that have traditionally proposed that the answer to the problem of poverty is to get rid of poor people. On this score, John Paul is adamantly liberal as in *liberalis*—meaning that he favors an order that is fitting for people who are free, generous, and motivated by an inclusive understanding of the human community. The marginalized, far from being the enemy, are potential collaborators in the building of a more just world order. "Man . . . is God's gift to man" (¶ 38). The new culture for which he hopes is "one that fosters trust in the human potential of the poor and consequently in their ability to improve their condition through work or to make a positive contribution to economic prosperity" (¶ 52).

The Pope drives the point home at every opportunity. "Justice will never be fully attained unless people see in the poor person who is asking for help in order to survive not an annoyance or a burden, but an opportunity for showing kindness and a chance for greater enrichment" (¶ 58). The idea that we should show kindness to the poor is derided by many as "paternalism," "noblesse oblige," and, worst of all, "charity." Justice is the opposite of charity, they claim. What is needed, they say, is "structural and system change"—and, it is often added, "revolutionary change." This Pope has little patience with such tired and tattered sloganeering. From hard experience, he knows better. He knows that Dives can call in the police. He knows that to incite Lazarus to storm the gates is probably to ensure Lazarus' death or more brutal oppression. Just as bad, were the Lazaruses to establish a new regime by violence, it would be as unjust and as economically unproductive as the regime it replaced, possibly more so.

THE GREATEST OF THESE IS LOVE

This Pope is definitely not what in the 1990s came to be described as "politically correct." Among other offenses against fashionable thinking, he wants to rehabilitate the concept of charity. Only at the price of our own humanity can we move "beyond charity." Charity is but another word for love, and without love there is no solidarity, no justice. "Love for others, and in the first place love for the poor, in whom the Church sees Christ himself, is made concrete in the promotion of justice" (¶ 58). Justice is love in social practice. Without love there is no reason to seek justice. At least, there is no reason for the materially privileged to seek justice. Not to put too fine a point on it, from a narrow calculus of economic self-interest, most of us would be no worse off if a billion poor people in the world and ten million of the underclass in our own cities were simply to disappear tomorrow morning. The argument might be made that we would be better off. That argument is being made in some quarters, as John Paul knows all too well.

The Pope is by no means averse to systemic and structural change, rightly understood. But such change must capitalize on "the potential of the poor" and have as its goal that the marginalized "enter into the sphere of economic and human development" (¶ 58). Again, he is saying that this is challenge enough for our lifetime and for generations to come. It will require all the ardor for social justice motivated by love that we can possibly muster. This is the "new capitalism," what Berger calls "the capitalist revolution," that is now to be embraced as the cause of social justice. The unfashionable argument of John Paul cuts to the right and to the left of conventional wisdoms.

If the poor are viewed as a nuisance, burden, and threat, certain policies quite naturally follow. John Paul repeatedly mentions the plight of immigrants, for instance. Ours is a time of massive population movements, exceeding even the great migrations from the Old World to the New in the nineteenth century. War and famine play their dolorous part in motoring these migrations but, as frequently, people are seeking opportunities to "enter the sphere of economic and human development." The argument of the Pope would seem to have a direct bearing on the millions of migrant laborers moving about Europe and, even more directly, on Latin Americans seeking opportunities in the United States. While not denying the legitimate and necessary reality of nation-states, an understanding that "the earth is the Lord's" disposes one to an open and liberal view of the fluidity of national boundaries. *Centesimus* positions itself against all forms of nativist sentiment. Catholics, Jews, and others, we might note, do well to remember that a century ago they were the "unwashed immigrant hordes" who were viewed with alarm by "old stock" Americans.

In the Third World, millions gravitate to sprawling urban centers in search of opportunity. Whether it is Calcutta, Mexico City, or Buenos Aires, Westerners visiting the urban slums with their appalling conditions are inclined to conclude that the problem is "too many people." If that is the problem, the remedy would seem obvious, and it is not surprising that "there are attempts to eliminate them from history through coercive forms of demographic control that are contrary to human dignity" (¶ 33). John Paul later returns to this lethally wrongheaded response to the marginalized: "Human ingenuity seems to be directed more toward limiting, suppressing or destroying the sources of life—including recourse to abortion, which unfortunately is so widespread in the world—than toward defending and opening up the possibilities of life" (¶ 39).

An Act of Faith in Life

Centesimus is not so much offering specific policy prescriptions as it is challenging our *habit of mind* in thinking about poverty. First, we are challenged to think about poverty not in terms of *exploitation* by the free market of work and capital but in terms of *exclusion* from that market. Thus, poverty equals marginalization. Then we are challenged to think of the marginalized not in terms of *threat* or *burden* but in terms of *potential* and *opportunity*. One has to make a basic decision about these alternative habits of mind, for from that decision flows a diametrically opposed set of policies. Walking through the shantytowns of the Third World or the drug-plagued streets of black Brooklyn, it requires an act of faith to think of these people in terms of potential and opportunity. But the alternative to that act of faith is despair, and the lethal policies that necessarily attend despair.

Consider Communist China. The sclerotic despots of that country try to impose a policy of "one child per family." Pregnant women are dragged off in tears and subjected to abortion. Infanticide is widespread. There are an estimated 500,000 "missing girls" each year, as families kill girl babies in the hope that the next pregnancy will produce a boy. If a couple can have only one child, better that it be a boy who can continue the family line and take care of parents in old age. Were such a policy to succeed, imagine a society in which nobody has brothers or sisters, brothers-in-law or sisters-in-law, uncles or aunts. And yet this callous coercion and closing of the heart to new life is hailed by some experts in the West as China's "realistic" and "courageous" response to the threat of "population explosion." This reflects a habit of mind disposed toward a culture of closure and of death. As John Paul writes, "In the face of the so-called culture of death, the family is the heart of the culture of life" (¶ 39).

The arguments about Third World population growth are, mutatis mutandis, the arguments employed by the "pro-choice" side in our domestic debate over abortion. In the 1960s, before he became embroiled in presidential politics, Jesse Jackson insisted that with the promotion of abortion, the war on poverty had been replaced by a war against the poor. In the pro-abortion literature one regularly finds the proposal that by the calculus of personal and societal interest, abortion is a bargain. They note that over its lifetime it "costs society" $200,000 or more to support a child born into poverty, while an abortion can be procured for a piddling $150. The assumption, of course, is that those born in poverty will remain in poverty. Never being productive, these parasites will dangerously diminish "our scarce resources." Thus does despair of the poor logically invite the elimination of the poor.

It is perhaps only fair that this author confess to a deep-seated bias on these questions. When I was for seventeen years pastor of a low-income black parish in Brooklyn, many were the white middle-class visitors, well-intended folk no doubt, who opined that "life would not be worth living" in the circumstances endured by the people of St. John the Evangelist. By the 1970s, courts were making awards in "wrongful life" suits, judging that it would have been better for them if severely handicapped children had been killed in the womb.

The idea of a "quality of life index" gained currency. According to this way of thinking, those lives were worth living that were assured certain medical, psychological, educational, and financial securities. I recall at the time looking out over the hundreds of people at Sunday liturgy and pondering that by these measures, not one of the people of St. John's was living a life that these experts deemed worth living. The Nazis used a marvelous phrase, *lebensunwertes Leben*—lives not worthy of life. *Of course* our society is not Nazi Germany, but only the obtuse will fail to see the chilling similarity in both logic and rhetoric. Surely John Paul does not exaggerate when he posits "the culture of life" against "the culture of death."

In 1968, Paul Ehrlich published *The Population Bomb*, a book that had an enormous impact on our political culture. It popularized the notion that the poor of the Third World are a threat and a burden. The key to the problem was "the population explosion," and the key to its remedy was "population control," by which Ehrlich and many others left no doubt that they meant *coercive* population control and, where necessary, the elimination (at least by deliberate neglect) of excess populations already born. The literature of the time was replete with apocalyptic scenarios of the impoverished masses overrunning the sanctuaries of the rich. The favorite example was India, a hopeless "basket case" where only mass starvation could bring the population down to manageable size.

Today India, with 200 million more people, is agriculturally self-sustaining and indeed a food-exporting nation. Never mind. In the past twenty years Ehrlich and his like have published many identical alarms and "studies," bothering only to change the predictions that have been so embarrassingly falsified by history. As some people are political pilgrims, ever in search of the revolution that works, so others are *apocalyptic pilgrims*, ever in search of the catastrophe that will vindicate the logic of closure and death.

In 1991 the German Bishops Conference issued an important study on population and poverty that corresponds to the argument being set out by John Paul. "The main problem," the bishops wrote, "is the fact that children begotten in conditions of poverty are in many cases the sole safeguard against destitution. To reduce the number of children without removing the causes of people's desire to have a large family would be to deprive the poor of their only hope. At the same time, the 'blessing of children' becomes a problem for society as a whole. Thus freedom to procreate is to a large extent restricted by the prevailing conditions and falls within the realm of population policy. This central problem, which affects the people in all developing countries and the solution of which is vital to the poorest among them, must be given priority. The solution, in a nutshell, is: *fewer people through less poverty, not less poverty through fewer people.*" After a careful examination of various expert projections, the bishops recognize that there is no agreement on the size of global population that can be supported in prosperity. It is expected that by the third millennium the global population will be six billion. Many experts believe that given present and foreseeable patterns of production in food and other necessities, the top sustainable population is twelve billion. But, of course, nobody knows for sure.

THE ULTIMATE RESOURCE

The dire predictions about population explosion were closely linked to ecological alarms that the environment could simply not support any more poor people, and certainly not billions of people living at the level of prosperity enjoyed by us few. In 1971, I wrote *In Defense of People*, the first book-length critique of the skewed logic and practical excesses of certain environmentalists. I said then: "The chief resources available to us are human knowledge and imagination, and while history demonstrates their notorious fallibility it also suggests their eminent renewability . . . If cataclysm impends, it is invited more by the failure of human imagination and nerve and not by the exhaustion of nature's resources." In 1981, Julian Simon elaborated that argument with careful scientific documentation in *The Ultimate Resource*. The ultimate resource is humanity or, as John Paul puts it, "God's gift to man is man himself."

In recent years there has been a growing interest in "animal rights," often motivated by a moral and aesthetic revulsion against egregious cruelty toward the creatures with whom we share this earth. In its harder ideological form, however, this movement challenges the "anthropocentric" assumption that humanity has a privileged status among the creatures. Those who subscribe to that assumption are accused of "speciesism"— of elevating the human species above others. In the lexicon of the politically correct, this "ism" is in a condemned category, along with "sexism," "racism," "ageism," and other social vices. It has often been noted that most of those who avidly press for greater legal protection of snail darters and spotted owls are equally determined that the human fetus should remain entirely vulnerable to the whims of human behavior and preference.

Against that ideological turn, John Paul positions himself as an unapologetic "speciesist." At several points he cites the teaching of Vatican Council II and contends that "man is the only creature on earth that God willed for its own sake, and for which God has his plan, that is, a share in eternal salvation" (¶ 53). Human beings are the only culture-forming creatures. As the late Rabbi Abraham Joshua Heschel declared, "Man is the caretaker and cantor of the universe." What the animal rights ideologists and the devotees of the goddess Nature usually seem to miss is that only by affirming the biblical view of human beings as the stewards of the creation can the other creatures be protected. It is certainly right that we are called to greater respect and care for nature and other creatures. The fact that the call is, of necessity, directed to human beings, however, only underscores the utterly singular status and responsibility of the human in the order of creation. Were we to allow, for the sake of argument, that animals have rights, it is obvious that animals do not respect the rights of animals; only human beings can do that. In other words, the well-being of all the creatures of the earth depends upon the "speciesism" and "anthropocentrism" that are today so frequently derided.

Another word for "speciesism" is humanism. And again, a Christianity that declares that God became man can take second place to none in its devotion to the human. Resistance to the radical nature of the Christian proposition about the dignity of the human takes many forms. Today many are impressed by a science that would seem to accent the insignificance of the human. The Jesuit Christopher Mooney notes that the human species is one of about two and a half million known species, a relatively recent arrival in the cosmos, living on a medium-sized planet orbiting an average star in the outer regions of an ordinary spiral galaxy that has about a hundred billion other stars in it, and that exists in a universe with at least a billion other galaxies. Alpha Centauri, the nearest star to our sun in our Milky Way galaxy, is four light years away, which is the distance light travels in four years at the rate of 186,282 miles per second, or about 23 trillion miles. "The traditional Christian message that humans are the ones for whom the material world primarily exists, when delivered in this context of overwhelming vastness," Father Mooney notes with nice understatement, "is not easily heard."

INFINITE REALITY, FINITE US

The message that the story line of the divine drama of creation, redemption, and eternal life is centered in the human has never, one might suggest, been easily heard. The Copernican revolution that spatially displaced man from the center of the universe deeply disturbed many committed Christians, but one may wonder whether that was not an understandable misunderstanding. The scandal of the Christian message is not in what cosmology tells us about the vastness of the universe but in the claim that the infinite God became, in Christ, finite. Even apart from the incarnation, in the Hebrew Scriptures, the testimony is one of wonder at the role of humanity in God's drama. The Psalmist declares, "When I look at your heavens, the work of your fingers, the moon and the stars that you have established; what are human beings that you are mindful of them, mortals that you care for them?" (Psalm 8).

Infinite, after all, is infinite. Having perceived that the stars are "beyond numbering," the ancient biblical writers may have thought that little substantively new is added by the knowledge that there are thousands of trillions of them. Again, it is not the vastness of the universe but the concept of infinity—a concept perfectly familiar to ancient Greeks and Hebrews alike—that makes difficult the biblical casting of humanity in the central role of the divine drama. Although the findings of modern science have great emotive force, they were not required philosophically to arrive at the oft-quoted conclusion of geneticist Jacques Monod: "The ancient covenant is in pieces; man at last knows that he is alone in the unfeeling immensity of the universe out of which he emerged only by chance." Many in the past have thought that they knew what Monod says we only know now. The Psalmist had them in mind when he wrote, "The fool has said in his heart, 'There is no God' " (Psalm 14).

The point is not to suggest that science has not posed new questions and new wonders to us moderns, nor to deny that Christian thought in the past and at present has sometimes been lamentably slow to engage the findings and theories of science. It is only necessary to note that the charge of "anthropocentricity" lodged against biblical teaching is hardly new. At various times, it takes scientific, cultural, and explicitly religious forms. The literary Romanticism of the nineteenth century, the blood-

and-soil ideology of National Socialism, radical feminism's promotion of the worship of the great goddess Gaia, plus current "ecophilosophies" and "ecotheologies" are all at war with the presuppositions of, for example, *Centesimus.*

These various movements are no doubt complex and have many parts, but they have in common a rejection of the biblical view of human dignity and responsibility. And that, in turn, has a strong bearing on our disposition toward the poor. If humanity is indeed "lost in the cosmos," having emerged by chance and heading for annihilation, we who are momentarily in charge are free to arrange things as we see fit. And what we see fit will almost certainly be what fits our security, pleasure, and convenience. In that case, John Paul's vision of an ever-expanding community of solidarity with the poor is a piece of arrant, inconvenient, and probably very dangerous, sentimentalism.

Like Martin Luther King, Jr., John Paul has a dream. His dream, however, is what many others call a nightmare. If we act upon the potentiality rather than the threat of the poor, he says, the goal should be "raising all peoples to the level currently enjoyed by the richest countries." He knows that it will take time, no doubt a very long time, to achieve that. Meanwhile, the marginalized are by no means without hope. "The apex of development is the exercise of the right and duty to seek God, to know him and to live in accordance with that knowledge" (¶ 29). The achievement of that "apex" is not "pie in the sky" but the reality of what is available to all here and now. That spiritual reality sustains both the marginalized and the rich in striving toward an ever-more-inclusive prosperity.

Lifestyles and Sacrifice

The end result of that striving will be "an overall human enrichment of the family of nations." The Pope calls for a "concerted worldwide effort to promote development," noting that this "also involves sacrificing the positions of income and power enjoyed by the more developed economies" (¶ 52). The latter observation might at first seem to be a regression to zero-sum thinking about economic development, implying that more for the marginalized means less for the prosperous. That interpretation, however, would seem to contradict many other explicit statements in the encyclical and, indeed, the entire structure of its argument.

Reading it within the context of that argument, the more accurate interpretation would appear to be that *relative* positions of income and power would be sacrificed in achieving broader development. For instance, comparing the situation of the United States after World War II and today, America's relative position of income and power has sharply declined. That is in no way to be deplored. On the contrary. The United States was then relatively unscathed in a world otherwise devastated by war. The economic recovery of Europe and Japan was precisely an American aim, in the full knowledge that it would reduce America's temporary and unnatural advantage in income and power. This interpretation of the statement that advantages will have to be sacrificed comports with the goal of "raising all peoples to the level currently enjoyed by the richest countries." If the raising of the marginalized requires that the rich become poorer, it is obvious that *nobody* would enjoy the prosperity "currently enjoyed by the richest countries."

The goal of global development, John Paul writes, "may mean making important changes in established lifestyles in order to limit the waste of environmental and human resources" (¶ 52). One could no doubt go further and say that it would certainly mean making such changes, just as such changes have been made in the past and are constantly being made. Change is the one constant in "the capitalist revolution." Most scenarios of ecological apocalypse depend upon extrapolations from present practices. If we continue to do such and such at the present rate, it is said, then such and such will be the dreadful outcome in the Year X. In 1883 one could extrapolate from the existing transportation system that our cities today would be covered by six feet of horse manure. Our urban areas have many problems, but that is not one of them. Similarly, economic self-interest and technology, together with popular sentiment and political regulation, have in only the last few years dramatically increased the number of miles automobiles go on a gallon of gas. A free economy in a free society will virtually guarantee that there will continue to be many such "important changes in established lifestyles."

Talk about changing established lifestyles in order to achieve justice or sustain the planet is a commonplace in political rhetorics, both on the left and the right. The single use of that language in *Centesimus* does tend to stick out. There is nothing in the argument that prepares the reader for it, and there is no follow-through to explain what the Pope means by it. It has, in short, all the appearances of being a throwaway line. Should we all consume less and, if so, consume less of what? And how will that help to include the poor within the circle of production and exchange? Or perhaps the statement means that we should switch to nuclear energy, away from exhaustible or polluting energy sources such as oil or coal.

The very leftist Center of Concern, based in Washington, seizes on this line, almost as though it were the very heart of the encyclical: "The challenge to Western capitalist societies should be painfully clear. The pope points out that it will take major sacrifices of income and power by the more developed economies to mount a serious effort at providing realistic opportunities to the poor individuals and nations of the world." As the Center of Concern recognizes, there is so very little in this encyclical for the comfort of the left that it is perhaps churlish of us not to allow them a sentence or two with which to shore up their badly sagging worldview. As much as we are inclined to be generous, however, honesty requires our saying that the sentence about changing "established lifestyles" is most likely a vestigial rhetorical fragment that somehow wandered into the text and is notable chiefly for its incongruity with the argument that the Pope is otherwise making.

That argument is an argument for a dream. Among those who view John Paul's dream as a nightmare are environmental ideologists who describe population as "popollution." Their purpose is not simply to reduce the number of poor people. Even more earnestly, they are determined to prevent the birth of those who would be prosperous. In the developed countries, each new baby, we are told, is a greedy little glutton who will in a lifetime consume 26 million tons of water, 11,000 pounds of meat, 28,000 pounds of milk and cream, and 9,000 pounds of wheat, among other robberies from our precious inventory of "nonrenewable resources."

Every schoolchild is told that six percent of the world's population consumes 50 (or 60 or 70) percent of the world's goods. They do not as often learn that the same six percent produces a comparable percentage of the world's goods. This focus on consumption to the exclusion of production might be described as another kind of "consumerism" in economic analysis. It is imperative that children learn that there is something radically wrong with so few having so much and so many having so little. The point of teaching that is not to produce guilt feelings about prosperity but, if John Paul is to be believed, to point us toward the inclusion of all peoples in the circle of exchange and productivity.

ALWAYS TO DEVELOP, NEVER TO BETRAY

One section of *Centesimus*, and it is among the shortest sections, deals with the environment. Human beings use resources in "an excessive and disordered way." They forget that while they are to "transform" and even "create" the world through work, their efforts depend "on God's prior and original gift of the things that are." We are indeed called to dominate the earth, but in a way that respects "a prior God-given purpose, which man can indeed develop but must not betray." We are urged to overcome a poverty of outlook that is devoid of gratitude and lacks an "aesthetic attitude that is born of wonder in the presence of being and of the beauty that enables one to see in visible things the message of the invisible God who created them" (¶ 37).

After that brief section on the natural environment, John Paul moves immediately to "the more serious destruction of the human environment" (¶ 38). What he calls "human ecology" includes an understanding of social structures, beginning with the family and extending to the other institutions that make and keep life human. The comparatively slight attention given the natural environment in *Centesimus* should not, I think, be taken as indifference to legitimate environmental concerns. John Paul has to be deeply conscious of the disaster of socialism also in its devastation of the environment, a devastation far exceeding the environmental threats that rightly concern us in the Western democracies. His beloved city of Kraków, for instance, which is in many ways the spiritual and cultural center of Poland, suffers under a weight of air pollution that is today unthinkable in our cities. At the same time, however, the Pope is aware of the antihumanistic turns taken by some forms of environmentalism. He insists that God has placed his good earth in the service of humankind, the cocreator and cantor of the universe who is to redirect everything back to the glory of God.

There are, one may suggest, three faces, or three forms, of contemporary environmentalism. First and most obviously, it is a housekeeping movement that cleans up our natural habitat, teaches industry better toilet habits, and inculcates greater modesty and caution in the technological rush to what is sometimes uncritically called progress. Second, it is the old conservationism, once a patrician preoccupation that has now gone middle-class. Here the concern for preserving wilderness space and endangered species is largely aesthetic, although often agitated with intense moral passion. The third face of environmentalism is harsher. It is a movement determined to rid the world of the error of "anthropocentrism" and impose coercive control over what is viewed as the "cancerous growth" of human population, among both the rich and the marginalized.

John Paul affirms the second environmentalism, encouraging as it does an "aesthetic attitude that is born of wonder." He was until recently an inveterate skier and outdoorsman, and one may imagine that as he was writing this paragraph, he had in his mind's eye the landscape of rural Poland and the slopes of the Italian Alps. He firmly endorses the first environmentalism as well, emphasizing that we are to "develop but not betray" God's gift of nature.

He is no Luddite, however, opposing technological development and change. On the contrary, we have earlier considered his high praise for technology and know-how, as well as his encouragement of the virtue of prudent risk. In so strongly endorsing the first environmentalism, *Centesimus* would seem to be cautioning against both hubris and timidity, both of which are forms of faithlessness. Against the third environmentalism, however, John Paul positions himself with adamant determination. This is the ultimate faithlessness—to assume a world of stasis, to think that history has come to an end, to permanently exclude the poor and vulnerable, to despair of the continuing interaction of divine presence and human freedom that is providence.

If the cause of poverty is marginalization, the cure is inclusion. "Even in recent years," John Paul writes, "it was thought that the poorest countries would develop by isolating themselves from the world market and by depending on their own resources." That, he makes clear, was a mistake. The mistake often traveled under the name of "dependency theory." The argument was that in the world economy of capitalism the "metropolitan areas" sucked the resources of the poor nations and subjected them to an ever-deeper servitude. In place of dependency theory, John Paul proposes what might be called *participation theory*. Experience shows, he says, that countries that isolated themselves, often adopting curious mixes of socialism and nationalism, "have suffered stagnation and recession." On the other hand, "the countries that experienced development were those that succeeded in taking part in the general interrelated economic activities at the international level" (¶ 33).

"It seems therefore that the chief problem is that of gaining fair access to the international market," he writes (¶ 33). People in both the marginalized and developed economies have the responsibility of achieving that. The Pope proposes no grand program. He does not claim to know precisely how that goal is to be achieved. He has no doubt, however, about its imperative character. It requires intellectual and moral changes—different habits of mind and habits of heart in our attitude toward the poor, especially different habits of heart. "Thus the first and most important task is accomplished within man's heart," he declares. "No one can say that he is not responsible for the well-being of his brother or sister" (¶ 51). Put differently, people can say that they are not responsible, but they do so at the price of debasing their own humanity and becoming guilty of neglecting the neighbor's need.

THE GUILTY AND THE RESPONSIBLE

Unlike so many religious declarations about the poor, *Centesimus* is not "laying a guilt trip" on the reader. In pondering the sorry conditions of the world, Rabbi Abraham Joshua Heschel was given to saying, "Some are guilty, all are responsible." The distinction is important. John Paul most particularly addresses those in the business community, reminding them that their decisions are not *only* moral decisions, but they are *also* moral decisions. The impact upon people, and especially on the marginalized, must be taken into account in taking care of business. He would evoke the creative imagination to find the ways to wed taking care of business and taking care of one another. It might be said that *Centesimus* is easy on capitalism but hard on capitalists. Yet more accurately, it is powerfully affirmative of the free economy and unwilling to accept the idea that the free economy cannot be made to work for everyone.

The encyclical does not blink the fact that the poor nations also have responsibilities that they have not adequately faced. It simply will not do for them to blame their plight on colonialism, neocolonialism, imperialism, and the such. While foreign states and corporations have taken and do take unjust advantage, Third World leaders are firmly told to put their own houses in order. "Also lacking [in these countries] is a class of competent professional people capable of running the state apparatus in an honest and just way, nor are there qualified personnel for managing the economy in an efficient and responsible manner" (¶ 20). Embracing the mentality of victimhood that dwells obsessively upon real or imagined injuries is not the way toward participation in the world economic order.

In addition, some Third World countries made the mistake of thinking that "Marxism can offer a sort of shortcut for building up the nation and the state" (¶ 20). They adopted a mishmash of socialist, nationalist, and traditional ideas in jerry-built political systems that were typically despotic and almost always economically disastrous. To be sure, many who followed a Marxist or quasi-Marxist course were caught up in the cold war between the "competing blocs" that John Paul so excoriated in *Sollicitudo Rei Socialis.* But now that the socialist bloc that seduced and subsidized them is itself collapsed, it is time for these Third World countries to recognize that they were taken in. Is capitalism "the model that ought to be proposed to the countries of the Third World that are searching for the path to true economic and civil progress?" the Pope asks. After clearly defining what he means by capitalism, he does not hesitate: "The answer is clearly in the affirmative" (¶ 42). The promise of a global order that will benefit everyone depends upon the shared determination to help "entire peoples that are presently excluded or marginalized to enter into the sphere of economic and human development" (¶ 58).

In this chapter, as in the encyclical itself, the discussion of the marginalized has focused mainly on the global picture. At several points, however, John Paul talks about the "Fourth

World" marginalized, meaning the very poor within the developed economies of democratic capitalism. For Americans, this requires that much more careful and sustained attention be given the urban underclass in our midst. Because this is very largely a black underclass, and because white Americans are increasingly weary of hearing about race, there is powerful, and in some ways understandable, resistance when this question is raised. The price of not paying attention, however, could be intolerable, and not only for the black and poor.

THE RADICALLY ISOLATED

William Julius Wilson of the University of Chicago offers one of the most detailed and compelling descriptions of the plight of the underclass in *The Truly Disadvantaged.* The most accurate way of thinking about the underclass, he contends, is that they are the people who are "radically isolated" in our society. That, of course, is another way of saying marginalized. They are isolated or marginalized not only from the mainstream economy but also from those blacks who are "making it" in the mainstream economy. It is important to keep in mind that the majority of black Americans are as fully and successfully participating in the economy as are their white counterparts. But they have, for the most part, now removed themselves from the blacks who are marginalized. In the 1950s, the Bedford-Stuyvesant section of Brooklyn included many middle-class and quite a few wealthy blacks. Black communities such as Bedford-Stuyvesant had earlier been created by massive "white flight." The last three decades have witnessed a massive "black flight," as most of those who can leave have left. Leaving behind, of course, those who are now even more radically isolated.

The ever-provocative social critic Charles Murray worries in more general terms that America may be turning into a "caste society." There are an increasing number of Americans who are rich, which is to say they have very large discretionary incomes.

And increasingly they are learning to live in ways that effectively marginalize the less rich, and most particularly the underclass. At the end of the Korean War, Murray notes, less than one family in fifty thousand had an income of $100,000 or more. In 1988, almost four families per *hundred* had an income that large. (The comparison is in constant 1988 dollars.) Murray is not the least interested in equality of income. He is very interested, and very anxious, about patterns of social behavior that could create a caste society. A few super-rich people at the top of the economic heap have always tended to isolate, even radically isolate, themselves from the common run of humanity. It is a very different thing when a large sector of the society (as in "caste") isolates itself from those who are not so well off.

The number of rich people will likely grow rapidly in the coming years. A major factor is the increasing monetary value of "cognitive skills"—of the ability to use one's head in exploiting the technology and know-how that figures so prominently in *Centesimus*. Murray notes that in 1980 a male college graduate made about 30 percent more than a male high school graduate. By 1988, he made 60 percent more. In only eight years, the premium for a college degree doubled in comparison with a high school diploma. The comparison with those who did not even graduate from high school is truly stark, giving us some idea of why the radically isolated may become more radically isolated yet.

While the value of first-class cognitive skills will skyrocket, says Murray, it seems likely that real wages for low-skill jobs will increase slowly, if at all. Efforts to increase such wages artificially by, for instance, raising the minimum wage will not work because technology will provide employers with more and more affordable alternatives to human labor. Recall our earlier discussion about the increasing number of people who are, by routine calculations of economic interest, simply not needed. Those who run the huge financial and insurance institutions in New York say that they interview fifty or even a hundred young people in order to find one who possesses the elementary skills needed for entry-level positions. As for the others, who needs them? Several insurance companies have resorted to flying to Ireland the huge amount of paperwork, in the form of insurance claims, that comes in each day. There it is processed overnight and sent back to New York by satellite the next morning. The companies obviously do not want to publicize such a politically sensitive practice, but it is part of a pattern that should be worrying to all of us.

As companies seek both alternative human labor and alternatives to human labor, the marginalized become increasingly irrelevant to the economy. By the usual calculations of utility, they are eminently expendable. Meanwhile, the rich will constitute an ever-larger portion of the population. Just as John Paul fears, they may more and more adopt lifestyles designed to isolate themselves, and protect themselves, from the marginalized. Anyone with even a cursory knowledge of the connection between crime and the urban underclass will appreciate that such isolation is not entirely irrational. Murray asks us to consider "what happens when 10 or 20 percent of the population has enough income to bypass the social institutions it doesn't like in ways that only the top fraction of one percent used to be able to do."

THE SECESSION OF THE SUCCESSFUL

Some social critics are now talking about a "secession of the successful" from the social order. Cities such as New York and Chicago are not America, for which most Americans are grateful. But the cities may tell us something important about emerging patterns of caste in American life. The British author Jonathan Raban writes wittily and disturbingly about his time in New York. He discusses the "air people" and the "ground people." The air people are the rich. They live and work and socialize in great towers accessible only by elevator and secured by private police forces. When they need to get from one air space to another, they quickly scurry by cab or limousine, avoiding the ground people as much as possible, until they reach the security of the next well-guarded tower and rejoin the other air people.

Raban is not averse to a bit of hyperbole, but his description rings true. In terms of class stratification, and its complicated connections with race, Manhattan is quite precisely defined by means of transport. Caste membership is denoted, moving from bottom to top, by whether one travels by subway, bus, taxi, or limousine. The real air people—a privileged few that includes the mayor—use helicopters when possible. (Raban notwithstanding, a redeeming feature of Manhattan is the perduring popularity of walking a great deal. Not after dark, of course, and certainly not alone after dark.)

The secession of the rich is evident not only in the great cities but in "gated communities" of the suburbs that are, for all practical purposes, private preserves or republics of the privileged. There are other examples, such as the use of fax machines, modems, and overnight mail. The rich have, for communications that really matter, simply bought out of the U.S. Postal Service. And almost nobody in our major cities who can afford an alternative sends their children to the public schools. The great majority of teachers in the public schools send their children to voluntary, usually church-related, schools. At the end of the twentieth century urban public schools have come full circle; they are once again the "poor schools" that they started out to be in the early nineteenth century.

Murray wonders whether, as the country becomes increasingly conservative, American conservativism might follow the Latin American model, "where to be conservative means to preserve the mansions on the hills above the slums." The American model used to be one of openness, opportunity, and participation, very much along the lines so vigorously pressed by *Centesimus*. But that may be changing, says Murray. "Conservatives are now being joined by defectors from urban liberalism who have been mugged—sometimes figuratively, often literally . . . Their political agenda is weighted heavily toward taking care of number one, using big government to do so whenever it suits their purposes. More broadly, the culture of the urban underclass, increasingly violent and bizarre, fosters alienation. As each new social experiment fails to diminish the size of the underclass, our increasing national wealth will make it tempting to bypass the problem by treating the inner city as an urban analogue of the Indian reservation."

Is this alarmist? Unfortunately, no. Last year and the year before that and the year before that, going back at least ten years now, more than 80 percent of the children born in the black underclass were born, not simply out of wedlock, as it used to be said, but without adult males who accept responsibility for them. In a sector of the American population that includes five to eight million people, the institution of the family has almost disappeared. It is doubtful that this has ever happened on such a scale in all of human history. Since it is unprecedented, we cannot know whether the institution of family can be reestablished. It is, for the most part, not a matter of reviving the institution but of *reintroducing* it. In many cases, there is now a second and third generation that does not remember it, although they do occasionally watch functioning families on television. They view such families as part of the way "they" live. This is marginalization with a vengeance.

In 1961, Michael Harrington wrote *The Other America*, which played an important part in preparing the country for the war on poverty launched by Lyndon Johnson. The other America was "other" in that they had a lot less money. Harrington and those like him did not hesitate to promote a frankly socialist "remedy" of redistributing the wealth. In fact, some programs of the war on poverty worked very well in lifting people out of poverty, notably the elderly. But the underclass, with its "increasingly violent and bizarre" behavior, is also part of that legacy. As it is said that no good deed goes unpunished, so it seems that no well-intentioned program fails to backfire. William Julius Wilson observes that even the end of racial discrimination in areas such as housing accelerated the isolation of the underclass. Blacks who could afford it moved to where they could not move before, leaving behind those who could not afford to move. Wilson quickly adds, of course, that the answer is not to reintroduce legal discrimination.

But a growing number of people despair of any answer at all. If the rich constitute 10 or 20 percent of the population, they will, of course, look out for themselves and their families. Their political power will quite thoroughly transform our public life. "The Left has been complaining for years that the rich have too much power," Murray writes. He adds, "They ain't seen nothing yet." Many among the rich may be wonderfully compassionate and caring but if there are no credible answers to the question of what to do about the underclass, their options are limited. Daniel Patrick Moynihan got in deep political trouble two decades ago when he proposed a policy of "benign neglect" in connection with the problems of race. His critics misunderstood him (sometimes deliberately, it seems) to be urging benign neglect of the problems of poverty. In the view of more and more Americans today, benign neglect begins to look like the best that can be done. That is manifestly unacceptable.

Murray's analogy of the Indian reservation is apt. Or we might think of a sandbox surrounded by a high chainlink fence. There, at a safe distance from our world, the unruly children are permitted to play with one another, rut with one another, drug one another, kill one another. They will have their "leaders" who strut and shuffle and threaten and bluff—you know, the way black folks do. They demand new toys for the sandbox, and politicians who are accountable to the rich, who know that it is in their interest to pacify the marginalized, will toss the toys over the big chainlink fence. A rich society can afford to do that. After all, benign neglect is by no means the worst of final solutions that might be proposed.

Lazarus sits at the gates of our gated communities in a gated world. John Paul insists that we owe him, and we owe ourselves, much better than that. In the next chapter we examine *Centesimus* in search of clues to a better way.

NOTES

Page 211. "Instruction on Certain Aspects of the 'Theology of Liberation' " issued by the Congregation for the Doctrine of the Faith, September 3, 1984 (English translation reprinted in *Origins*, September 13, 1984). "Instruction on Christian Freedom and Liberation" issued by the Congregation for the Doctrine of the Faith, April 5, 1986 (English translation reprinted in *Origins*, April 17, 1986).

Page 217. For a discussion of the similarities and dissimilarities between Nazi Germany and policy directions in the United States, see the author's "Bioethics and the Holocaust," *First Things*, March 1991. Also Chapter Three, "Die Buben Sind Unser Unglueck," of James Burtchaell's *Rachel Weeping*, Harper and Row, 1982.

Page 218. The German bishops' study, "Population and Poverty," is published in *Catholic International*, October 1991.

Pages 218–19. See the author's *In Defense of People*, Macmillan, 1971. Also Julian Simon, *The Ultimate Resource*, Princeton, 1981.

Page 219. On the dubious notion of animal rights, see "Animal Rights, Human Rights," by Thomas Derr in *First Things*, February 1992.

Page 220. Christopher Mooney, "Theology and Science," *Theological Studies*, June 1991.

Page 221. Quote by Jacques Monod in *Chance and Necessity*, Knopf, 1971.

Page 224. On changing lifestyles and economic sacrifices required of capitalism, see *Center Focus*, August 1991.

Page 230. William Julius Wilson, *The Truly Disadvantaged*, Chicago, 1987. While Wilson's analysis of the urban underclass is masterful, his proposed solutions are, for the most part, liberal nostrums that have been tried and, in the view of most experts and generalists alike, found wanting. Wilson wisely contends that policies designed to help the poor should be crafted in a way that is perceived to help the middle class as well. Unfortunately, this tends to move him in the direction of a more comprehensive social control of the economy, the very direction that *Centesimus* rightly warns against. The sobering fact about poverty in the United States is not so much that we lack the political will to "solve" the problem. It is, first, that the problem is widely misunderstood and, second, that we have learned from bitter experience that many policies aimed at remedying poverty have only exacerbated it. It is an important part of the argument of this book that on both scores *Centesimus Annus* is a richly suggestive proposal.

Page 230. Charles Murray on poverty is in "The Conservative Future," *National Review*, July 8, 1991.

Page 232. Jonathan Raban, *Hunting Mister Heartbreak*, HarperCollins, 1991.

Chapter Nine

. . .

SOCIETY AND STATE

It is obvious by now that John Paul's understanding of the social order intends to be of a piece. His manner is not to throw out scattered dicta of do's and don'ts, of rights and wrongs. He proposes, rather, a coherent way of thinking about politics, and therefore about morality. Politics and morality are inseparable, as Aristotle said when he declared that *the* political question is, "How ought we to order our life together?" The "ought" in that question clearly requires a moral point of reference.

The way to think about society, says John Paul, is by primary reference to the acting person, and the acting person in community. Thus the controlling concept becomes that of the "subjectivity of society." A healthy society is ordered by the free interaction of subjects who must never be viewed and should never view themselves as objects. This idea of the acting, thinking, creating person makes democracy both possible and necessary. *Centesimus* is by no means the first authoritative Catholic document to affirm the democratic project, but it does so with a force and nuance that is perhaps unprecedented. A crucial part of that project, as we have seen, is an economy that is marked by free-dom, enterprise, and participation. That kind of capitalism is the economic corollary of the Christian understanding of human nature and destiny.

In this chapter we want to bring *Centesimus* into even closer conversation with questions that are perennially agitated in the American political culture. These questions continue the last chapter's discussion of the relationship between the prosperous and the marginalized, and cluster around the concepts of state and society. John Paul insists upon the limited nature of state power, one of the key concepts of democratic governance. In that sense he is antistatist, but he is not antistate. It is not enough to be opposed to the inflation of state power that is called statism. Indeed, unless one embraces anarchy, resisting such inflation requires a strong and positive understanding of the appropriate role of the state. *Centesimus* offers such a strong and positive understanding.

At the same time, John Paul is opposed to the "politicizing" of the entire social order, while knowing that the acting person is also political by nature and must be trained in the virtues of politics. Here his argument is very similar to the well-known claim of Edmund Burke: "To be attached to the subdivision, to love the little platoon we belong to in society, is the first princi-ple (the germ as it were) of public affection." Many have ob-served that *Centesimus* moves in a direction remarkably sympa-thetic to an understanding of the social order that has long been associated with the American experiment. From his observation of the American experiment, Alexis de Tocqueville concluded, "In democratic countries the science of association is the mother of science; the progress of all the rest depends upon the progress it has made." The science—and, we would add, the art—of asso-ciation is of the essence in understanding the subjectivity of soci-ety.

Here and elsewhere it is evident that John Paul's is a thor-oughly modern way of thinking about state and society. Or, as we suggested earlier, it might better be described as a postmodern viewpoint. That is to say, it has internalized the modern understanding of the state, and then it goes beyond that modern understanding to bring political theory back into conversation with classical and biblical appreciations of the common good. Earlier Catholic discussions typically relied heavily on the concept of "natural law" in thinking about society and state. The almost complete absence of any explicit reference to natural law in *Centesimus,* and its very limited place in the Pope's other writings, is noteworthy. In addition, and unlike many earlier Catholic discussions, John Paul does not discuss the state in the terms of divinely established hierarchies of order. Rather, his conceptual framework is hinged upon the acting person, the acting person in community, the subjectivity of society, and the state as an instrument in giving effect to the personal and communal quest for the good. This way of thinking about society and state does not fit easily into our familiar patterns of thought regarding political philosophy and practice.

GOVERNMENT BIG AND SMALL

In our political culture there is a running debate over "big government." Conservatives decry it and liberals are allegedly in favor of it. The reality is considerably more complex than that. Another way of putting it is to say that most people are, on this question, a little conservative *and* a little liberal. There are two apparently conflicting tendencies in American public life. People desire an expansive definition of government responsibility and an increase of those government services that benefit them while, at the same time, they desire to reduce the bureaucratic, depersonalizing, and exceedingly costly operations of big government. The concept of society and state proposed by *Centesimus* may point to a way out of this apparent contradiction, while satisfying what is legitimate in both desires.

The encyclical consistently distinguishes between the society and the state. For instance, in discussing unemployment and necessary economic safeguards, it typically talks about what society should do, what the state should do, and, frequently, what is to be done by "society and the state" (cf. ¶ 15). The goal, if we take seriously the subjectivity of society, is an open process in which society organizes itself (¶ 16). The state is in the service of that goal. The key presupposition here is that society is prior to the state—prior in terms of both time and dignity. Agreeing with Tocqueville, John Paul declares that "the right of association is a natural right of the human being, which therefore precedes his or her incorporation into political society." He cites Leo XIII, who wrote that "the state is bound to protect natural rights, not to destroy them; and if it forbids its citizens to form associations, it contradicts the very principle of its own existence" (¶ 7).

In the modern world we frequently encounter a mind-set that tends to equate and confuse society and state. Most of us are susceptible to that error at times. Seeing some social need, people say that "we" or "they" should do something about it, meaning that the state should do something about it. Whether they say "we" or "they" depends in large part upon their social placement. Those with government power or ready access to it are the more inclined to speak of the state in the first person plural.

But the state is not the society. The subjectivity of society means that people—the acting persons who are closest to the need in question—need to act. Sometimes they are not able to act in addressing the need. They need help. In most cases, the help is to be sought from other acting persons through *free associations*. Sometimes government policies hinder individuals and associations from acting. Sometimes government policies can enable or empower them to act. In all instances, the government is to be in the service of society, helping society to organize itself. The state, then, is not to be equated with the society. The state is one very important actor *within* society, and it is always to act as the servant, never as the master.

The subjectivity of society is protected and enhanced by *the principle of subsidiarity*. Subsidiarity was first articulated by Pius

XI in *Quadragesimo Anno* (1931) but has seldom been expounded with the nuance and force to be found in the present encyclical. This principle is so foundational that it is fair to say that almost everything else in this chapter is but an unfolding of the principle of subsidiarity. We therefore put in italics John Paul's way of formulating the principle of subsidiarity: *"A community of a higher order should not interfere in the internal life of a community of a lower order, depriving the latter of its functions, but rather should support it in case of need and help to coordinate its activity with the activities of the rest of society, always with a view to the common good"* (¶ 48).

That sentence rewards a close rereading. The state is "higher" and the family, for instance, is "lower" with respect to the hierarchy of organized power in society. But the family is higher in terms of priority and rights. The word "subsidiary" suggests an auxiliary agent that supplies aid and support. Or we speak of subsidiary in the sense of one thing being derived from and subordinate to another—for instance, a stream that is a subsidiary of the larger river. In understanding the principle of subsidiarity, it is of utmost importance to know what is subsidiary to what. The state, "a community of a higher order," is in fact of a lower order. The state is subsidiary to the society in service, as it is also derived from the society in its moral legitimacy.

A PRINCIPLE SUBVERTED

In the words of the American Founders, society is "We the people." The state is not "We the people," and "We the people" are not the state. The Preamble to the Constitution declares, "We the people of the United States . . . do ordain and establish this Constitution for the United States of America." In other words, the political order is the creature and the servant of the civil society. It thus becomes obvious that the principle of subsidiarity is inseparably linked to a proper understanding of democratic theory and practice. One of the most critical expressions in the events that led up to 1989 in Eastern Europe was "civil society." The constituting premise of totalitarianism is that there is only one society and it is embodied in the ruling party. There may be purely private "societies," but they are not public, they are not civil, they are not permitted to influence the *civitas*, which is the sphere that in totalitarian theory belongs exclusively to the party-state.

The principle of subsidiarity is frequently subverted by confusions. Some confusions result in turning it quite precisely on its head. For example, it is said that subsidiarity means that government functions should be "devolved" or "decentralized" to the lowest possible levels of society. Such thinking is no doubt well-intended, but it inadvertently attacks the principle at its core. The notion of devolving or decentralizing state functions assumes that the functions belong to the state in the first place. Subsidiarity is based on precisely the opposite assumption. In the concept of the subjectivity of society, the point is that these functions—such as economic activity, education, health, and social services—properly belong to the free associations of the people of the society. The state has an important *ancillary* role in providing a framework of law and order in which people can attend to the business that is properly theirs.

In current American discussions, the principle of subsidiarity is commonly addressed in terms of "mediating structures." When Peter Berger and this author first wrote about mediating structures in *To Empower People* (1977), we observed, "Taken seriously, they could become the basis of far-reaching innovations in public policy, perhaps of a new paradigm for at least sectors of the modern welfare state." As we noted at the time, we were working out the implications of subsidiarity within the context of American society. The mediating-structures argument, dubbed the "New Paradigm," was subsequently adopted by some political leaders and social policy experts and is today being advanced with varying energy and effect at both the federal and state levels of public policy.

Centesimus is intensely concerned about mediating structures. John Paul calls them intermediary or mediating groups. He writes that "the social nature of man is . . . realized in various intermediary groups, beginning with the family and including economic, social, political, and cultural groups that stem from human nature itself and have their own autonomy, always with a view to the common good" (¶ 13). Berger and I defined mediating structures as those institutions that stand between, and mediate between, the isolated individual and the megastructures of society, including the state. John Paul speaks of "intermediate communities" that provide a zone of freedom for the individual who "is often suffocated between two poles represented by the state and the marketplace" (¶ 49). The idea in both cases is that these communal structures give the individual an identity and leverage over against the massive anonymous forces that would otherwise control the entire social order, turning people into objects rather than subjects.

There are many such intermediate groups in society. When the Pope speaks of freedom of association, for instance, he several times makes favorable mention of trade unions or the labor movement. Unions are favored "certainly not because of ideological prejudices or in order to surrender to a class mentality, but because the right of association is a natural right of the human being, which therefore precedes his or her incorporation into political society" (¶ 7). Nobody should deny that labor unions have played an exceedingly important role in the American context. At the same time, it is commonly acknowledged that unions are today in deep trouble. In recent decades, many leaders of organized labor have not hesitated to call it a crisis.

UNIONS IN CRISIS

A steadily declining portion of the American work force is unionized. Most workers seem to think that the labor movement is obsolete, and are prepared to dismiss it with thanks for past services rendered. *Centesimus* may also be helpful in providing insight to some of the difficulties in contemporary unionism. First, organized labor is frequently infected by "ideological prejudices" and a "class mentality" that is hostile to the free economy urged by John Paul. In significant sectors of labor leadership there is still a zero-sum mind-set with respect to economic exchange and productivity. Second, labor's organizing methods and structures would seem to be in conflict, or at least in tension, with what John Paul calls "free association." One may wonder whether an association is free if people are forced to belong to it and are taxed by it without their consent. At the very least, these are questions that are still awaiting satisfactory resolution, and the questioning would seem to find considerable support in the argument of *Centesimus*.

The third reason for the contemporary "crisis" of organized labor would seem to be almost beyond dispute. The sector of the union movement that is growing is in government employment. Some of the most powerful organizations, such as the National Association of Education and other public-service unions, are now clearly in alliance with the megastructure of the state that is, to use the Pope's word, "suffocating" individuals and their mediating institutions. It is in the perceived self-interest of unionized government employees to secure and ever expand the reach of the state. Certainly it is in the interest of the leaders of such government unions. That is, so to speak, the business they are in. Unfortunately, this leads to the labor union, which is ideally a model of the intermediate groups that the Pope says are so necessary, becoming the enemy of such mediating structures.

According to some studies, the number of workers on state payrolls grew twice as fast as the population at large during the decade of the eighties. In Illinois, it was four times as fast, in Massachusetts, six times, and in New York, fourteen times. While overall union membership is down a third from its 1975 peak, the government-sector unions have gained 1.2 million members. The bulk of this dramatic increase is related to social-service functions that, if John Paul is right, properly belong to the mediating institutions that government tends to displace. We cannot be delayed here by a fuller discussion of the current problems of trade unionism. Suffice it that the leaders and friends of organized labor have every reason to study *Centesimus* with self-critical care.

To Learn to Love

The foremost model of what mediating structures do when they function well is the family. "The first and fundamental structure for 'human ecology,' " John Paul writes, "is the family, in which man receives his first formative ideas about truth and goodness, and learns what it means to love and to be loved, and thus what it actually means to be a person" (¶ 39). This is what the intermediate structures uniquely do—they provide "meaning systems" by which people acquire their own identities and an understanding of their duties to others. These "little platoons" do what the state cannot do, unless it becomes authoritarian or totalitarian. Remember the Communist claim—the phraseology of which goes back to earlier utopianisms—that it was producing the New Man in the New Society. Nazism, similarly, boasted that it was producing not only a new German but a New Man to advance the global mission of the Thousand-Year Reich.

We earlier discussed John Paul's description of different cultures being different ways of understanding personal existence. Recall also his insistence that culture is the most important factor in determining the social order. The culture-forming tasks do not belong to the state. They belong to the mediating institutions, to the free communities of identity, memory, and mutual aid. The family is such an institution, as is the church for those who freely adhere to it. When politicians, whether on the right or the left, begin to speak of the political order as a family, it is time to take alarm. It is a step toward turning the state into a church.

That temptation is endemic to the modern state with its

voracious appetites. The most dangerous ambition of the state is not to expand and consume an ever-increasing share of a society's wealth. The most dangerous ambition is to become the "meaning bestowing" institution within society. For many Americans, politics and the state *are* their church. It is the enterprise of their primary identity. The state is the public institution about which they most easily say "we." As Saint Augustine taught sixteen hundred years ago, those who have no citizenship in the City of God will inevitably order their ultimate loves and allegiances in the City of Man. The proper word for that, in the Christian view of things, is idolatry.

Centesimus is fairly described as antistatist, but not antistate. The encyclical has a good deal to say about the appropriate and *necessary* function of the state within society. The theory of the state that is propounded sometimes sounds very much like what political scientists call the "night watchman" state or "umpire" state. That is to say, the state is to make sure that people play fairly in the public arena, it is to keep an eye out for brigands, and, when necessary, adjudicate conflicts over the rules. Leo XIII, says this Pope, understood that "the state has the duty of watching over the common good and of ensuring that every sector of social life, not excluding the economic one, contributes to achieving that good while respecting the rightful autonomy of each sector."

Then, as though fearful that this may be granting too much authority to the state, John Paul immediately adds: "This should not, however, lead us to think that Pope Leo expected the state to solve every social problem. On the contrary, he frequently insists on necessary limits to the state's intervention and on its instrumental character inasmuch as the individual, the family, and society are prior to the state and inasmuch as the state exists in order to protect their rights and not stifle them" (¶ 11). Catholic social teaching has frequently been interpreted in a statist direction. John Paul is obviously determined to make it indelibly clear that that is a misinterpretation. He acknowledges that in some societies necessary reforms "were carried out in part by states," but then he moves immediately to the critical role played by mediating institutions and the "open process" by which society organizes itself (¶ 16).

Subsidiarity and Solidarity in Tandem

The state contributes "directly and indirectly" to ensuring certain social goals. Here the Pope envisions the principle of subsidiarity and the principle of solidarity working in tandem. The state contributes "indirectly and according to the principle of subsidiarity by creating favorable conditions for the free exercise of economic activity, which will lead to abundant opportunities for employment and sources of wealth." The state contributes "directly and according to the principle of solidarity by defending the weakest by placing certain limits on the autonomy of the parties who determine working conditions and by ensuring in every case the necessary minimum support for the unemployed worker" (¶ 15). Some may see more tension than tandem in the relationship between those two propositions. If the state is going to "ensure" everything in the second proposition, would it not be undermining "the free exercise of economic activity"? To the extent that there is a tension here, other passages in the encyclical indicate how John Paul proposes that that tension be resolved.

The state, he writes, "has the task of determining the juridical framework within which economic affairs are to be conducted and thus of safeguarding the prerequisites of a free economy." For instance, monopolies and cartels that exclude people from economic activity or prevent them from participating fully must be precluded by "the juridical framework." That is because the free economy "presumes a certain equality between the parties such that one party would not be so powerful as practically to reduce the other to subservience" (¶ 15). Here we encounter a rare reference to equality in connection with "a certain equality" of participation or, as it is said in American discussions, equality of opportunity. The state serves the "open process" of societal functioning by devising laws and regulations aimed at making sure that the process is indeed open to all.

There is particular concern in *Centesimus* for "the nightmare of unemployment." "Society and the state will both assume responsibility" for protecting workers from unemployment. As he later makes explicit, this cannot mean that the state guarantees employment. It does mean, however, policies "aimed at ensuring balanced growth and full employment or through unemployment insurance and retraining programs capable of ensuring a smooth transfer of workers from crisis sectors to those in expansion" (¶ 15). Obviously, the state cannot ensure such measures by edict. Given John Paul's understanding of the free economy, he would seem to be addressing himself chiefly to business leaders, who are reminded that also with respect to unemployment, their decisions have moral consequences. At the same time, the "juridical framework" provided by the state can be designed in a way that encourages decision-makers to do the right thing.

Like the biblical prophets, John Paul calls for justice to roll down like mighty waters, but he does not take it upon himself to prescribe the irrigation system. At several points he does indicate the kind of interaction between state, society, and economy that he has in mind. We noted earlier the three social virtues of "free work, of enterprise, and of participation." And we recall again his answer to his own question as to whether capitalism is the model for world development: "If by capitalism is meant an economic system that recognizes the fundamental and positive role of business, the market, private property, and the resulting responsibility for the means of production, as well as free human creativity in the economic sector, then the answer is certainly in the affirmative . . ." (¶ 42).

In an earlier section, where he is commending the democratic reconstruction of societies after World War II, we are offered a more detailed depiction of the goal he proposes. "In this context, an abundance of work opportunities, a solid system of social security and professional training, the freedom to join trade unions and the effective action of unions, the assistance provided in cases of unemployment, the opportunities for democratic participation in the life of society—all these are meant to deliver work from the mere condition of 'a commodity' and to guarantee its dignity" (¶ 19). Some commentators have suggested that this description best fits the West (now united) German "social market economy." Others say the Pope has in mind the American system of democratic capitalism. The Pope does not say. As is the way with models, it is less important to locate them geopolitically than to act upon them as a guide. Certainly the several indications of the model that John Paul has in mind all require a sure but restrained measure of state intervention.

A market economy "cannot be conducted in an institutional, juridical, or political vacuum" (¶ 48). An economic system of itself cannot assure a healthy society. Moral and cultural decisions must be made, consumers must be educated to make wise discriminations, the mass media must inculcate responsibility, and, he mentions at the end, there must also be "the necessary intervention by public authorities" (¶ 36). "There are collective and qualitative needs that cannot be satisfied by market mechanisms." Protecting the environment, for instance, is a "task of the state." "[In] the new capitalism, the state and all of society have the duty of defending those collective goods that, among others, constitute the essential framework for the legitimate pursuit of personal goals on the part of each individual" (¶ 40).

GOVERNMENT HELPING THE HELPERS

In every case, the state is ancillary and instrumental to the natural functioning of society. Subsidiarity assumes that most people best understand their own needs and how to meet them. In any society, there will always be some people who are in desperate need of help. In his much-discussed work, *The Unheavenly City*,

Edward Banfield proposes that as much as 6 percent of any population is made up of the socially incompetent. The severely
handicapped, the mentally ill, the criminally disposed, the very
old—they cannot take care of themselves, they must be cared
for. Six percent may be too high, but if the figure is only 3
percent, that means millions of people in a society such as ours.
Underneath all such people there must be a safety net of care,
and an economic floor of decency. What constitutes "decency"
cannot be determined by the market but is an inescapably political and moral decision that is always open to democratically
decided revision.

That the needs of the socially incompetent are to be addressed is a *public* concern. The state is properly involved in
seeing to it that these needs are met. That does *not* mean that
the state is to meet these needs. In some rare instances, John
Paul suggests, the state might directly intervene to meet such
needs. But that would only be appropriate if the mediating
structures and other institutions of society were not in place or
were not doing their job. As with the functioning of the free
economy, the state is to provide a "juridical framework" within
which the subjectivity of society can flourish in meeting human
needs.

Here a clear distinction is called for between what is *public*
and what is *governmental*. Common prejudices to the contrary,
"public" and "governmental" are not synonyms. There are
many tasks connected with the *res publicae* (public things) that
are not the tasks of the state. In areas such as education, for
instance, we are accustomed to talking about "public" schools as
distinct from "private" schools—or, if they are church-related,
"sectarian" schools. Rather than calling them public schools, it
would be more accurate to speak of government schools or state
schools. All schools that serve the public purpose of socializing
children are public schools. The penchant of subsuming the entirety of the *res publicae* under the control of the state and to
relegate what remains to the realm of "the private" must be

resisted. John Paul observes that the free exercise of religion, for instance, has a public status, "notwithstanding the general opinion even in [Leo's] day that such questions pertained exclusively to an individual's private life" (¶ 9). It is a matter of public justice whether people are enabled to freely exercise their religion in, for instance, the education of their children. Civil society is public society. It is not enough to say that the state *shares* public space with civil society. The only justification for the state's existence at all is that it *serves* civil society.

Relatively few Americans want to turn back the New Deal development of an expanded understanding of what constitutes legitimate public concerns. The emphasis of *Centesimus* on the subjectivity of society and intermediate groups does not call for a constricting of the responsibilities that we call public. *Centesimus* does suggest a conceptual and practical paradigm for reform by which society is better able to deal with human problems. The unfortunate equation of "public" with "governmental" has locked especially the poor into patterns of dependency upon the state. Policies designed in accord with the principle of subsidiarity have the promise of bringing "the radically isolated" into the mainstream of opportunity and endeavor.

In this connection, we recall John Paul's persistent accent on the *potentiality* of the poor. Government social policies tend to focus on human *pathology* rather than potentiality. There are understandable reasons why public policy gets fixated on the pathological. Things that go wrong are much more likely to catch public attention than things that go right. As it is said, good news is no news, and politics is driven by what is in the news. The focus on social pathologies, including the exaggeration of their incidence, also serves those who have an interest in expanding government programs. Especially is this the case if the statement "We should do something about it" is translated into "The government should do something about it." All too often, "doing something about it" does not mean that the state should provide a juridical framework that empowers mediating institutions (the family, for instance) to attend to the problem. More typically, it means that a government program should displace the role of the family.

DISPLACEMENT AND DEPENDENCY

These patterns of displacement and resulting dependency are often driven by the best of intentions. In many cases, we are confronted by a vicious circle. For instance, in urban school systems where students are predominantly, if not exclusively, from poor families, it is commonly said that the schools must take over the functions of the failed or nonexistent families. The vicious circle goes to work in that by displacing these families, the school system further weakens whatever viability these families still have. School administrators say, for instance, that children should learn morality in the family and in the church but, since they don't, the schools must take over their moral education. This frequently results in a moral formation (often in the name of "value-neutrality") that is in direct conflict with the moral formation favored by family and church. This pattern undermines the civil virtues on which civil society depends, and it further alienates citizens from the state, thus weakening the democratic order.

In 1991, under most particular pressure from homosexual activists, the New York City school system adopted a policy of distributing free condoms to its students. That might strike some readers as bizarre, but it follows logically enough from a set of distorted assumptions. The state, through its schools, displaces family authority, thereby further eroding family authority. Parents are "disempowered" as they are deprived of responsibility for their children. The New York program explicitly excludes the need for parental notification or permission. Such deprivation, of course, is justified by state officials who claim that parents have in fact abdicated their responsibility. (Which is often, sad to say, true.) Moreover, as state institutions, the schools are vulnerable to the pressure of sundry interest groups that may or may not have the well-being of children in mind. A reinforcing rationale for the policy is that the pathological is taken to be normative. "We all know," it is said, that adolescents are "doing it" anyway. Since they are going to behave like rutting animals no matter what we do or say, better that they rut with the "safety" of condoms. (In the New York program, volunteers, including volunteers from homosexual organizations such as ACT-UP—AIDS Coalition to Unleash Power—instruct the young people in the joys of "safe sex." Among the many doleful consequences of this program is the almost certain increase in the number of young people who will contract AIDS.)

The concepts of subsidiarity and the subjectivity of society do not give us precise instructions on when or how state intervention is legitimate. They do provide a conceptual framework, a paradigm, that helps us understand what has gone wrong in so many areas of social policy, and what might be done about it. They are not a panacea for the problems of the urban underclass, but they can put us on the road toward that "moral reconstruction" that John Paul says is so necessary in formerly socialist countries and is no less necessary in our own society. Key to such a reconstruction is changing our mental habits—to understand the state as the servant of society and its mediating institutions, to understand the distinction between what is public and what is governmental, and to understand that the promise of improvement depends on policies built not upon the pathologies but upon the potentialities of the poor.

John Paul illustrates his understanding of the right relationship between state and society by giving examples of the wrong relationship. Just as it is neither proper nor possible to meet every public need by government action, so not every *right* is to be satisfied by the government. This, too, counters some common ways of thinking in our political culture. There are even those who argue, for instance, that if there is a right to abortion, the state has the obligation to pay for abortions. Most people understand, however, that there is a necessary difference between rights and the satisfaction of rights. The constitutional guarantee of freedom of the press does not require the state or anyone else to provide a printing press for everybody who wants to promulgate their opinions. The fallen and skewed condition of the world is such that not every right can be satisfactorily exercised.

Centesimus clearly claims that there is a right to work. "The obligation to earn one's bread by the sweat of one's brow also presumes the right to do so." It is equally clear that a society that systematically denies people the opportunity to work "cannot be justified from an ethical point of view, nor can that society attain social peace" (¶ 43). At the same time, John Paul explicitly rejects the idea—an idea frequently promoted in some Catholic circles—that the government should be the "employer of last resort." "The state could not directly ensure the right to work for all its citizens unless it controlled every aspect of economic life and restricted the free initiative of individuals," he writes (¶ 48).

ATTENDING TO CONSEQUENCES

Disagreeing with "those who argued against any rules in the economic sphere," the Pope does not let the state off the hook. "Rather, the state has a duty to sustain business activities by creating conditions that will ensure job opportunities, by stimulating those activities where they are lacking or by supporting them in moments of crisis" (¶ 48). As in the discussion of when ownership of property is morally legitimate or illegitimate, John Paul again invites our attention to the probable consequences involved. This does not make the Pope a moral "consequentialist" or "pragmatist" in the sense that those terms are sometimes used to describe someone who does not believe in universal principles. It does make him what he is—a phenomenologist who attends to "concrete" persons, institutions, and patterns of behavior with a keen respect for how the world works.

While the state should sometimes intervene, it should not interfere. John Paul might well subscribe to the American political maxim, "If it ain't broke, don't fix it." Even when social institutions are not working the way they should, the remedy, he suggests again and again, is cultural, moral, and spiritual. The state is often the clumsiest of instruments, producing a remedy that is "worse than the sickness." At places he seems to be suggesting that the first axiom for the state might be taken from the Hippocratic Oath, "Do no harm." The state is not to "absorb" but to "defend" the mediating institutions of society, recognizing that such institutions "enjoy their own spheres of autonomy and sovereignty" (¶ 45). (The references to spheres of autonomy and sovereignty is noteworthy. The phrase has long been associated with the Dutch Calvinist theologian, politician, and public philosopher Abraham Kuyper, who died in 1920. While John Paul may have hit upon the phrase by himself, it is not unreasonable to expect that he has some familiarity with the distinguished body of political theory known as "Kuyperism." Certainly the understanding of state and society in *Centesimus* is strikingly similar at many points to the arguments advanced by Kuyper and his disciples today.)

The principle of "Do no harm" and the distinction between intervening and interfering require prudential judgments. There are times when maybe the state has to temporarily take over certain functions that rightly belong to other social institutions, but John Paul is exceedingly cautious on this score. "[I]n exceptional circumstances the state can also exercise a substitute function when social sectors or business systems are too weak or are just getting under way and are not equal to the task at hand" (¶ 48).

Even in the case of societies that are just at the beginning stages of economic, social, and political development, John Paul is vigorously skeptical about state intervention. "Such supplementary interventions, which are justified by urgent reasons touching the common good, must be as brief as possible so as to avoid removing permanently from society and business systems the functions that are properly theirs and so as to avoid enlarging excessively the sphere of state intervention to the detriment of both economic and civil freedom" (¶ 48). When the decision is between state intervention or letting "society and business systems" address the problem at hand, the benefit of the doubt is to be given the latter. Of course, resolving problems takes time. There is a powerful attractiveness—not only for politicians and those with a vested interest in expanding the sway of government—in the claim that the state can more quickly and directly "solve" the problem. On the basis of both political philosophy and practical experience, *Centesimus* urges us to resist the temptation posed by that claim.

In his analysis of state and society, John Paul deals with formerly socialist countries as well as the societies of the marginalized in the Third World. Once again, however, this thoroughly reformist Pope is not about to give a clean bill of health to the Western democracies. He observes that "such intervention"—meaning the kind of state intervention he criticizes—has "vastly expanded" also in the developed societies. He recognizes that the creation of the welfare state, or the "social assistance state" as it is sometimes called in Europe, came about "in order to respond better to many needs and demands by remedying forms of poverty and deprivation unworthy of the human person." He notes, however, that the "excesses and abuses" of the welfare state have come under increasingly harsh criticism. Also in the developed societies, "enlarging excessively the sphere of state intervention" could result and has resulted in doing damage to "both economic and civil freedom" (¶ 48).

"Malfunctions and defects" in the welfare state are not simply the result of policy errors, design failures, or technical inefficiencies, although there are no doubt plenty of each. When the social order goes out of whack, it is not an engineering problem, and certainly not a problem for government engineers. When the spheres of sovereignty are not respected, when mediating institutions are undermined or displaced, the root problem is philosophical. "Malfunctions and defects in the social assistance state are the result of an inadequate understanding of the tasks proper to the state" (¶ 48).

The Need for Neighbors

"By intervening directly and depriving society of its responsibility, the social assistance state leads to a loss of human energies and an inordinate increase of public agencies that are dominated more by bureaucratic ways of thinking than by concern for serving their clients, and that are accompanied by an enormous increase in spending." John Paul does not call for a dismantling of the welfare state, and certainly he does not recommend a more constricted sense of the human needs that are part of the *res publicae* touching on the common good. Rather, and precisely for the sake of the common good, he urges that we explore public policies that can better assist those who are in the best position to meet human needs. "In fact," he writes, "it would appear that needs are best understood and satisfied by people who are closest to them and who act as neighbors to those in need" (¶ 48). And that, of course, is another way of saying subsidiarity.

It is in this context that he again proposes that old and yet new paradigm, and his words might be as good a way as any to end this chapter's discussion of society and state: *A community of a higher order should not interfere in the internal life of a community of a lower order, depriving the latter of its functions, but rather should support it in case of need and help to coordinate its activity with the activities of the rest of society, always with a view to the common good.*

NOTES

Page 244. Peter Berger and Richard John Neuhaus, *To Empower People: The Role of Mediating Structures in Public Policy*, American Enterprise Institute, 1977.

Page 246. On unions and the government sector, see "Services Sag, Budgets Soar," *Forbes*, May 13, 1991.

Pages 251–52. Edward Banfield, *The Unheavenly City*, Little, Brown, 1968.

Pages 254–55. For a fuller discussion of the New York City "AIDS prevention" program, see "AIDS: Deadly Confusions Compounded," *First Things*, February 1992.

Page 257. Abraham Kuyper's political philosophy is kept in circulation today by a number of Calvinist thinkers both here and in the Netherlands. For Kuyper's thought and variations on it, see Bob Goudzwaard, *Capitalism and Progress*, Eerdmans, 1979, and James Skillen and Rockne McCarthy, editors, *Political Order and the Pluralistic Structure of Society*, Scholars Press, 1991.

Chapter Ten

. . .

THE MANY AND
THE ONE

Because the economic, the political, and the cultural are so intimately intertwined, we should not be surprised that the argument of *Centesimus* moves back and forth between capitalism, democracy, and the truths by which we order our life together. We have said that the argument is "of a piece." That does not mean that John Paul is proposing a monistic view of the social order. Exactly the opposite is the case. The argument that is of a piece is an argument that society is composed, as it were, of many pieces. The opposite of monism is pluralism, and *Centesimus* is a veritable manifesto in defense of pluralism.

The word "pluralism" has not been spared the abuse to which most of our public vocabulary has been subjected. We often hear it said that we must downplay or deny our differences "because ours is a pluralistic society." This is most frequently heard in connection with religious and ethnic differences. But the denial of differences is not the way of pluralism but the way of monism. If civil society requires that we pretend that our deepest differences make no difference, our common life is corrupted by a fundamental falsehood. The much-discussed "melting pot" of American society then turns out to be a process of homogenization that produces a tasteless social stew of anonymous ciphers. More favored today is the image of society as a "mosaic," but that, too, has been spoiled for many because of its associations with racial and ethnic separatism. Pluralism is the alternative to both homogenization and separatism.

Pluralism is engaging our deepest differences within the bond of civility. The motto *E Pluribus Unum* (out of many, one) is inscribed on the Great Seal of the United States of America. "We the People" are one, but not at the price of the many. The "one" is not the enemy of the "many." The "one" is not the national goal that is to be achieved by conquering or dissolving the "many." Were that the goal, ours would be a monistic and not a pluralistic society. The American experiment is to sustain the *unum* within which myriad *plures* can flourish. Monism is reductionistic and fearful of difference. Pluralism is adventurous, requiring confidence and, yes, even faith. Pluralism is derived from "plural," which means more. Pluralism is more.

In America, unity is supposed to be on friendly terms with particularity. Maintaining the bond of civility requires making accommodations, but it does not ask that we give up the many worlds that form, define, and sustain us. Precisely the opposite is the case. It is in the "little platoons" that the taste for civil society is cultivated, and the arts for living together in the *polis* are acquired. And, of all the little platoons, the littlest and the greatest is the family. As John Paul puts it, "The first and fundamental structure for 'human ecology' is the family, in which man receives his first formative ideas about truth and goodness, and learns what it means to love and to be loved, and thus what it actually means to be a person" (¶ 39).

Wrongheadedness Foiled, a Saving Grace

The free economy is a sustained turmoil of innumerable particularities of interest interacting in a maddeningly unmanageable mix of competition and cooperation. John Paul says that the state cannot arrange to give everyone a job because to attempt to do so would mean taking control of the entire society. That, of course, is what totalitarianism attempts to do. In the ideological guise of "workers working for themselves," everybody works for the ruling party that operates by the fantastic conceit that its interests embody the interests of all. A saving grace of totalitarianism is that it always fails in its ambition to control the entirety of society. The fact that their mad ambition always eludes them makes those in power all the more brutal in the pursuit of their goal, and as a consequence millions beyond numbering have been impoverished, imprisoned, and killed. The monistic dream has, in the course of human history and most especially in this most lethal of centuries, produced rivers of blood and mountains of corpses.

But surely, one may object, it is a great hyperbolic leap from government-guaranteed jobs to mountains of corpses. Yes, of course. In our society, those who propose grand schemes for expanded government control—they always say "services" rather than "control"—are not usually cryptototalitarians set upon "rationalizing" society according to their version of reason. Of course not. But well-intended schemes are often driven by a mind-set that is, at least implicitly, monistic. And monism, given its head, lurches toward totalitarianism. That the totalitarian reach always exceeds its grasp is, as we said, a saving grace. Under Communism, for instance, there were stubborn zones of freedom, especially freedom of the mind and of the spirit, that the masters were not able to bring to heel. And the day came when those little platoons grew into irrepressible divisions of human beings who stood up and said they were not going to take it anymore.

The free economy and the free society resist rationalization. Remember the young Harvard economist who said that he stopped being a socialist and became a capitalist when he decided that he could not respect an economic system that he could understand? In socialist critiques of democratic capitalism, one of the most frequent complaints is that capitalism is irrational and therefore wasteful. A homely illustration of the point that one runs across again and again is that in the supermarket there are forty-eight (or sixty-five or eighty-seven) brands of breakfast cereal. After all, who really needs twelve kinds of raisin bran? The answer is that we almost certainly do not *need* forty-eight brands of breakfast cereal. But it is the answer to a wrong question. There are other questions to be put to that question. How many kinds of breakfast cereal should be available in the supermarket? Which ones? How should we decide? And, most important, *who* would decide? *Somebody* would have to decide. The somebodies who decided would say, of course, that "Society" decided. But that is not right. It is much closer to the truth to say that society—through the subjectivity of millions of producers, suppliers, advertisers, retailers, and buyers—has decided to have forty-eight (or sixty-five or eighty-seven) brands of breakfast cereal for sale in the supermarket.

"The state," John Paul writes, "could not directly ensure the right to work for all its citizens unless it controlled every aspect of economic life and restricted the free initiative of individuals" (¶ 48). Is that really true? Surely it would be better for the government to provide jobs, or even put people into jobs, rather than maintaining them on the demeaning dole of welfare. But a large number of people are not interested in work; they do not see work as something that is in their interest. Efforts to turn welfare into "workfare" have been disappointing to date. To say someone is unemployed assumes that he is normally employed, but there are millions of Americans who have never been gainfully employed and have no serious intention of being so in the future. While public policy can modulate economic incentives and disincentives, it is hard to see how people could be "put into" jobs without the use of coercion.

In addition, economists tell us that half or more of the people listed as unemployed at a given time are, in fact, between jobs. The "free initiative of individuals" who leave jobs to look for higher-paying or more satisfying work is what makes them temporarily unemployed. If work is not to be meaningless, if skills and interests are to be at least roughly matched with jobs that need doing (and who will decide what needs doing?), it takes little imagination to see that a state program to directly ensure the right to work would indeed end up by undermining the free economy.

One may argue that in ensuring the right to work, the government would be only, as it is said, "the employer of last resort." Both theoretically and practically, however, it would be exceedingly difficult to construct and maintain a definition of "last resort." If the jobs involved are not make-work or drudgery, if they provide financially rewarding and personally satisfying work, they would be in competition with work opportunities in the wealth-producing sector of the society. They would in many instances become jobs of first resort, and therefore the state would become, at least in many instances, the employer of first, last, and in-between resort.

The principles of economic pluralism supported by *Centesimus* certainly do not preclude further and vigorous efforts to move people from welfare dependency to productive work. In fact, as we have seen, the entire argument regarding the marginalized is aimed at encouraging efforts to include them in the circle of the free economy. John Paul emphasizes the *duty* of the state to help sustain business and thus create opportunities for work. Beyond that, there would seem to be no objection to, but every support for, energetic programs in job training and social policies designed to provide incentives for the marginalized to move into the work force. These problems sometimes seem intractable, but that is no reason to despair of discovering more efficient remedies. We have not the right to despair. In all of our experimenting with social policy, however, we are to be guided by the imperative necessity of sustaining, and never stifling, the free economy and the initiative of persons within the free economy.

WHY WE CANNOT KNOW OR CONTROL

If we have truly internalized the concept of the subjectivity of society, it becomes obvious that not only should we not try to eliminate the sometimes maddening diversities of economic initiative but that it is impossible to do so. At the risk of belaboring the point, consider only the one aspect of the free economy that is the financial market itself. On a given day on Wall Street, as many as 200 million stocks and bonds are traded. Add to that the action on the London, Tokyo, Zurich, and other exchanges. Every day, millions of decisions are made by hundreds of thousands of people about what to buy and sell. True, relatively few people may make decisions about millions of trade, but their decisions are contingent upon the innumerable decisions of others responsible for the enterprises traded. All of these decisions together engage factors of interest and risk so numerous as to reach toward infinity.

It becomes patently preposterous to propose that this turbulent commotion, bordering on apparent chaos, should be "rationalized." We have but to imagine the task of trying to understand any one day's market activity—what decisions were made, why they were made, and their probable consequences. Even if, after monumental labor, we got a secure cognitive fix on that day's activity, the whole thing has gone and happened again several times over in the time that has elapsed while we were figuring out what happened on the day in question. Keep in mind, also, that what happens on the formal financial markets is but a small part of the deciding, exchanging, buying, selling, haggling, risking, promoting, investing, and general agitation that is the daily life of the free economy. Billions of capitalist acts between consenting adults take place every day. Nobody understands it. Nobody can understand it.

The economic pluralism that is the lifeblood and heartbeat of democratic capitalism is offensive to those who want the world to be tidy, or want to tidy it up according to their ideological tastes. The free economy is permanently and of necessity untidy. The same is to be said of democracy. It is no accident, as our Marxist friends used to say, that *Centesimus* joins its analysis of the free economy to a strong affirmation of democratic governance. The linkage between pluralism in the economic sphere and pluralism in the political sphere is, to say the obvious, complex. That does not mean that connections cannot be made. Once again, Berger's *The Capitalist Revolution* is helpful. Among his carefully, one might almost say elegantly, nuanced fifty propositions about prosperity, equality, and liberty are these:

- Capitalism is a necessary but not sufficient condition of democracy under modern conditions.

- If a capitalist economy is subjected to increasing degrees of state control, a point (not precisely specifiable at this time) will be reached at which democratic governance becomes impossible.

- If a socialist economy is opened up to increasing degrees of market forces, a point (not precisely specifiable at this time) will be reached at which democratic governance becomes a possibility.

- If capitalist development is successful in generating economic growth from which a sizable proportion of the population benefits, pressures toward democracy are likely to appear.

DEFIANCE BEYOND FEAR

In reading the signs of the times surrounding the great events of 1989, John Paul notes that the way was prepared by a democratizing force that was evident in many places around the world as peoples pressed "toward more participatory and more just political institutions" (¶ 22). This worldwide movement had many parts—the manifest economic failures of socialism, the experiments in market alternatives, the growing attention to human rights, the heroism of individuals and communities who stood up in defiance of apparently immovable tyrannies. The most critical factor, he insists, was cultural. People asserted their identities, which means that people asserted their differences, which means that people forced a new social order marked by pluralism.

A somewhat longish quotation is in order:

> Man is understood in a more complete way when he is situated within the sphere of culture through his language, history, and the position he takes toward the fundamental events of life such as birth, love, work, and death. At the heart of every culture lies the attitude man takes to the greatest mystery: the mystery of God. Different cultures are basically different ways of facing the question of the meaning of personal existence. When this question is eliminated, the culture and moral life of nations are corrupted. For this reason the struggle to defend work was spontaneously linked to the struggle for culture and for national rights [¶ 24].

The message of pluralism as it relates to economics, democracy, and culture is as applicable to our society as it is to those of Eastern Europe or Latin America. Against the schemes of social engineering that would smooth out the wrinkles by ignoring or eliminating differences, against those who, in the words of the late British political philosopher Michael Oakeshott, design public policy "as the crow flies," John Paul insists that we pay respectful attention to the particularities of real people on the ground. The hardest social reality, the reality that we ignore at our peril, is the reality that crackpot realists think so "soft"— namely, how people face "the question of the meaning of personal existence." Admittedly, the multifarious ways of the communities of meaning, memory, and mutual aid can be frustrating. But their stubborn perdurance only frustrates those who do not like them. John Paul likes them very much, because they are the way of humankind and "man is the way of the Church."

The most marginalized—refugees, immigrants, the poor, the elderly, the sick, the addicted—most need the institutions of a pluralistic society. They need the face-to-face institutions, the people-sized institutions, the mediating institutions where people "act as neighbors to those in need." It is not enough to supply "the necessary care" without a community of caring that offers "genuine fraternal support" (¶ 48). Here the role of religious communities is indispensable. Ministry to and with the needy is a permanent part of "the mission received from Christ." Such "active charity" is not a stopgap measure, simply a case of the Church filling in until we achieve a more "just society" and the state takes over (¶ 49). In the most possibly just society, there will be innumerable needs to be addressed, and the justice of the society will be measured by its nurturing of the innumerable ways in which individuals and communities respond to those needs.

Religious communities in particular can and do respond to those in need "in ways that neither humiliate nor reduce them to mere objects of assistance." Against current patterns of professionalizing and monetarizing all social services, John Paul praises volunteer work. He calls for social policies that will empower families in taking care of their elderly "so as to avoid distancing the latter from the family unit and in order to strengthen relations between generations" (¶ 49). In the American context, all this will strike many people as being very old-fashioned. Some will no doubt scorn it as a nostalgia-tainted invitation to "return to a past that never was." In fact, despite the claim of some that work without wages is exploitation, voluntarism in America, always strong, has dramatically increased in recent years. In fact, despite the claim that the three-generation family is dead, the overwhelming majority of the elderly in America are not institutionalized but live with their children or by themselves near their children.

To Care Is to Prefer

Also in our society we must contend with a deep-seated hostility to the multiplication of points of initiative in caring for those in need. "Good government" and "reformist" movements dating from the nineteenth century instilled a mind-set that defines progress in terms of the centralizing, rationalizing, professionalizing, and governmentalizing of social services. The advocates of progress, who then and now dominate the mass media, highlighted the instances in which families, church-related agencies, and other voluntary agencies neglected and even abused those in their care, especially children and the elderly. Nobody could deny that there was frequent neglect and abuse. But, again, this is an approach that builds on pathologies rather than strengths.

One must ask whether the instances of neglect and abuse are any fewer or less severe among the needy who are the "objects of assistance" in state-operated programs. Are people better off when they are no longer members of a community but "clients" of professional caregivers? The answer is almost certainly no. All too often professionals regard those they serve as clients in the rather unfortunate sense the Latin word originally implied. The clients of a Roman patrician were but one step above his slaves in the social hierarchy, not entirely unlike some of today's servile dependents upon professionals. Such degrading of people in need has no place in a society that aspires to being decent and democratic.

We may agree that, as John Paul says, "needs are best understood and satisfied by people who are closest . . . and act as neighbors to those in need" while at the same time also agreeing that these mediating institutions often fail. But what is the alternative? The alternative is not, the argument of *Centesimus* suggests, to replace those institutions but to strengthen them. In education, child care, and care of the elderly, for instance, devices such as tax credits and vouchers can financially enable families to better assume responsibility for their own.

Genuine "fraternal support" is most likely among those who are, or those who relate to one another, as brothers and sisters, rather than as professional care dispensers relating to clients. Consider parenting. Put an advertisement in the classified section for the job of parent, honestly listing the open-ended duties involved, and nobody in his right mind would apply. Unless he knew the children and loved them. Love is very unprofessional. For understandable reasons, codes of professional ethics caution against "excessive emotional involvement" with clients. But the support that those in need most desperately need is precisely the love that defies calculations of utility and the rational distribution of services. They need the love that cannot help but seem excessive.

In large areas of public policy today, it is common to talk about "the delivery of social services." The phrase is derived from an economic model of supply and demand and, as John Paul repeatedly insists, there are many needs that must elude the mind-set of the market. Education, the sustained embrace of the handicapped and the elderly, and kindness to the bedridden—these things cannot be "delivered." Things are delivered to dependent objects. The things that the needy most need are not commodities called "services" but the sustaining experiences provided by communities of character and virtue. Quantitatively, qualitatively, and in terms of historical experience, the intermediate groups are the "normal" givers of care and communities of sustaining nurture.

Pluralism Recovered

The direction pointed by *Centesimus* may seem radical to us to-day, but it is well to remember that for many centuries the entirety of what we now call social services was in the domain of families, churches, voluntary associations, and small communities. It is relatively recently that progressive thought succeeded in turning the normal into the exceptional. Now it is proposed that social service is normally "public," while exceptions are made for "the private sector." The contention, no doubt advanced sincerely, was that this change would benefit both those in need and society as a whole. Whether in Warsaw or New York City, we now know that that claim has been falsified by hard experience.

Anyone familiar with the actual operation of state social services would not be inclined to deny that despite the system, there are many instances of caregiving that evidence the genuine fraternal support and love that John Paul calls for. But neither would such a person be inclined to dissent from his more general observation: "By intervening directly and depriving society of its responsibility, the social assistance state leads to a loss of human energies and an inordinate increase of public agencies that are dominated more by bureaucratic ways of thinking than by concern for serving their clients, and that are accompanied by an enormous increase in spending" (¶ 48).

The state is the great universalizer, and therefore easily becomes the enemy of authentic pluralism. It becomes that not because the people in charge are maliciously motivated, but simply because there is no other way of rationally devising programs of general applicability. "Equal treatment" and "general applicability" are maxims essential to state programs. Particularity, preference, and pluralism are obstacles to be overcome. Yet the care that people most need—as in parents' love for their children or children's love for their parents—is by definition unequal, particular, and preferential.

Also in the area of human services, the progressive mind-set is impatient with what it dismissively calls the "parochial." Modernity and parochialism, it is suggested, are antithetical. The challenge posed by *Centesimus* is to rehabilitate the concept of the parochial. Like the word "parish," "parochial" is related to the Greek *para* plus *oikos*, meaning the place next door. The parochial is essential to neighborhood, and to being neighbors to one another. The parochial is the constellation of particularities that sustains communities of meaning, memory, and mutual aid. Without the parochial, there is no pluralism. And without a commitment to pluralism, the *unum* becomes the enemy of the *plures* that provide us with the "different ways of facing the question of the meaning of personal existence."

In a letter addressed to the universal Church, the Pope obviously cannot address all the problems of, for instance, the American situation. However, his understanding of the subjectivity of society and of the consequent need for the state to respect other spheres of sovereignty in the social order has a direct and urgent bearing upon what we in this country call church-state relations. In America, "the separation of church and state"—an important concept strongly supported by Catholic teaching—has been widely misunderstood to mean the separation of religion from public life.

In education, medicine, child care, and other areas, the chief (although not the only) alternatives to state-controlled programs in our society are those sponsored, directly or indirectly, by religious communities. In recent decades, a certain reading of the "no establishment" provision of the First Amendment has forced a serious erosion of the religious genius that made those institutions so distinctive and valuable. In order to receive state funds, they are told that they must give up their religious distinctiveness and become more like state institutions. Across the country there are innumerable colleges, hospitals, nursing homes, and other agencies that are called Jewish, Lutheran, Presbyterian, or Catholic but are otherwise indistinguishable from their government-run counterparts. In fact, they are, for most practical purposes, government-run.

CAPITULATIONS,   CRAVEN   AND   OTHER

In many cases, this happened because the leaders of such agencies unnecessarily surrendered religious distinctiveness in order to obtain state funding. In other cases, they were embarrassed by their religious identity. Driven by a professionalizing and progressive bias, they desperately wanted to fit into "the larger picture of American society." At a recent conference sponsored by the Institute on Religion and Public Life, the president of a nominally Methodist university that still receives funds from the United Methodist Church allowed that he might be able to get away with calling his institution a Methodist university but it would be intolerably "sectarian" for him to say it was a Christian university. Examples of the craven accommodations made to the perverse formula that public = government = secular could be multiplied ad nauseam.

The core problem, however, is with the legal doctrine that "the separation of church and state" means that wherever the writ and coin of government run, religion must retreat. Today the writ and coin of government run almost everywhere, and almost everywhere religion is in institutional retreat from our public life. The damage to pluralism, and therefore to democracy, and therefore to the vibrant subjectivity of society is immense. The "no establishment" provision of the Constitution's religion clause has been turned into the enemy of the "free exercise" provision. Since, as John Paul insists, the free exercise of religion is "the source and synthesis" of all human freedoms, the consequence undermines, both conceptually and practically, the structure of a free society.

In the courts and in the law schools, there are today heartening signs of reconsideration. There is a growing recognition that —as Madison, Tocqueville, Lincoln, and a host of other worthies warned long ago—the separation of religion from public life will inevitably result in the undoing of the American experiment in democratic governance. But those who have come to, or returned to, that recognition are still in a relatively small minority in the councils of American jurisprudence and public policy. And the damage already done to thousands of institutions that once possessed the virtues of religious identity and inspiration is probably beyond repair. Pluralism and democracy have been crippled and are being crippled. As almost the entire world aspires to the freedom that they believe is exemplified by America, we are, in large sectors of our public life, becoming less free.

THE TRUTH AND OTHER TRUTHS

As in the black spiritual about Ezekiel and the bones, the ligaments of pluralism are all connected. Economic pluralism is connected to political pluralism is connected to cultural pluralism. That brings us to the matter of democracy and a number of remarkable assertions about why democracy is the appropriate political expression of the subjectivity of society. Churchill famously said that democracy is the worst possible form of government, except for all the others that have been tried. John Paul would seem to go considerably beyond that. Without apotheosizing any particular form of democracy, he suggests that the democratic idea is integral to a theologically and historically informed understanding of human nature.

Totalitarianism, the antithesis of democracy, "arises out of a denial of truth in the objective sense." Or it arises out of the claim of a partisan group that they "are exempt from error and can therefore arrogate to themselves the exercise of absolute power" (¶ 44). The logic suggested here is important. The claim to possess an absolute monopoly on absolute truth is, in fact, a denial of truth. That is because truth is transcendent; we mere mortals are always subject to the judgment of truth. In the Christian view, mortality and the transcendent truth were perfectly conjoined in the God-man Jesus Christ. To know him is to know the truth that makes us free (John 8). There are lesser truths—for instance, truths about the right ordering of society—but nobody has a monopoly on them. The truth by which Christians are made free requires the continuing and free contention over these lesser truths.

The democratic polity itself must be pluralistic. John Paul notes that *Rerum Novarum* presents the polity in terms of what Americans call the "checks and balances" of legislative, executive, and judicial powers. He says that at the time that was "a novelty in church teaching." After Vatican Council II, it is no longer novel. It is important "that each power be balanced by other powers and by other spheres of responsibility that keep it within proper bounds." Not only should the polity be internally pluralistic, but the "spheres of responsibility" external to the state help keep the pluralistically structured state "within proper bounds" (¶ 44).

"The Church values the democratic system inasmuch as it ensures the participation of citizens in making political choices, guarantees to the governed the possibility both of electing and holding accountable those who govern them and of replacing them through peaceful means when appropriate" (¶ 46). It may not be the most elegant definition of democracy, but the ability to throw the rascals out is no little thing. Democracies do not always work as they should. Sometimes egregiously unfair advantages are given to incumbents. In recent American history, up to 98 percent of the members of Congress who run for reelection are reelected. Few would explain that by the highly improbable claim that they are doing such a great job. The political expression of pluralism no doubt requires a greater measure of honest contestation, and we may well wonder whether American democracy at present meets the test of the "inasmuch as" in John Paul's affirmation of democracy.

Perhaps the reader will hold still for one more longish quotation. It is important because it deals directly with some of the most hotly contested issues in our own political culture:

Authentic democracy is possible only in a state ruled by law and on the basis of a correct conception of the human person. It requires that the necessary conditions be present for the advancement both of the individual through education and formation in true ideals, and of the "subjectivity" of society through the creation of structures of participation and shared responsibility. Nowadays there is a tendency to claim that agnosticism and skeptical relativism are the philosophy and the basic attitude that correspond to democratic forms of political life. Those who are convinced that they know the truth and firmly adhere to it are considered unreliable from a democratic point of view, since they do not accept that truth is determined by the majority or that it is subject to variation according to different political trends. It must be observed in this regard that if there is no ultimate truth to guide and direct political activity, then ideas and convictions can easily be manipulated for reasons of power. As history demonstrates, a democracy without values easily turns into open or thinly disguised totalitarianism. Nor does the Church close her eyes to the danger of fanaticism or fundamentalism among those who, in the name of an ideology that purports to be scientific or religious, claim the right to impose on others their own concept of what is true and good [¶ 46].

Truth Imposed and Proposed

That excerpt warrants a book in its own right. John Paul is here throwing down the gauntlet to those who claim that religion poses a danger to democracy. Not only Christians but all people "who are convinced that they know the truth and firmly adhere to it are considered unreliable" because it is feared that they want to impose their truth upon others. We are wearily familiar with that claim in American public life. But democracy is precisely a free and open-ended contestation between different, and often conflicting, claims about the truth of "how we ought to order our life together." Those who want to exclude from the contest the truth claims with which they disagree—such as those derived from religious conviction—would call a halt to the democratic process itself.

Remember the statement from the earlier encyclical, *Redemptoris Missio*, "The Church imposes nothing; she only proposes." Convinced Christians and Jews are certainly among those "who are convinced that they know the truth and firmly adhere to it." So also are philosophers who belong to schools as various as those of Aristotle, Locke, Kant, and Leo Strauss. They believe that there are universal truths or principles applicable to the right ordering of public life. Within the arena of democratic discourse and debate, all propose and contend for the truths that they hold. The very idea could hardly be more American. "We hold these truths," the Founders asserted in the Declaration of Independence. Those constituting truths brought forth what Lincoln at Gettysburg called "a nation so conceived and so dedicated." How astonishing it should be to us that today there are those who claim that truth is the enemy of democracy. Yet, as John Paul says, there are many who make that claim.

Part of the truth that Christians hold is that truth cannot be coercively imposed. Truth must be freely adhered to. Assent to the truth that is extracted by force is contrary to truth. Did Christians, and Catholics in particular, always understand this in theory and practice? By no means. The horror of the Spanish Inquisition is inevitably thrown up by the secular-minded to prove the threat that religious conviction poses to public life. Horror it was, although it is worth keeping things in comparative perspective by remembering that as many people died in three hundred years of the Spanish Inquisition as died on any routine afternoon in one of Stalin's busier gulags. The fact that can be resisted only by the willfully ignorant or obtuse is that in this century—notably at Vatican II and reinforced by numerous authoritative statements in this pontificate—the Catholic

Church has become the most vigorous, sophisticated, and effective institutional proponent of religious liberty in the world.

Admittedly, the teaching of the magisterium has not penetrated the practice of the Church everywhere. In Latin America, for example, historically entrenched Catholic establishments face massive challenges from evangelical Protestants and are tempted to reconsider the merits of religious freedom for what they call "the sects." There are still Catholic voices, also in official positions, that resist and confuse this Pope's call for democratic freedom and, especially, his affirmation of the free economy. It should not be expected that developments in social doctrine are immediately embraced by all. But the official teaching of the Church, the almost uniform practice of the Church, and the historical impact of the Church is emphatically on the side of democracy and, at the heart of democracy, religious freedom. (Recall Samuel Huntington's discussion of the "third wave" of democracy.) This is not a grudging accommodation to democracy, nor is it understood as a necessary compromise of the truth. On the contrary, it is precisely Christian truth and the freedom to contend for Christian truth that require democracy.

CONTENTION AND CIVILITY

On the question of democracy and truth, John Paul turns us from the defensive to the offensive. Who are these people who "claim that agnosticism and skeptical relativism" are required for democratic life? On what basis do they make that truth claim against the making of truth claims? Against the Founders, they declare, in effect, "We hold this truth against the holding of truths." They frequently, and implausibly, claim that the Founders did not really believe what the Founders insisted that they did believe. Their argument is not with those who democratically contend for the truths of which they are convinced. Their argument is with the history of the American experiment.

Since the dawning of the modern democratic idea, the greatest and bloodiest assaults on that idea have been directed by the declared enemies of biblical religion. From the enthronement of the Goddess of Reason by the French Revolution, to Hitler's divinizing of blood and soil, to Stalin's assertion of "the objective will of the people" as determined by "scientific" Marxism, the monsters of tyranny have been the declared enemies of the God of Abraham, Isaac, Jacob, and Jesus. Of course Robespierre, Hitler, and Stalin are, in viewpoint and personal style, very unlike the sophisticated and ironic liberals who today tell us that "agnosticism and skeptical relativism are the philosophy and basic attitude that correspond to democratic forms of political life." But without truth and values grounded in truth, John Paul contends, democracy "easily turns into open or thinly disguised totalitarianism." The naked public square does not and cannot remain naked.

Again, upward of 90 percent of the American people claim to believe, however confusedly, that morality, personal and public, is derived from the traditions of religion. They are not always agreed on what they might be, but they are agreed that there are such things as moral truths. Some of the most impressive secular thinkers in American life have recognized that democracy cannot be sustained in a cultural context of pervasive agnosticism and skeptical relativism. Figures such as John Dewey and John Rawls, along with many lesser imitators, have tried to construct a public philosophy for the American experiment that is not dependent upon the biblical tradition. Such efforts have not been democratically legitimated and stand little chance of being democratically legitimated. In a democracy, that is a weakness of no small proportions. A philosophy of democracy that is not understood or is not accepted by the people who constitute that democracy is, no matter how intellectually elegant, stillborn.

Centesimus does not preclude the development of such a secular philosophy for democratic governance. Almost inevitably, many will continue the attempt to construct secular alternatives to the biblically-grounded truths that most Americans hold and that, we would suggest, hold Americans together. Only let those who have alternatives to propose freely and honestly contend for their truths against the truths of others. Pluralism requires such engagement of differences within the bond of civility. Nobody should be surprised or feel threatened if, by the same token, Christians and Jews contend for truths that, they are convinced, make imperative the bond of civility that makes possible continued democratic contention.

Human freedom that is detached from truth is human freedom detached from duty to others. "The essence of freedom then becomes self-love carried to the point of contempt for God and neighbor, a self-love that leads to an unbridled affirmation of self-interest and that refuses to be limited by any demand of justice" (¶ 17). Not everybody agrees that there is a necessary connection between duty to God and duty to neighbor. In answer to the question of why we should care about others or treat them justly, however, those who disagree must give some account of "the truth" of the matter. If there is no truth of the matter that guides public life, says John Paul, "then ideas and convictions can easily be manipulated for reasons of power" (¶ 46).

The truth of the matter that is proposed by *Centesimus* is not "determined by the majority or subject to variation according to different political trends" (¶ 46). According to Christian teaching, the ultimate truth of the matter is, not to put too fine a point on it, revealed by God. After thousands of years of pondering that truth as it has made its tortuous way through history, the conclusion has been reached that the truth requires a social order in which it is possible for individuals and even the majority to decide against the truth. That conclusion makes possible the open-ended process in which truth, when provisionally rejected, can contend more effectively another day. That conclusion is the firmest foundation for a social order of sustainable pluralism—economic, political, and cultural.

Now we have touched on many subjects, all of them no doubt treated too briefly. There is obviously much more to be said about Christian social teaching and the Catholic tradition in particular. Indeed there are concerns and nuances in *Centesimus* that we have touched only lightly, and I hope the reader will go on to study the words of the encyclical in the appendix to this book. For the nearly 60 million American citizens who are Roman Catholic, the document has a peculiarly authoritative weight, but the premise of this book is that it has a compelling argument that can enrich and reform the ways in which all of us think about our life together. There are better ways of ordering our life together—better for us, and better for the millions in this country and the billions in other countries who are marginalized from the benefits of a social order structured by freedom and directed to truth.

Some may complain that this discussion has been long on ideas and short on ways to implement those ideas. I can understand that, but perhaps I will be forgiven if I do not apologize for it. As is the case in *Centesimus*, some self-denying ordinances were at work in the writing of this book. (Other readers may think they were not self-denying enough!) We should not move too quickly from moral argument to policy prescription. It is the argument that counts here, and, if it is persuasive, it can no doubt be applied in quite different ways. "Ideas have consequences," as the American philosopher Richard Weaver wrote and as many of us are given to repeating. If we could get our thinking straight about a seminal concept such as the subjectivity of society, for instance, the possible policy implications would begin to flow readily enough. It is said that politics is the art of the possible, and I would not argue with that. Except to say that it is also the art, and the courage and the imagination, of exploring what might be possible. It should not be beyond us to find better ways of taking care of business and taking care of one another.

Each of us is responsible for only a small piece of all that needs doing. Our best-intended efforts to solve problems will sometimes produce new problems, just as we now have to cope with the problems created by the best-intended efforts of the past. The challenges are formidable, and our wisdom even more limited than our time. But, if the biblical story got things right, we are not alone and our effort is not the final word. "Grace, in cooperation with human freedom, constitutes that mysterious presence of God in history that is providence" (¶ 59).

So we end on that grace note, remembering the juggler who did not have much to offer. But what he had he offered gratefully, joyfully, bravely, faithfully.

God loveth adverbs.

NOTES

Page 274. For a more comprehensive discussion of confusions about "the separation of church and state," see the author's *The Naked Public Square*, Eerdmans, 1984. Also his "A New Order of Religious Freedom," *First Things*, February 1992. On the inversion of "no establishment" that pits it against the "free exercise" of religion, see Mary Ann Glendon and Raul F. Yanes, "Structural Free Exercise," *Michigan Law Review*, December 1991.

Appendix

* * *

Centesimus Annus[*]
THE ECONOMICS OF
HUMAN FREEDOM

John Paul II

This is a condensation of Centesimus Annus *("The Hundredth Year"), Pope John Paul II's ninth encyclical. Words added for continuity are in square brackets. (Reprinted from* First Things, *August/September 1991.)*

1. The centenary of the encyclical *Rerum Novarum* ["New Things"] by my predecessor Leo XIII is of great importance for the present history of the Church and for my own Pontificate. I wish to satisfy the debt of gratitude that the whole Church owes to this great Pope and his "immortal document." I also mean to show that *the vital energies* rising from that root have not been spent with the passing of the years, but rather *have increased even more.*

2. [This occasion] honors also those encyclicals and other documents of my predecessors that have helped to make *Rerum Novarum* live in history, thus constituting what would come to be called the Church's "social doctrine," "social teaching" or even "social magisterium."

3. I propose a "rereading" of Pope Leo's encyclical by issuing an invitation to "look back" at the text itself, but also to "look around" at the "new things" that surround us, very different from the "new things" at the final decade of the last century. Finally, it is an invitation to "look to the future" at a time when we can glimpse the third millennium of the Christian era, so filled with uncertainties but also with promises. A rereading of this kind confirms *the permanent value of such teaching,* but also manifests *the true meaning of the*

Church's Tradition, which, being ever living and vital, builds upon the foundation laid by our fathers in the faith.

The Lord compares the scribe to "a householder who brings out of his treasure what is new and what is old" (Matt. 13:52). The treasure is the Church's tradition, which contains "what is old" and enables us to interpret the "new things" in the midst of which the life of the Church and the world unfolds. Millions of people, spurred on by the social Magisterium, have sought to make that teaching the inspiration for their involvement in the world. [They] represent a *great movement for the defense of the human person* and the safeguarding of human dignity, [and have] contributed to the building up of a more just society, or at least to the curbing of injustice.

The present encyclical involves the exercise of [the Church's] teaching authority. But pastoral solicitude also prompts me to propose *an analysis of some events of recent history*. Such an analysis is not meant to pass definitive judgments since this does not fall *per se* within the Magisterium's specific domain.

I. CHARACTERISTICS OF *RERUM NOVARUM*

4. Towards the end of the last century the Church faced a historical process that was reaching a critical point. In politics, the result of these changes was a *new conception of society and of the state*, and consequently *of authority itself*. A traditional society was passing away and another was [emerging]. In economics, a *new form of property* had appeared—capital; and a *new form of labor*—labor for wages, characterized by high rates of production that lacked due regard for sex, age, or family situation, and was determined solely by efficiency, with a view to increasing profits.

Labor became a commodity freely bought and sold on the market, its price determined by the law of supply and demand, without taking into account the minimum required for the support of the individual and his family. Moreover, the worker was not even sure of being able to sell "his own commodity," continually threatened as he was by unemployment. The result of this transformation was a society "divided into two classes, separated by a deep chasm." At the same time, another conception of property and economic life was beginning to appear in an organized and often violent form, one that implied a new political and social structure.

At the height of this clash, fanned by ideals that were then called "socialist," Pope Leo intervened with a document dealing with the "condition of the workers." [Papal teaching] called attention to the essential bond between human freedom and truth, so that freedom that refused to be bound to the truth would fall into arbitrariness and end up submitting itself to the vilest of passions, to the point of self-destruction. Indeed, what is the origin of all the evils to which *Rerum Novarum* wished to respond if not a kind of freedom that cuts itself off from the truth about man?

5. The "new things" [that the Pope addressed] were anything but positive. The Church was confronted, as was the civil community, by a society that was torn by a conflict all the more harsh and inhumane because it knew no rule or regulation. It was *the conflict between capital and labor.* The Pope's intention was certainly to restore peace, and the reader cannot fail to note his severe condemnation of the class struggle. However, the Pope was very much aware that *peace is built on the foundation of justice.*

The Church has something to say about [such] specific human situations. She formulates a genuine doctrine, a *corpus* that enables her to analyze social realities, to make judgments about them, and to indicate directions for the just resolution of problems. In Pope Leo's time such a concept of the Church's right and duty was far from being commonly admitted. [His] approach in publishing *Rerum Novarum* gave the Church "citizenship status," as it were, amid the changing realities of public life. Her social doctrine pertains to the Church's evangelizing mission, and is an essential part of the Christian message.

The "new evangelization" which the modern world urgently needs must include *a proclamation of the Church's social doctrine.* This doctrine indicates the right way to respond to the great challenges of today when ideologies are being increasingly discredited. We repeat that there can be *no genuine solution of the "social question" apart from the Gospel.* In the Gospel we find the context for proper moral perspective on the "new things."

6. Pope Leo affirmed the fundamental rights of workers. Indeed, the key to reading the encyclical is the *dignity of the worker* as such, and [therefore] the *dignity of work.* Work belongs to the vocation of every person; indeed, man expresses and fulfills himself by working. Another important principle is that of the *right to "private property."* Private property is not an absolute value. [There are] necessary complementary principles, such as the *universal destination of the earth's goods.* The type of private property that Leo mainly considers is land ownership. [But the same principles apply] in the face of the changes we are witnessing in systems formerly dominated by collective ownership of the means of production, as well in the face of the increasing instances of poverty or, more precisely, of hindrances to private ownership in many parts of the world.

7. *Rerum Novarum* affirms *other rights* as inalienable and proper to the human person. Prominent among these is the "natural human right" to form private associations. This means above all *the right to establish professional associations* of employers and workers, or of workers alone, and the establishment of what are commonly called trade unions. The right of association is a natural right of the human being, which therefore precedes his or her incorporation

into political society. The encyclical also affirms the right to the "limitation of working hours," the right to legitimate rest, and the right of children and women to be treated differently with regard to the type and duration of work.

8. The Pope adds *another right* that the worker has as a person, the right to a "just wage." If work *as something personal* belongs to the sphere of the individual's free use of his own abilities and energy, *as something necessary* it is governed by the obligation to ensure "the preservation of life." "It necessarily follows," the Pope concludes, "that every individual has a natural right to procure what is required to live, and the poor can procure that in no other way than by what they can earn through their work." A workman's wages should be sufficient to enable him to support himself, his wife, and his children. The Pope attributed to the "public authority" the "strict duty" of providing properly for the welfare of the workers, because a failure to do so violates justice; indeed, he did not hesitate to speak of "distributive justice."

9. Leo XIII adds another right, namely the right to discharge freely one's religious duties. The general opinion, even in his day, [was] that such questions pertained exclusively to an individual's private life. He affirms the need for Sunday rest so that people [may offer] the worship they owe to Almighty God. [We] see in this statement a springboard for the principle of the right to religious freedom, which was to become the subject of many solemn *International Declarations* as well as of the Second Vatican Council's *Declaration* and of my own repeated teaching.

10. Another aspect is the relationship between the state and its citizens. *Rerum Novarum* criticizes two social and economic systems: socialism and liberalism. "When there is question of defending the rights of individuals, the defenseless and the poor have a claim to special consideration. The richer class has many ways of shielding itself, and stands less in need of help from the state." [Such] passages [speak today to] the new forms of poverty in the world.

The principle of solidarity, both within each nation and in the international order, is clearly seen to be one of the fundamental principles of the Christian view of social and political organization. Leo uses the term "friendship," [while] Pius XI refers to it as "social charity," and Paul VI speaks of a "civilization of love."

11. Rereading the encyclical in the light of contemporary realities enables us to appreciate *the Church's constant concern for and dedication to* categories of people who are especially beloved to the Lord Jesus. [There is] the continuity within the Church of the "preferential option for the poor." The encyclical is thus [about] the poor and the terrible conditions to which the new and often violent process of industrialization had reduced great multitudes of people. Today, in many parts of the world, similar processes of economic, social, and political transformation are creating the same evils.

The state has the duty of ensuring that every sector of social life, not excluding the economic one, contributes to achieving the common good, while respecting the rightful autonomy of each sector. Pope Leo did not expect the state to solve every social problem. On the contrary, he frequently insists on necessary limits to the state's intervention and on its instrumental character, inasmuch as the individual, the family, and society are prior to the state, and inasmuch as the state exists in order to protect their rights and not stifle them. The guiding principle of all the Church's social doctrine is a *correct view of the human person*. God has imprinted his own image and likeness on man (Gen. 1:26).

II. TOWARDS THE "NEW THINGS" OF TODAY

12. The prognosis of *Rerum Novarum* has proved to be surprisingly accurate. This is especially confirmed by the events near the end of 1989 and at the beginning of 1990. Pope Leo foresaw the negative consequences of the social order proposed by "socialism," which at that time was still only a social philosophy and not yet a fully structured movement. He correctly judged the danger posed to the masses by the attractive presentation of this simple and radical solution to the "question of the working class."

[He demonstrated] great clarity, first, in perceiving, in all its harshness, the actual condition of the working class; second, in recognizing the evil of a solution [that] was in reality detrimental to the very people whom it was meant to help. The remedy would prove worse than the sickness. By defining socialism as the suppression of private property, Leo arrived at the crux of the problem. His words deserve to be reread: "Were the contentions [of the socialists] carried into effect, the working man himself would be among the first to suffer. They are moreover emphatically unjust, for they would rob the lawful possessor, distort the functions of the state, and create utter confusion in the community." The evils caused by what would later be called "real socialism" could not be better expressed.

13. The fundamental error of socialism is anthropological. Socialism considers the individual simply as an element, so that the good of the individual is completely subordinated to the socioeconomic mechanism. Socialism maintains that the good of the individual can be realized without reference to his free choice in the face of good or evil. A person who is deprived of something he can call "his own," and of earning a living through his own initiative, comes to depend on the social machine and those who control it.

In the Christian vision, the social nature of man is not completely fulfilled in the state but is realized in various intermediary groups, beginning with the family and including economic, social, political, and cultural groups that stem from human nature itself and have their own autonomy, always with a view to the common good. This "subjectivity" of society, together with the subjectivity of the individual, was cancelled out by "real socialism."

The first cause of socialism's mistaken concept of the person is atheism. It is by responding to the call of God contained in the being of things that man becomes aware of his transcendent dignity. This response constitutes the apex of his humanity, and no social mechanism or collective subject can substitute for it. Such atheism is also closely connected with the rationalism of the Enlightenment, which views human and social reality in a mechanistic way.

14. From this atheistic source, socialism derives the means of action [that it calls] class struggle. The Church recognizes the positive role of conflict when it takes the form of a "struggle for justice." What is condemned in class struggle is the idea that conflict is not restrained by ethical or juridical considerations or by respect for the dignity of others (and consequently of oneself). Conflict becomes "total war." Marxist class struggle and militarism have the same root, namely, atheism and contempt for the human person, which place the principle of force above that of reason and law.

15. The state's task is to determine the juridical framework within which economic affairs are to be conducted, and thus to safeguard the prerequisites of a free economy, which presumes a certain equality between the parties, such that one party is not so powerful as to reduce the other to subservience. Society and the state assume responsibility for protecting the worker from unemployment. Historically, this happens in two converging ways: either through policies [of] balanced economic growth and full employment, or through unemployment insurance and retraining that ensures a smooth transfer of workers from crisis sectors to those in expansion.

The society and the state must ensure wage levels adequate for the worker and his family, including a certain amount for savings. Improving workers' training will [make them] more skilled and productive. [Measures are needed to protect] especially the most vulnerable workers—immigrants and those on the margins of society. The role of trade unions in negotiating salaries and working conditions is decisive. Trade unions serve the development of an authentic culture of work and help workers to share in a fully human way in the life of their place of employment. The state must contribute to these goals both directly and indirectly. Indirectly and according to the *principle of subsidiarity*, by creating conditions for the free exercise of economic activity. Directly and according to the *principle of solidarity*, by defending the weakest and ensuring support for the unemployed.

The Church's social teaching had far-reaching influence in the numerous reforms introduced in the areas of social security, pensions, health insurance, and [creating a] framework of greater respect for the rights of workers.

16. *The role of the workers' movement* was important in these reforms. Later,

this movement was dominated to a certain extent by the Marxist ideology that *Rerum Novarum* criticized. The reforms were also a result of *an open process by which society organized itself* through instruments of solidarity that sustained economic growth more respectful of the person. We thank God that the encyclical was not without an echo in human hearts and indeed led to a generous response on the practical level.

17. The encyclical points to the error [of] an understanding of freedom that detaches it from obedience to the truth, and consequently from the duty to respect the rights of others. This error had extreme consequences in the wars that ravaged Europe and the world between 1914 and 1945. There was no hesitation to violate sacred human rights, with the extermination of entire peoples and social groups. Here we recall the Jewish people in particular, whose terrible fate has become a symbol of the aberration of which man is capable when he turns against God.

18. Since 1945, there has been in Europe and the world a situation of non-war rather than genuine peace. Half of the continent fell under the domination of a Communist dictatorship, while the other half organized itself in defence against this threat. Many peoples were [contained] within the suffocating boundaries of an empire [that attempted] to destroy their historical memory and the centuries-old roots of their culture. An insane arms race swallowed up the resources needed for development. An ideology, a perversion of authentic philosophy, was called upon to provide doctrinal justification for [this] new war. We must repudiate the idea that the effort to destroy the enemy, confrontation, and war itself are factors of historical progress. [When we do that] the concepts of "total war" and "class struggle" must necessarily be called into question.

19. After World War II, [we saw] the spread of Communist totalitarianism over more than half of Europe and other parts of the world. The war, which should have reestablished freedom and restored the right of nations, [did not] attain these goals. Following the war, we see in some countries an effort to rebuild a democratic society inspired by social justice. Such attempts preserve free market mechanisms, ensuring, by means of a stable currency and the harmony of social relations, the conditions for economic growth in which people through their own work can build a better future for themselves and their families.

[Other countries] set up systems of "national security" aimed at controlling the whole of society in order to make Marxist infiltration impossible. They run the grave risk of destroying the freedom and values of the person, the very things for whose sake it is necessary to oppose Communism. Another response, practical in nature, is represented by the affluent society or the consumer society. It seeks to defeat Marxism on the level of pure materialism by showing how a free-market society can [better satisfy] material needs. Insofar as [such a society] denies morality, law, culture, and religion, it agrees with Marxism by reducing man to the sphere of economics and the satisfaction of material needs.

20. After "decolonization," many countries gained state sovereignity but find themselves merely at the beginning of the journey toward genuine independence. Decisive sectors of the economy and political life itself are controlled by foreign powers. Also lacking is a class of competent professional people capable of running the state and managing the economy in an honest and just way. Many think that Marxism offers a shortcut for building the nation and the state, [and] thus Marxist-Leninist concepts mingle with militarism and popular traditions in many variants of socialism.

21. After World War II, there arose a more lively sense of human rights [expressed] in *International Documents*. The focal point of this evolution has been the United Nations Organization. While we note this with satisfaction, policies of aid for development have not always been positive. Moreover, the United Nations has not yet established alternatives to war for the resolution of international conflicts. This seems to be the most urgent problem that the international community has yet to resolve.

III. THE YEAR 1989

22. In the course of the eighties, certain oppressive regimes fell one by one in some countries of Latin America and also of Africa and Asia. A decisive contribution was made by *the Church's commitment to defend and promote human rights*. In situations [under Communist] ideology, the Church affirmed forcefully that every individual bears the image of God and therefore deserves respect. From this process, new forms of democracy have emerged that offer hope for change in [societies] weighed down by injustices and resentments, and by a heavily damaged economy and serious social conflicts. I thank God for the often heroic witness borne in such circumstances by many pastors, entire Christian communities, individual members of the faithful, and other people of goodwill.

23. The decisive factor in the fall of oppressive regimes was the violation of the rights of workers. The crisis of systems claiming to express the dictatorship of the working class began with the great upheaval in Poland in the name of solidarity. On the basis of a hard, lived experience of oppression, it was they who recovered the principles of the Church's social doctrine. The fall of this empire was accomplished almost everywhere by means of peaceful protest, using the weapons of truth and justice. It seemed that the order resulting from the war and sanctioned by the *Yalta Agreements* could only be overturned by war. Instead, it has been overcome by people who [found] effective ways of

bearing witness to the truth. This disarmed the adversary, since violence always needs to justify itself through deceit.

24. The second factor in the crisis was the inefficiency of the economic system, which is not simply a technical problem but a consequence of the violation of the human rights to private initiative, to ownership of property, and to freedom in the economic sector. To this must be added the cultural and national dimensions; it is not possible to understand man on the basis of economics alone. Man is understood within the sphere of culture through his language, history, and the position he takes towards the fundamental events of life, such as birth, love, work, and death. At the heart of every culture lies the attitude man takes to the greatest mystery: the mystery of God. The true cause of the new developments was the spiritual void brought about by atheism. Marxism had promised to uproot the need for God from the human heart, but it is not possible to succeed in this without throwing the heart into turmoil.

25. The events of 1989 are a warning to those who, in the name of political realism, wish to banish law and morality from the political arena. Only by trust in the Lord of history is man able to accomplish the miracle of peace and to discern the often narrow path between the cowardice that gives in to evil and the violence that, under the illusion of fighting evil, only makes it worse. [We can see] that not only is it ethically wrong to disregard human nature, which is made for freedom, but in practice it is impossible to do so.

Moreover, man, who was created for freedom, bears within himself the wound of original sin. Man tends toward good, but he is also capable of evil. He can transcend his immediate interest and still remain bound to it. The social order will be the more stable the more it takes this fact into account and does not place in opposition personal interest and the interests of society as a whole, but rather seeks to bring them into fruitful harmony. Where self-interest is suppressed, it is replaced by a burdensome system of bureaucratic control that dries up the wellsprings of initiative and creativity. [There is no] perfect social organization that makes evil impossible. No political society can ever be confused with the Kingdom of God. God alone can separate the subjects of the Kingdom from the subjects of the Evil One, and this judgment will take place at the end of time. By presuming to anticipate [that] judgment, man puts himself in the place of God and sets himself against the patience of God.

26. The events of 1989 [involved] *an encounter between the Church and the workers' movement.* For about a century, the workers' movement had fallen in part under the dominance of Marxism. The crisis of Marxism does not rid the world of the injustice and oppression that Marxism itself exploited. To those searching for a new and authentic theory and praxis of liberation, the Church offers her social doctrine, her teaching about the person redeemed in Christ, and her concrete commitment and material assistance in the struggle against marginalization and suffering.

In the recent past, many believers sincerely sought an impossible compromise between Marxism and Christianity. Beyond all that was short-lived in these attempts, circumstances are leading to an authentic theology of integral human liberation. [In this way], the events of 1989 are important also for countries of the Third World.

27. In Europe, many injustices were committed during and prior to the years in which Communism dominated; much hatred and ill-will have accumulated. It is hoped that all people will grow in the spirit of peace and forgiveness. Between nations, international structures are needed to arbitrate conflicts, especially in Europe, where nations are united in a bond of common culture and an age-old history. A great effort is needed to rebuild morally and economically the countries that have abandoned Communism.

28. For some countries of Europe, the real postwar period is just beginning. They need the help of Western Europe. They find themselves in [such need] not as a result of free choice or mistakes that were made, but as a consequence of tragic historical events that were violently imposed on them. Assistance, especially from countries of Europe that bear responsibility for that history, represents a debt in justice. It is also in the interest of Europe as a whole.

This must not lead, however, to a slackening of efforts to assist the countries of the Third World. What is called for is a special effort to mobilize resources, which are not lacking in the world, for the purpose of economic growth and common development. Enormous resources can be made available by the disarmament of huge military machines. It is above all necessary to abandon a mentality in which the poor are considered a burden, as irksome intruders trying to consume what others produce. The advancement of the poor constitutes a great opportunity for the moral, cultural, and even economic growth of all humanity.

29. Development is not only a question of raising all peoples to the level currently enjoyed by the richest countries but of building a more decent life [appropriate to] man's vocation from God. The apex of development is the exercise of the right and duty to seek God, to know him and to live in accordance with that knowledge. Total recognition must be given to *the rights of human conscience*, which is bound only to the truth, both natural and revealed. The recognition of these rights is the primary foundation of every authentically free political order. In some countries, religious fundamentalism denies to citizens of [other] faiths the full exercise of their civil and religious rights. No authentic progress is possible without respect for the right to know the truth and live according to that truth.

IV. PRIVATE PROPERTY AND THE UNIVERSAL DESTINATION OF MATERIAL GOODS

30. The natural right to private property, which is fundamental for the autonomy and development of the person, has always been defended by the Church. [But] the possession of material goods is not an absolute right. The "use" of goods, while marked by freedom, is subordinated to their original common destination as well as to the will of Christ.

31. The original source of all that is good and sustains human life is the very act of God who created [all] and gave the earth to man to have dominion over it by his work and enjoy its fruits (Gen. 1:28). This is *the foundation of the universal destination of the earth's goods*. It is through work that man, using his intelligence and exercising his freedom, dominates the earth and makes it a fitting home. This is *the origin of individual property*. Individuals [must] not hinder others from having their own part of God's gift; indeed, they must cooperate so that together all can dominate the earth.

At one time, *the natural fruitfulness of the earth* was the primary factor of wealth. In our time, *the role of human work* is increasingly the productive factor both of nonmaterial and material wealth. Also, more than ever work is *work with others* and *work for others*; it is a matter of doing something for someone else.

32. In our time, another form of ownership is becoming no less important than land: *the possession of know-how, technology, and skill*. The wealth of the industrialized nations is based much more on this kind of ownership than on natural resources. A person produces something so that others may use it after they have paid a just price, mutually agreed upon through free bargaining. The ability to foresee both the needs of others and the factors [best fit] to satisfying those needs is another source of wealth in modern society. In this way, the role of disciplined and creative *human work* and *initiative and entrepreneurial ability* become increasingly decisive.

Besides the earth, man's principal resource is *man himself*. Disciplined work in collaboration with others creates the ever more extensive *working communities* that transform man's natural and human environments. Important virtues are involved in this process, such as diligence, industriousness, prudence in undertaking reasonable risks, reliability and fidelity in interpersonal relationships, as well as courage in carrying out decisions that are difficult and painful but necessary, both for the overall working of a business and in meeting possible setbacks.

33. [There are] risks and problems connected with this process. Many people do not have the means enabling them to take their place within a productive system. Thus, if not actually exploited, they are to a great extent marginal-

ized; economic development takes place over their heads, so to speak. Allured by the dazzle of an opulence beyond their reach, these people crowd the cities of the Third World without the possibility of becoming integrated. Their dignity is not acknowledged and there are even attempts to eliminate them from history through coercive forms of demographic control.

Many others, while not completely marginalized, live in situations in which the rules of the earliest period of capitalism still flourish. In other cases the land is still the central element in the economic process, but those who cultivate it are excluded from ownership and reduced to a state of quasi-servitude. In these cases, it is still possible to speak of inhuman exploitation. In fact, for the poor, to the lack of material goods has been added a lack of knowledge and training that prevents them from escaping their state of humiliating subjection.

Countries isolating themselves from the world market have suffered stagnation, while the countries that experienced development take part in economic activities at the international level. The chief problem is that of gaining fair access to the international market. [At the same time,] aspects typical of the Third World also appear in developed countries, where [market] transformation devalues skills and expertise, thus requiring continual retraining. Those who fail to keep up with the times can easily be marginalized.

34. It would appear that *the free market* is the most efficient instrument for utilizing resources and effectively responding to needs. But there are many human needs that find no place on the market. It is a strict duty of justice and truth not to allow fundamental human needs to remain unsatisfied. It is also necessary to help needy people acquire expertise, to enter the circle of exchange, and to develop their skills to make the best use of their capacities and resources. Prior to the logic of a fair exchange of goods, there exists *something that is due to man because he is man,* by reason of his lofty dignity.

35. In [one] sense, it is right to speak of a struggle against an economic system, if that system upholds the absolute predominance of capital, the possession of the means of production and of the land, in contrast to the free and personal nature of human work. The alternative is not the socialist system, which in fact turns out to be state capitalism, but rather *a society of free work, of enterprise, and of participation.*

The Church acknowledges the legitimate *role of profit* as an indication that a business is functioning well. But profitability is not the only indicator of a firm's condition. It is possible for the financial accounts to be in order, and yet for the people—who are the firm's most valuable asset—to be humiliated and their dignity offended. This is morally inadmissible [and] will eventually have negative repercussions on the firm's economic efficiency. The purpose of a business firm is to be a *community of persons* endeavoring to satisfy basic needs at the service of the whole of society.

It is unacceptable to say that the defeat of "real socialism" leaves [the present operation of capitalism] as the only model of economic organization. It is necessary to break down barriers and monopolies in the international community. Stronger nations must offer weaker ones opportunities for taking their place in international life, and the latter must learn how to use these opportunities by making the necessary efforts and sacrifices, by ensuring political and economic stability, by the improvement of workers' skills, and [by] the training of competent business leaders conscious of their responsibilities.

Positive efforts along these lines are affected by the unsolved problem of the foreign debt of the poorer countries. The principle that debts must be paid is certainly just. However, it is not right to demand payment at the price of unbearable sacrifices. In such cases it is necessary to find—as in fact is partly happening—ways to lighten, defer, or even cancel the debt.

36. In the more advanced economies, the problem is also one of responding to a *demand for quality:* the quality of goods and services, the quality of the environment, and of life in general. A given culture reveals its understanding of life through the choices it makes in production and consumption. Here *the phenomenon of consumerism* arises. Of itself, an economic system does not possess criteria for correctly distinguishing new and higher forms of satisfying needs from artificial new needs that hinder the formation of a mature personality. *Thus a great deal of educational and cultural work* is urgently needed, including the education of consumers in the responsible use of their power of choice. A striking example of artificial consumption contrary to the health and dignity of the human person is the widespread use of drugs. Drugs, pornography, and other forms of consumerism exploit the frailty of the weak.

It is not wrong to want to live better; what is wrong is a style of life presumed to be better when directed towards "having" rather than "being." Even the decision to invest in one place rather than another, in one productive sector rather than another, is always *a moral and cultural choice.* The decision to invest, that is, to offer people an opportunity to make good use of their own labor, is also determined by an attitude of human sympathy and trust in providence that reveals the human quality of the person making such decisions.

37. Closely connected to consumerism and equally worrying is *the ecological question.* Desiring to have and to enjoy rather than to be and to grow, man consumes the earth and his own life in an excessive and disordered way. Man thinks that he can make arbitrary use of the earth, as though it did not have its own prior God-given purpose, which man can develop but must not betray. Instead of being a cooperator with God in creation, man sets himself in place of God, provoking a rebellion on the part of nature, which is more tyrannized than governed by him.

38. Yet more serious is the destruction of the *human environment.* People are rightly worried about the extinction of animal species, but too little effort is made to *safeguard the moral conditions for an authentic "human ecology."* God gave

the earth to man, but man too is God's gift to man. Here attention should be given a "social ecology" of work.

39. The first and fundamental structure for "human ecology" is *the family*, in which man receives his first ideas about truth and goodness and learns what it means to love and be loved, and thus what it means to be a person. But it often happens that people are discouraged from creating the proper conditions for human reproduction and are led to consider their lives as a series of sensations to be experienced rather than as a work to be accomplished.

The result is a lack of freedom that causes a person to reject a commitment to enter into a stable relationship and to bring children into the world, or that leads people to consider children as one of the many "things" that an individual can have or not have, and that compete with other possibilities. The family is indeed sacred. In the face of the so-called culture of death, the family is the heart of the culture of life. Human ingenuity seems directed more towards limiting or destroying the sources of life—including recourse to abortion—than towards defending and opening up the possibilities of life. [I have] denounced systematic antichildbearing campaigns that, on the basis of a distorted view of the demographic problem, subject people to a new form of oppression.

These criticisms are directed not so much against an economic system as against an ethical and cultural system. The economy is only one aspect of the whole of human activity. If material goods become a society's only value, the reason is to be found not so much in the economic system itself as in the fact that the entire sociocultural system, by ignoring the ethical and religious dimension, has been weakened.

40. It is the task of the state to preserve common goods that cannot be safeguarded simply by market forces. In the time of primitive capitalism, the state had the duty of defending the basic rights of workers, and so now, with the new capitalism, the state and all of society have the duty of *defending those collective goods* that constitute the framework for the legitimate pursuit of personal goals. There are important human needs that cannot be satisfied by market mechanisms. There are goods that by their very nature cannot and must not be bought or sold. [Forgetting this] carries the risk of an "idolatry" of the market.

41. Marxism affirms that only in a collective society can alienation be eliminated. However, historical experience has sadly demonstrated that collectivism increases alienation, adding to it a lack of basic necessities. Alienation—and the loss of the authentic meaning of life—is a reality in Western societies too. In consumerism people are ensnared in a web of false and superficial gratifications. Alienation is found in work when it is organized so as to ensure maximum profits with no concern for the worker.

The gift [of authentic life] is made possible by the person's "capacity for transcendence." Man cannot give himself to a purely human plan for reality, to an abstract ideal or to a false utopia. A man is alienated if he refuses to transcend himself in self-giving and in the formation of human community oriented toward his final destiny, which is God. A society is alienated if it makes it more difficult to offer this gift of self. Exploitation, at least in the forms analyzed by Karl Marx, has been overcome in Western society. Alienation, however, exists when people use one another, ignoring *obedience to the truth* about God and man, which obedience is the first condition of freedom.

42. Can it perhaps be said that, after the failure of Communism, capitalism is the victorious social system, and that capitalism should be the goal of the countries now making efforts to rebuild their economy and society? Is this the model that ought to be proposed to the countries of the Third World?

If by "capitalism" is meant an economic system that recognizes the fundamental and positive role of business, the market, private property, and the resulting responsibility for the means of production, as well as free human creativity in the economic sector, then the answer is certainly in the affirmative, [although it is] perhaps more appropriate to speak of a "business economy," "market economy," or simply "free economy." If by "capitalism" is meant a system in which freedom in the economic sector is not circumscribed within a strong juridical framework that places it at the service of human freedom in its totality, and that sees it as a particular aspect of that freedom, the core of which is ethical and religious, then the reply is certainly negative.

Vast multitudes live in conditions of great material and moral poverty. The collapse of Communism removes an obstacle to facing these problems, but it is not enough to bring about their solution. There is a risk that a radical capitalistic ideology could refuse even to consider these problems, blindly entrusting their solution to market forces.

43. The Church offers her social teaching as an *indispensable and ideal orientation* that recognizes the positive value of the market and of enterprise when [they are] oriented towards the common good. In the light of today's "new things" we have reread *the relationship between individual or private property and the universal destination of material wealth.* Man works in order to provide for his family, his community, his nation, and ultimately all humanity. He collaborates in the work of his fellow employees, of suppliers, and in the customers' use of goods in a progressively expanding chain of solidarity. Just as the person fully realizes himself in the free gift of self, so too ownership morally justifies itself in the creation of opportunities and human growth for all.

V. STATE AND CULTURE

44. *Rerum Novarum* presents the organization of society according to the three powers—legislative, executive, and judicial. It is preferable that each

power be balanced by [the] others. This is the "rule of law" in which the law is sovereign and not the arbitrary will of individuals. This concept has been opposed by Marxist-Leninist totalitarianism, which maintains that some people are exempt from error and can therefore exercise absolute power. The root of totalitarianism is the denial of the transcendent dignity of the human person who, as the visible image of the invisible God, is by his very nature the subject of rights that no one may violate.

45. Totalitarianism also involves a rejection of the Church. The state sets itself above all values [and] cannot tolerate the affirmation of an *objective criterion of good and evil* beyond the will of those in power. The state tends to absorb within itself the nation, society, the family, religious groups, and individuals themselves. In defending her own freedom, the Church is also defending the human person, who must obey God rather than men (cf. Acts 5:29).

46. The Church values the democratic system [that] ensures the participation of citizens in making political choices, guarantees to the governed the possibility of electing and holding accountable those who govern and of replacing them through peaceful means when appropriate. Nowadays, there is a tendency to claim that agnosticism and skeptical relativism are the philosophy and attitude that correspond to democratic forms of political life. It must be observed [however] that if there is no ultimate truth to direct political activity, then ideas can easily be manipulated for reasons of power. A democracy without values easily turns into open or thinly disguised totalitarianism.

Christian truth does not claim the right to impose on others [one] concept of what is true and good. Since it is not an ideology, the Christian faith does not imprison changing sociopolitical realities in a rigid schema. Human life is realized in history in conditions that are diverse and imperfect. Further, reaffirming the transcendent dignity of the person, the Church's method is always that of respect for freedom. While paying heed to every fragment of truth he encounters [elsewhere], the Christian will not fail to affirm in dialogue with others all that his faith and the correct use of reason have enabled him to understand.

47. Today we are witnessing a predominance of the democratic ideal, together with lively attention to human rights. Those rights [are] the solid foundation of democracy. Among the most important is the right to life, an integral part of which is the right of the child to develop in the mother's womb from the moment of conception. The source and synthesis of [all such rights] is religious freedom, the right to live in conformity with one's transcendent dignity as a person. The Church respects *the legitimate autonomy of the democratic order* and is not entitled to express preferences for this or that institutional or constitutional solution. Her contribution to the political order is her vision of the dignity of the person revealed in all its fullness in the mystery of the Incarnate Word.

48. The market economy cannot be conducted in an institutional, juridical, or political vacuum. The role of the state is to guarantee individual freedom and private property, as well as a stable currency and efficient public services. The state also oversees the exercise of human rights in the economic sector. However, primary responsibility in this area belongs not to the state but to individuals and to the groups and associations that make up society. The state could not directly ensure the right to work for all its citizens unless it controlled every aspect of economic life and restricted the free initiative of individuals. The state has a duty to sustain business activities by creating conditions that will ensure job opportunities.

The state has the right to intervene when monopolies create obstacles to development. In exceptional circumstances the state can also exercise a *substitute function*, when social or business sectors are too weak or just getting under way. Such supplementary interventions must be as brief as possible, so as to avoid removing permanently from society and business the functions that are properly theirs, and so as to avoid enlarging excessively the sphere of state intervention to the detriment of both economic and civil freedom.

In recent years, such intervention has vastly expanded, creating the "welfare state." Excesses and abuses have provoked very harsh criticisms of the welfare state, dubbed the "social assistance state." Malfunctions in the social assistance state result [from] an inadequate understanding of the tasks proper to the state. *The principle of subsidiarity* must be respected: a community of a higher order should not interfere in the internal life of a community of a lower order, depriving the latter of its functions, but rather should support it in case of need and help to coordinate its activity with the activities of the rest of society, always with a view to the common good. Needs are best understood and satisfied by people who are closest to them, and who act as neighbors to those in need.

49. The Church has always been present and active among the needy. Active charity has never ceased to be practiced, and today it is showing a gratifying increase. Special mention must be made of *volunteer work*, which the Church favors and promotes. To overcome today's individualistic mentality we require *a concrete commitment to solidarity and charity*, beginning with the family. It is urgent to promote family policies for [among other tasks] looking after the elderly, so as to avoid distancing them from the family unit and in order to strengthen relations between generations. Apart from the family, other intermediate communities, communities [that function between] the state and the marketplace, exercise primary functions and give life to networks of solidarity.

50. From the open search for truth *the culture of a nation* derives its character. *Evangelization plays a role in the culture of the various nations*, sustaining culture in its progress to truth. When a culture becomes inward-looking and

tries to perpetuate obsolete ways by rejecting any exchange with regard to the truth about man, it becomes sterile and is heading for decadence.

51. The first and most important [cultural] task is accomplished within man's heart. The way in which he builds his future depends on the understanding he has of himself and his destiny. It is on this level that *the Church's specific and decisive contribution to true culture* is to be found. The Church renders this service to human society *by preaching the truth* whereby the Son of God has saved mankind and united all people, making them responsible for one another. No one can say that he is not responsible for the well-being of his brother or sister (cf. Gen. 4:9, Luke 10:29–37, Matt. 25:31–46). Concern for one's neighbor is especially important in searching for alternatives to war in resolving international conflicts.

52. On the occasion of the recent tragic war in the Persian Gulf, I repeated the cry: "Never again war!" As in individual states a system of private vendetta and reprisal has given way to the rule of law, so too a similar step is now needed in the international community. Another name for peace is *development.* As there is a collective responsibility for avoiding war, so too there is a collective responsibility for promoting development. This is the [international] culture that is hoped for, one that fosters trust in the human potential of the poor, and in their ability to improve their condition through work. They need to be provided opportunities [through a] *concerted worldwide effort to promote development*, an effort that also involves [surrendering the advantages] of income and power enjoyed by the more developed economies.

VI. MAN IS THE WAY OF THE CHURCH

53. For a hundred years the Church has expressed her thinking [on] the social question, [but] not in order to recover former privileges or to impose her own vision. Her sole purpose has been *care and responsibility* for man, who has been entrusted to her by Christ himself. The horizon of the Church's wealth of doctrine is man in his concrete reality as sinful and righteous.

54. The human sciences and philosophy are helpful for interpreting *man's central place within society*. However, man's true identity is only fully revealed to him through faith, and it is from faith that the Church's social teaching begins. The Church's *social teaching* is itself a valid *instrument of evangelization.*

55. Christian anthropology is really a chapter of theology, and the Church's social doctrine [as I earlier wrote] "belongs to the field of theology and particularly of moral theology." The theological dimension is needed both for interpreting and solving present-day problems in society. This is true in contrast to both the "atheistic" solution and to permissive and consumerist solutions. On the eve of the third millennium the Church continues to be "a

sign and safeguard of the transcendence of the human person," walking together with man through history.

56. I wish this teaching to be applied in the countries that, following the collapse of "real socialism," are experiencing a serious lack of direction. The Western countries, in turn, run the risk of seeing this collapse as a one-sided victory of their own economic system, and thereby failing to make necessary corrections in that system. Third World countries experience more than ever the tragedy of underdevelopment.

57. The social message of the Gospel [is] not a theory but a basis and motivation for action. That message will gain credibility from the *witness of actions*. This awareness is also a source of the Church's preferential option for the poor, which is never exclusive or discriminatory toward other groups. This option is not limited to material poverty, [for] there are many other forms of poverty—not only economic but cultural and spiritual. In the West there are forms of poverty experienced by groups that live on the margins, by the elderly and the sick, by the victims of consumerism, by so many refugees and immigrants. In developing countries tragic crises loom on the horizon.

58. Justice will never be attained unless people see in the poor person who is asking for help in order to survive not an annoyance or a burden but an opportunity for showing kindness and a chance for greater enrichment. It is not merely a matter of "giving from one's surplus," but of helping entire peoples that are presently excluded or marginalized to enter into the sphere of economic and human development. Today's "globalization" of the economy can create unusual opportunities for greater prosperity. In order to direct the economy to the common good, increased coordination among the more powerful countries is necessary, with international agencies [to assure that] the interests of the whole human family are equally represented.

59. For the demands of justice to be met, what is needed is *the gift of grace*. Grace in cooperation with human freedom constitutes that mysterious presence of God in history that is providence.

60. Solving serious national and international problems is not just a matter of economic production or of juridical or social organization, but calls for ethical and religious values. There is hope that the many people who profess no religion will also contribute to providing the necessary ethical foundation. [But] the Christian churches and world religions will have a preeminent role in preserving peace and in building a society worthy of man.

61. After World War II, the Church put the dignity of the person at the center of her social messages. As she has become more aware of the too many people living in the poverty of the developing countries, she feels obliged to denounce this [marginalization] with absolute frankness, although she knows that her call will not always win favor with everyone.

62. I again give thanks to Almighty God, who has granted his Church the

light and strength to accompany humanity on its earthly journey toward its eternal destiny. In the third millennium, too, the Church will be faithful *in making man's way her own*. It is Christ who made man's way his own, and who guides him, even when he is not aware of it.

Given in Rome, at St. Peter's, on 1 May, the Memorial of Saint Joseph the Worker, in the year 1991, the thirteenth of my Pontificate.

Index

• • •

Abortion (the unborn), 85, 127, 155, 183, 215, 216–17, 219, 255–56
Acting person, the, 182–83, 188, 206, 207–8, 239, 241, 242
Adversary culture, 33, 34
Age of Innocence, The (Wharton), 32
Agnosticism, 279
"Aha experience," 83, 95
AIDS, 255
Alexy II, Patriarch, 144, 145
"American Catholicism and the Capitalist Ethic" (Weigel), 62–63, 64, 67, 69
American Founders, 3, 4, 6, 85, 154, 197, 243, 278, 279
Americanism, 64
Animal rights, 219–20, 226
Anthropocentrism, 219, 220–22, 226–27
Apocalyptic pilgrims, 218
Aquinas, Thomas, 89
Aristotle, 239, 278
Ash, Timothy Garton, 147–48, 161
Association, freedom of, 245, 246

Atheism, 152-53, 302
Augustine, Saint, 143, 248
Authority, papal teaching and tradition and, 75–105, 129–30, 136; self-denying ordinances and, 116–18, 119; and social doctrine, 107–32, 136–64 (*see also* Social doctrine)
Autonomy and sovereignty, spheres of, 173, 257–59, 273

Banfield, Edward, 252
Baptism, 125
Baptists, 86, 129
Barth, Karl, 48
Bedford-Stuyvesant section (Brooklyn, N.Y.C.), 230
Bellarmine, Robert, 89
Belloc, Hilaire, 50
Benedict, XIV, Pope, 76
Bennett, John, 48, 140–41
Berger, Peter, 53, 111–12, 198–99, 244, 267; on "economic culture," 198–99, 267

Bible, the, 86, 95, 107–8, 129, 221–22; on poverty and the wealthy, 171–72; on the Social Gospel, 107–8, 129. *See also* New Testament; Old Testament

"Big Business," 27

Bishops' Program for Social Reconstruction (1919), 67–68

Black Americans, 230–32, 234–35

Blake, William, 31

Bourgeois Gentilhomme, Le (Molière), 25–26

Brooks, Van Wyck, 35

Brothers Karamazov, The, 28–29

Brownson, Orestes, 65–66

Burke, Edmund, 240

Business, 26–30; as a source of wealth, 202, 203; being in, 26–30. *See also* Capitalism; Economics; Free Economy

Buttiglione, Rocco, 169, 177

Calvin, John, 89, 130

Calvinist Protestantism, 4, 31, 37

Canavan, Francis, 78

Capitalism, 54–56, 57, 140, 149, 197–98, 295–99; choice of two, 45–71; Christian economic behavior and responsibility and, 17–44 (*see also* Social doctrine); John Paul II's affirmation of, 54–56, 57; meanings of, 177–78, 179, 197, 299; new (democratic), and a free economy, 2, 9, 30–31, 38–39, 40, 43, 54–58, 80, 150–53 (*see also* Democracy; Free economy); property and creativity and, 187–208, 297; socialism and, 39–43, 45–71; society and the state and, 239–59, 261–83

Capitalist Revolution: . . . , The (Berger), 198–99, 267

Carroll family of Maryland, 64; Charles, 64; Archbishop John, 64

Caste patterns, 230–31, 232–35

Catherine of Siena, 89

Catholic Church (Catholics), 8–14, 63–71; capitalism and, 47–51 (*see also* Capitalism); Communism and, 142–63 (*see also* Communism); and human freedom and the free economy, 17–44, 167–85, 285–304 (*see also* Freedom; Free economy); and papal teaching authority and tradition, 75–105, 107–32; and pluralism, 261–83; and the poor, 209–35 (*see also* Poverty); and property and creativity, 190–208; and religious liberty, 253, 279, 294; and society and the state, 240–59; and the Social Gospel, 107–32, 136–63 (*see also* Social doctrine); wealth of, 199–201

Catholic cultures, democratic capitalism and, 37, 42–43, 47–51 *passim*, 198–99, 267

Catholic Moment, The, 89, 111

Catholic News Service, 13

Catholics, American, economic success of, 63–66

Ceausescu, Nicolae, 143

Center of Concert, 80–81, 84, 224; *Focus*, 81

Centesimus Annus ("The Hundredth Year"), 9, 12, 13, 30–31, 37, 40, 49, 52–71 *passim*, 285–304; condensed version of, 285–304; disputes and interpretations of, 184; and the Social Gospel, 107–32, 136–64 (*see also* Social doctrine)

Challenge of Peace, The, (pastoral letter), 113

Charity, 212, 213–15, 269, 308; "active," 269

Chesterton, G. K., 4, 50, 89

Child care, 270, 271, 272, 273. *See also* Family, the; Parents

China, Communist, 3, 138, 215–16

Christianity, 17–44, 45–71; as a comprehensive "meaning system," 18; choice of capitalisms and, 45–71; church and state and, 240–59; economic behavior and responsibility and, 17–44, 46–71 (*see also* Social doctrine); as eschatological, 41; human freedom and the free economy and, 167–85; pluralism and, 261–83; and the Social Gospel, 107–32 (*see also* Social doctrine); socialism and, 46–48 (*see also* Socialism); and tradition and papal teaching authority, 75–104; and truth claims, 18

Christianity and Communism Today, 141

Churchill, Winston, 45–46, 275

Church-state relations, 273–75

Class mentality and struggle, 157–60, 212, 245, 246

"Cognitive chart," 45–46, 47, 50

Cognitive skills, wages and, 231–32

Cold war, 2–4, 57, 140, 158, 159

Common good, society and the state and, 241, 243, 248, 259

Communism, 2–4, 28, 117, 138–63, 180, 181, 215–16, 263, 299; capitalism and, 45–71; collapse of, 2–3, 11, 39–40, 138–63; and the New Man, 247. *See also* Marxism; Socialism

Community, 6, 67, 222, 301; gated, the poor and, 233, 235; neighbors as, 259; society and the state and, 241, 243, 259, 269–70, 271, 301; and the Social Gospel, 109–10, 112–13, 155; tradition and papal teaching authority and, 104–5, 109–10, 125–26, 129, 130–31

Computers, 201

Condoms, distribution in schools of, 254

Conservatives, 169; and big government, 241; and the poor, 212–13, 226–27, 233. *See also* Neoconservatives

Constitution, U.S., 4–5, 243, 274; First Amendment, 273

Consumerism, 52–55, 160, 206, 225, 251, 302

Contingent historical judgments, 122–23

Council of Nicaea (325), 96

Council of Trent, 96
Counter-Reformation, 12
Creativity, 183–85; property and, 187–208; tradition and papal teaching authority and, 83; work and, 183–85
"Critical consciousness," Marxism and, 51
Cuba, 3
Culture: Catholic, democratic capitalism and, 37, 42–43, 47–71 *passim*, 198–99, 267; as determining the social order, 247–48; elite and popular, 32–34, 35–37; pluralism and, 261–83; the state and, 261–83, 299–302
Czechoslovakia, 203

Daniels, Anthony, 22–23
Day, Dorothy, 50
Democracy, 2–14, 150–53, 275–83; authentic, 276–77; democratic (free) capitalism and, 150–53 (*see also* Free economy); freedom and (*see* Freedom); ideas and ideals of, 2–14; making it more democratic, 150–53; papal authority and teaching and, 84–89, 117–18; pluralism and, 261–83; the Social Gospel and, 120–21, 123, 132, 136, 156–63 (*see also* Social doctrine); society and the state and, 239–59, 261–83; "third wave" of, 10–11, 279
Dependency: and displacement patterns, the state and, 254–56, 258–59, 264, 270–71; welfare and, 151–52, 254–56, 258–59, 264, 270–71
Despair, 119, 120
Development, global, 223–25, 227–30, 294, 302
Dewey, John, 38, 280; his "common faith" proposal, 5
Dignity, 120, 151, 153, 157, 169, 180–83, 189, 195, 204, 210, 220, 222, 251, 303
Diocletian, Emperor, 143
Displacement and dependency patterns, the state and, 254–56, 258–59, 264, 270–71
Distributive justice, 172
Dives (Biblical rich man), 211, 212
Docility, papal authority and, 99–101
Dominion et Vivificantem, 77–78
Donatists, 143, 146, 147
"Do no harm" principle, the state and society and, 257
Dostoevsky, Fedor, 28–29
Douglas, Ann, 36
Drugs (addictions), 205, 269
Dworkin, Ronald, 154

Eastern Europe, 268-69. *See also* specific countries
Economic Justice for All (1966 pastoral letter), 76, 113–14
Economics (economic behavior), 17–44, 167–85; being in business and, 26–30; choice of
capitalisms and, 45–71 (*see also* Capitalism); *Christianly* thinking about, 17–44; defined, 19–21; free, 2, 43, 56–71, 150–53 (*see also* Free economy); human freedom and, 285–304; potential of the poor and, 209–35, 253 (*see also* Poverty); property and creativity and, 187–208; society and the state and, 242–59; the Social Gospel and, 110–32 (*see also* Social doctrine); subjectivity of society and, 21–22, 24, 26; zero-sum, 172–73, 179, 223
Education (schools), 233, 252–53, 254–55, 271, 273, 274
Ehrlich, Paul, 217
Elderly, the care of, 269–70, 271
Eliot, T. S., *East Coker* by, 121
Elite culture, popular culture and, 32–34, 35–37
Emerson, Ralph Waldo, 38
Employment (unemployment), 230–32, 242–43, 249, 250–51, 256, 263–66
Encyclopedic Dictionary of Religion, The, 77
Enlightenment, the, 153–54, 156
Entrepreneurship (enterprise), 197–208 *passim*; potential of the poor and, 210–35; wealth and, 190–91
Environmentalism (ecology), 218–20, 223–24, 225–28, 297–98
Episcopal Church, 31–32, 37, 38
Equality, 156–57, 183, 194; of opportunity, 250, 253, 265; society and the state and, 249–50, 253, 265, 267–68, 272
Essay on the Development of Christian Doctrine, An (Newman), 82
Ethics (morality). *See* Morality
Evangelical/fundamentalist churches and communities, 8, 11, 38
Evangelical Lutheran Church in America (ELCA), 127
Evangelization, Catholic, 121–22, 125, 301–2

Factionalism, 129, 130–131, 171
Faith, 19, 174; potential of the poor and, 215–18; the Social Gospel and, 120–21, 123–24, 125; "structure" of, 88, 90–91, 102. *See also* Religion
Family, the, 247–49, 262, 269–70, 298, 301; as a mediating structure, love and, 247–49, 254–55, 262, 270, 271, 272; society and the state and, 243, 247–49, 254–55, 269–70
Fascism, 3, 68, 140. *See also* Totalitarianism; specific countries, individuals
Feminism, radical, 222
Feminization of American Culture, The (Douglas), 36
Founding Fathers. *See* American Founders
France, Anatole, 25, 202
Freedom, human (free societies), 1–14, 136,

137, 140, 163; of association, 245, 246;
democratic models of, 2–14 (*see also*
Democracy); economic (*see* Free economy);
morality and, 1–14; of religion, 253, 279,
294
Free economy (business economy; new
capitalism); 9, 30–31, 37, 40, 42, 43, 50,
150–53, 210; capitalism and (*see* Capitalism);
human freedom and, 167–85, 285–304;
pluralism and, 261–83; potential of the poor
and, 209–35; property and creativity and,
187–208; society and the state and, 240–59,
261–83; workers and (*see* Labor). *See also*
Economics
French Revolution, 156, 193, 280
Frossard, André, 148–49

Gallup polls, 27
Gated communities, the poor and, 233, 235
Gender, language and, 13
Genteel tradition, 35–37; hostility to capitalism
and, 35–37
"Genteel tradition in American Philosophy,
The," 35–36
German Bishops Conference (1991), study on
population and poverty of, 218
Germany, 158–59, 160, 162, 247, 251. *See also*
Nazism; West Germany; World War II
Gibbons, Archbishop James, 67–68
Gilder, George, 201–2; on "the overthrow of
matter," 201–2
God, 18, 19, 87–88, 89, 95, 102, 107, 108,
116, 118, 120–22, 125, 131, 132, 136, 153,
181, 189, 201, 204, 208, 213, 220, 221, 225–
26, 281, 283; adverbs and, 61–63; as the
continuing Creator, 183–84, 189, 203, 226;
economic behavior and responsibility and,
18, 19, 20, 26, 29, 41–42, 61–63
Goethe, Johann Wolfgang von, 105
Gompers, Samuel, 111–12
Gooden, Dwight, 193
Gorbachev, Mikhail, 11, 139–40
Government (the state), 239–59; big or small,
241–43; church-state relations and, 273–75;
and culture, 261–83, 299–302; intellectuals
and, 33–34; pluralism and, 261–83; *res
publicae* and, 252–53, 255, 259; society and,
239–59
"Government and Business: The Moral
Challenges," 29–30
Grace, 120–21, 124, 125, 132, 136, 283, 303
Greed (selfishness), capitalism and human
nature and, 27–37, 47–48, 161–62, 189–90,
293
Gulf War. *See* Persian Gulf War

Hall, Joseph, 61
Harrington, Michael, 234

Hauerwas, Stanley, 126–27
Hebrews, 221. *See also* Israelites; Jews
Hebrew Scriptures, 95, 221
Heschel, Abraham Joshua, 219, 228
"Hierarchy of truths," 88
Higgins, Msgr. George, 68
Hitler, Adolf, 98, 280
Holocaust, the, 137
Holy Spirit, 76, 78–79, 86, 97, 102
Holy Trinity, 86
Homo economicus, 25
Homosexuality, 255
"How Churches Crack Up," 128–29
Howe, Irving, 41
Hughes, Archbishop John, 65, 66
Humanae Vitae (encyclical), 77
Humanism and Capitalism, 35, 37
Human nature, 115, 120, 161–62, 178–80, 183,
184–85, 240, 275; economic behavior and
greed and, 27–37, 47–48, 161–62, 189–90,
293; self-interest and, 161–62, 189–90, 293
Hungary, 10
Huntington, Samuel P., 10–11, 279

Ignatius of Antioch, 89
Illicit speculation, 191–94, 196
Imitation of Christ, The, 20
Immigrants, 63–67, 128–29, 214–15, 269
In Defense of People, 218–19
India, population growth in, 217
Individualism, 151, 154–55; rugged, 179
Individual rights, 154–57; responsibilities and,
155–57. *See also* Freedom, human
Industrialization, 31, 64, 65
Infallibility, 129–30; encyclicals and, 76–105
passim
Intellectuals. *See* Knowledge class
Ireland, Archbishop John, 67
Irish Catholics, American, 63–65
Irony of American History, The, 121
Islam, 173; challenge of, 162–63
Israelites, 98. *See also* Hebrews; Jews

Jackson, Jesse, 216
Jackson, Michael, 193
Jefferson, Thomas, 4
Jesus Christ, 18, 19, 54, 78, 83–84, 88, 91, 95,
97, 98, 102–3, 108, 120, 122, 124, 125, 126,
146, 148, 152, 163, 171, 207, 221, 269, 275;
economic behavior and responsibility and,
18–19; new birth in, 125–26
Jews, 78, 137, 214–15, 273, 278, 281; anti-
Semitism and, 98; and tradition, 6, 8, 63. *See
also* Hebrews; Israelites
John Paul I, Pope, 137
John Paul II, Pope, 11, 12, 21, 24, 30–31, 49,
52, 69–70, 77–105 *passim*, 109–32, 136; and
affirmation of capitalism as a free economy,

42–43, 52–71 (*see also* Free economy); affirmation of democracy by, 275–83; and *Centesimus Annus*, 77–105 *passim*, 285–304 (*see also Centesimus Annus*); and Communism and "moral reconstruction", 143–50; and consumerism, 52–55, 160, 206, 225, 251, 302; and creativity and prosperity, 187–208; and environmentalism, 225–28; and human freedom and the free economy, 163, 167–85, 285–304; millennial vision of, 59–61; and modernity, 170–71, 173; and pluralism, 261–83; and the poor, 209–35; (*see also* Poverty); and "reading the signs of the times," 135–64; and the Social Gospel, 109–32, 135–63 (*see also* Social doctrine); and society and the state, 239–59; and reformist message, 169–85; and socialism and liberalism, 2, 40–43, 52–56, 57, 149–63, 168–69, 178 (*see also* Socialism); and tradition and papal teaching authority, 75–105 *passim*, 107–32; and utopianism, 41, 119, 121

Johnson, L. B., and "war on poverty," 234
John XXIII, Pope, 76, 82, 89, 137
Judaism, 6, 8, 78. *See also* Jews
Judeo-Christian tradition, 6, 8
Junk bonds, 192–93, 196
Justice (injustice). *See* Social justice
Just wages, 192–96, 290

Kerygma, the, 124
Keynes, John Maynard, 48, 206
King, Martin Luther, Jr., 6–7, 222; and "I Have a Dream" speech, 7
Kingdom of God, 41–42, 108, 209
Knights of Labor, 67–68
Knowledge class (intellectuals), 33–34, 35–37, 43; and hostility to capitalism, 33–34, 35–37, 43, 49–54; and symbolic knowledge, 33
Kuyper, Abraham (Kuyperism), 257

Labor (workers), 167–85, 256; Catholic Church and, 64–68; creativity and, 183–85, 188–207; dignity of, 169, 180–83, 189; human freedom and the free economy and, 167–85, 285–93 (*see also* Freedom; Free economy); just wages and, 192–96, 290; potential of the poor and, 209–35; prosperity and creativity and, 187–208; right to work and, 256, 263–66; social justice and, 155–63, 167–85; society and the state and, 239–59, 263–66; trade unions and, 67–68, 176, 245–47
Laborem Exercens (encyclical), 181–82
Labor priests, 68
Land ownership, 188, 197–98
Latin America, 10, 11, 37, 46, 47, 200, 214, 233, 268, 292

Lazarus, 209, 211, 212, 235; and Dives, 211, 212
Lefebvre, Archbishop, 130
Lenin, V. I., 179
Leo XIII, Pope, 30–31, 40, 68, 78, 93, 96, 110–11, 132, 137, 149, 150, 170, 176, 180, 187, 188, 207, 248, 286–89. *See also Rerum Novarum*
Liberalism, 39, 53, 68, 168, 173, 233, 241
Liberation theology, 46, 69, 211
Libertarians, 59, 168–69, 195
Libertas Praestantissimum (encyclical), 93
Lifestyles, global development and change in, 223–25
Lincoln, Abraham, 3, 6, 7, 8, 278
Lippman, Walter, his call for a "public philosophy," 5
Love, 196–97; and allegiances, work and, 196–97; the family and, 247–49, 254–55, 262, 271; of the poor, Church's, 209–35
Luce, Clare Boothe, 93
Luther, Martin, 89, 130, 146
Lutherans, 124, 127, 128–29; 131; Missouri Synod, 128–29

McCarthy, Joseph ("McCarthyism"), 140
Madison, James, 5
Madonna, earnings of, 193
Magisterium, 84, 88–89, 129, 131, 136; social, 100, 117, 131
Marcion (d. 160), 95
Marcos, Ferdinand, 10
Marginalization of the poor, 210–13, 215–18, 223, 227–35, 240, 269
Marriage, 174. *See also* Family, the
Marx, Karl, 49, 152, 182, 299
Marxism, 22–23, 39, 40–43, 47–71 *passim*, 122, 176, 178, 179, 210–211, 212, 229, 267, 293–94, 298–99; capitalism and, 47–71; class struggle and, 157–60, 212, 245, 246; "scientific," 280. *See also* Communism; Socialism
Mater et Magistra (encyclical), 82, 137
Matter, overthrow of, 201–2
Mediating (intermediary) structures, the state and, 244–45, 246–49, 252, 253–59; and the family, 247–49; and meaning systems, 247–48
Meilaender, Gilbert, 128–29
Methodists, 38, 274
Milken, Michael, 192–93, 196
Modernity (postmodernity), 66–67, 82–83, 170–71, 173, 241; parochialism and, 273; pluralism and, 173, 273; "spheres of sovereignty" and, 66
Monism, pluralism and, 173, 261–83
Monod, Jacques, 221
Mooney, Christopher, 220

Morality (ethics), 1–14, 171; choice of capitalisms and, 45–71; democracy and religion and, 1–14; economic behavior and responsibility and, 17–44; pluralism and, 261–83; politics and, 239–59; property and creativity and, 187–208; social doctrine and, 126–27, 171–85, 187, 239–59; society and the state and, 239–59
More Equality, 156
Morgan, J. P., 32
Moynihan, Daniel Patrick, and "benign neglect" policy, 235
Murchland, Bernard, 35, 37
Murray, Charles, 230–31, 233–34, 235
Mussolini, Benito, 3, 68, 153

National Review, 82; *Mater et Magistra* editorials in, 82
NATO, 161
Natural law, 241, 245
Natural resources, 197–98, 201–2, 225–28; humanity as, 197–98, 201–2, 219
Nazism (National Socialism; Third Reich), 217, 222, 247
Neoconservatism, 34, 39, 80
Neoliberalism, 39
New capitalism. *See* Free economy
Newman, John Henry Cardinal, 82
"New Paradigm," 244, 259
New Testament, 75, 170, 171; the Social Gospel and, 126–27. *See also* Bible, the
Niebuhr, Reinhold, 48, 89, 121
Novak, Michael, 37, 49, 50, 197
Novus ordo seclorum, 3, 8–9
Nuclear arms, 113, 158; pastoral letter on, 113

Oakeshott, Michael, 269
O'Connor, Flannery, 129
O'Connor, John Cardinal, 127
Oeconomicus, 19–20
Old Testament, 171. *See also* Bible, the
Orthodox Church, 143–44; and Caesaro-papism, 143
Other America, the (Harrington), 234
Ownership, private, 210, 256, 295–99; creativity and, 187–208; land, 188, 197–98. *See also* Property; Wealth

Pacem in Terris (encyclical), 137
Paleoconservatism, 168
Parents (parenting), 226, 271, 272. *See also* Child care; Family, the
Parochialism, pluralism and, 273
Participation theory, 227–28, 268
Pastoral letters, authority of, 76
Paul, Saint, 19, 89, 125, 174; letters of, 75–76, 107

Paul VI, Pope, *Populorum Progressio* encyclical of, 69, 137, 148
Pelikan, Jaroslav, 83
Persian Gulf war, 159, 302
Peter, Saint, 89, 97, 102; and Petrine Ministry, 97, 102–3, 104, 123, 130–31
Phenomenology, 181–82, 245
Philadelphia Enquirer, 85
Philippines, the, 10
Pius XI, Pope, 68, 176, 243
Pius XII, Pope, 76, 93, 129
Pluralism, monism and, 173, 261–83
Poland, 10, 11, 49, 146–48, 158–59; Kraków in, 182, 183, 226
"Political pilgrims," 135–36, 217–18
Politics, 167–85; creativity and, 204–5; equality and, 157; human freedom and the free economy and, 167–85 *passim*; morality and, 239–59; pluralism and, 261–83; the Social Gospel and, 110–32; society and the state and, 239–59
"Pope Affirms, The 'New Capitalism,'" 9
Popes, 108–9; as Holy Father, 108–9; and infallibility and encyclicals, 76–105, 129–30; and the Social Gospel, 107–32, 136–64; and tradition and teaching authority, 75–105, 107–32. *See also* individual popes
"Popes and the Economy, The" (Canavan), 78
Population Bomb, The (Ehrlich), 217
Population growth, 216–18, 225, 227
Populorum Progressio, 69, 137, 148
Pornography, 205
Poverty (the poor; the underclass), 55, 209–35, 303; *Centesimus Annus* on, 288; charity and, 212, 213–15, 269, 301; Christian behavior and responsibility and, 28–30, 34, 43, 52–53, 62, 63–67 (*see also* Responsibility; Social doctrine); Church's love and, 209–35; exploitation and, 210–11; human freedom and the free economy and, 187–208; marginalization of, 210–213, 215–18, 223, 227–35; population growth and, 216–18; potential of, 209–35, 253; property and creativity and, 187–208; society and the state and, 239–59
Prayer, 41, 42, 61, 62
"Preferential option for the poor," 211
Presbyterians, 37, 38, 273
Profit-seeking, 58–59, 189–208 *passim*, 296. *See also* Self-interest
Property, 187–208, 210, 295–99; creativity and, 187–208. *See also* Ownership
Prosperity. *See* Wealth
Protestants, 4, 8, 10, 65; and democracy, 10; and economy, 31, 36–39, 47, 63, 65; oldline, 37–39, 111, 116; and the Social Gospel, 110, 111, 116, 123–25, 127–29; and teaching authority, 84, 86–87, 94–95, 100, 104, 111,

127–29; and work ethic, 37. *See also* specific denominations
Proudhon, Pierre-Joseph, 187
Puritan-Lockean Synthesis, 4, 6, 7

Quadragesimo Anno, 78, 242–43
Qu'est-ce-que la Propriété? (Proudhon), 187

Raban, Jonathan, 232–33
Ramsey, Paul, 116
Rand, Ayn, *Atlas Shrugged* by, 168
Ranke, Leopold Von, 136
Ratzinger, Joseph Cardinal, 88, 123
Rawls, John, 5, 280
"Reading the signs of the times," 135–64
Reagan, Ronald, 6, 7, 48
Redemptoris Mater (encyclical), 77–78
Redemptoris Missio (encyclical), 92, 115, 162–63, 278
Religion (spirituality): church-state relations and, 273–75; democracy and, 4–14, 277–79; economic behavior and responsibility and, 17–44, 45–71 (*see also* Economics; Responsibility; Social doctrine); free exercise of, 253, 279, 294; pluralism and, 261, 269, 273, 274–75; property and creativity and, 200–1. *See also* Faith
Rerum Novarum ("The New Things"), 30–31, 38, 40, 53, 68, 78, 110, 126, 148, 168, 188, 207, 276, 286–289, 299–300
Responsibility (social responsibility), 222; pluralism and, 276; the poor and, 187–208, 228–30; rights and, 154–57; the Social Gospel and social justice and, 116, 120–21 (*see also* Social doctrine; Social justice); society and the state and, 241–59, 272, 276
Revolution of 1989, 2–3, 10, 12, 13, 39, 40, 41, 59, 70, 162, 244, 292–94; the end of Communism and, 2–3, 149–63
Ricoeur, Paul, 108
"Robber barons," 31–32
Rockefeller, Nelson, 29–30, 171
Romania, 142–43
Roosevelt, Franklin D., 159
Rorty, Richard, "liberal irony" espousal of, 5
Russia. *See* Soviet Union
Russian Orthodox Church. *See* Orthodox Church
Ryan, Msgr. John A., 68

St. George's (Episcopalian) church, 31–32
St. John the Evangelist parish, 216–17
Salvation, 119, 122, 125, 185, 219
Santayana, George, 35–36
Schlesinger, Arthur, Jr., 39
Schools. *See* Education (schools)
Schutz, Alfred, 26; on the "Aha experience," 26

Science and technology, 221–22, 227–28, 231, 233
"Secession of the successful," 232–35
Second Vatican Council. *See* Vatican Council II
Self-denying ordinances, 116–18, 119, 196, 282
Self-interest, 161–62, 224, 266; as natural and good, 189–90, 293; narrow, 214. *See also* Profit-seeking
Sexuality, 174. *See also* Abortion; AIDS; Condoms; Homosexuality
Simon, Julian, 219
Sin, 19, 113, 115, 120, 124, 125, 146, 161–62, 169, 190, 293
Smith, Adam, 179, 197
Social Darwinism, 179
Social doctrine (social teaching), 107–32, 136–64, 239–59, 285–304; *Centesimus Annus* on (*see Centesimus Annus*; specific aspects); God's Law on, 124–26; human freedom and the free economy and, 167–85, 285–304 (*see also* Freedom; Free economy); papal authority and teaching and, 75–105; and the poor, 209–35 (*see also* Poverty); prosperity and creativity and, 187–208; Protestant movements and, 111; and reforms, 167–85; the Social Gospel and, 107–32, 136–64; social justice and, 80, 90–91, 113 (*see also* Social justice); society and the state and, 239–59. *See also* specific concepts, individuals
Social Gospel, papal teaching authority and tradition and, 107–32, 136–64. *See also* Social doctrine
Socialism, 2, 22, 27–29, 39–43, 45–46, 64, 67, 68, 71, 122, 135–36, 149–63, 168–69, 180, 187–88, 207, 211, 226, 227, 229, 234, 264, 289–92; atheism and, 152–53; capitalism and, 39–43, 45–71; class struggle and, 157–60; errors of, 151–53; "real," collapse of, 50, 149–63 *passim*, 269, 296–297, 303. *See also* Communism; Marxism
Social justice, 60–61, 63–68, 80, 90–91, 113, 120, 155–63, 167–68; democracy and, 5; equality and, 156–57; pluralism and, 261–63; the poor and (*see* Poverty); property and creativity and, 187–208. *See also* Social doctrine
Social services, "delivery of," 271, 272–73
Society, 239–59; culture and, 299–302 (*see also* Culture); pluralism and, 261–83; the state and, 239–59; subjectivity of (*see* Subjectivity of society)
Solidarity principle, 176, 191, 192, 204, 212, 222, 249–51, 290
Sollicitudo Rei Socialis (encyclical), 122, 183, 212, 229
Solzhenitsyn, Aleksandr, 137–38
Soviet Union (Russia), 11, 139–40, 143–46, 159–63, 178, 278. *See also* Communism; specific developments, individuals

Spain, 10, 278; Inquisition, 278
"Speciesism," 219–20
Speculation, investing and, 191–94, 196
Spheres of sovereignty, 173, 257–59, 273
Spirit of Democratic Capitalism, The (Novak), 37, 49
Stalin, Joseph, 3, 4, 143, 159, 198–99, 278; and gulags, 280
State, the. *See* Government
Steinfels, Peter, 93–94, 96, 98–99
Stewardship (caretaking), 188, 219–20, 225–28, 302; economic responsibility and, 19–20 (*see also* Responsibility); safety net and, 252, 259; society and the state and, 251–59, 261–83. *See also* Social doctrine; Social justice
Strauss, Leo, 278
"Structure of faith," 88, 90–91, 102
Subjectivity of society, 21–22, 24, 26, 123, 151, 152, 154–55, 176, 183, 229, 240, 241, 244, 252, 253, 255, 264, 266, 273; meaning of, 26
Subsidiarity principle, 243–45, 249–54, 255, 259
Survivalism, fear of nuclear war and, 142, 148

Tawney, R. H., 48
Temple, William, 48
Theory of Justice, A (Rawls), 5
Third World, 158, 170, 176, 199, 215–17, 227–28, 229, 258, 296. *See also* specific countries
Thomas à Kempis, 20
Thoreau, Henry David, 35, 38
Tillich, Paul, on socialism, 47–48
Tocqueville, Alexis, 5
To Empower People, 244–45
Totalitarianism, 153, 162, 244, 263, 275–79, 300. *See also* specific kinds
Trade unions, 67–68, 176, 245–47; crisis in, 245–47
Tradition, papal teaching authority and, 75–105, 107–32, 135; creativity and, 83; the Social Gospel and, 107–32, 136–64; traditionalism *vs.*, 82
Traditores, 143, 144
Trilling, Lionel, 33
Truly Disadvantaged, The, 230
Trump, Donald, 192
Truth(s), 275–83; hierarchy of, 88; the Social Gospel and, 109–10, 118–32, 156, 163 (*see also* Social doctrine); totalitarianism and denial of, 275–79, 300; tradition and papal teaching authority and, 87–91, 93, 94–105, 109–10, 129–30, 135; universal, pluralism and democracy and, 275–83, 300

Ultimate Resource, The (Simon), 219
Unheavenly City, The (Banfield), 251–52

Unions. *See* Trade unions
United Methodist Church, 38, 274
United Nations, 292
United States (Americans): caste patterns in, 230–31, 232–35; church-state relations and, 273–75; Communism and, 159–60; democracy and, 2–13, 275–83; income in, 192–96; pluralism and, 261–83; and the poor, 223, 230–35 (*see also* Poverty); "secession of the successful" and, 232–35; society and the state and, 239–59
United States Catholic Conference, 68
Utopianism, 41, 119, 121

Vatican Council II (Second Vatican Council), 12, 68, 80, 84, 95, 102, 103, 130, 135, 163, 219, 276, 278; "Constitution on the Church," 76; "Declaration on Religious Freedom" 163; *Gaudium et Spes*, 183; "Pastoral Constitution on the Church in the Modern World," 68
Virgin Mary (Blessed Virgin), 76, 95, 148
Virtues, wealth and, 203, 206
Volunteer work, 269–70, 301

Ward, Harry, 48
War on poverty, Johnson's, 234
Wealth (the rich), 171–73, 210, 231–35; the Bible on poverty and, 171–72; just wages and, 192–96, 290; potential of the poor and, 209–35; production of, 172–73, 179; property and creativity and, 187–208, 295–99 (*see also* Creativity; Property)
Wealth and Poverty (Gilder), 201
Wealth of Nations, The (Smith), 197
Weaver, Richard, 282
Weber, Max, 37
Weigel, George, 62–63, 64, 67, 69
Welfare dependency, 151–52, 254–56, 258–59, 264, 270–71
West Germany, 160, 162. *See also* Germany
Wharton, Edith, 32
Whitehead, Alfred North, 108–9
Williams, Roger, 89
Wilson, William Julius, 230, 234–35
Wilson, Woodrow, League of Nations and, 6
Wojtyla, Karol, 116, 159, 181–83; on "the acting person," 182–83; and phenomenology, 181–82
Workers. *See* Labor (workers)
Work ethic, Protestant, 37
World Council of Churches, 40, 145
World War II, 3, 10, 40, 138, 158, 159–60, 223, 291–292

Yakunin, Gleb, 145
Yalta agreements, 159, 292